SALES MEETINGS THAT WORK:

Planning and Managing Meetings to Achieve Your Goals

by Richard Cavalier

ISBN: 0-7596-5735-1 (e-book)
ISBN: 0-7596-5736-X (Paperback)

This book is printed on acid free paper.

1stBooks-rev. 08/01/03

Some of the material in this volume originally appeared in the author's *Achieving Objectives in Meetings* published in 1973 by Corporate Movement, Inc. The original hardcover edition of this book was published by Dow Jones-Irwin in 1983.

Library of Congress
Catalog Card No. 82-72764

Printed in the United States of America.

Preface to the Third Edition

Because of the advent of two-way video conferencing, the world of corporate meetings will change drastically. Site-dependency will end. The change will not be made overnight. It will be made in the face of protest and stiff competition from the hotel and airline industries (which until now had absolute access to and control over the people moved for the purposes of better internal communication) and from other suppliers who profit from service to crowds. Disinformation in their interests and service probably will not end, but probably will become rampant. Their interests will not always (or often?) coincide with yours.

The immediate consequence of any video conferencing substitute for travel is that the emphasis will be back on the meeting purpose and content—where it has always belonged! Rather than being tied up with details of distant planning, Corporate Meeting Managers will now be free to specialize in the subject matter which concerns the given corporation, rather than in the stringencies of the travel trade and subsequent planning for the distant event. For purposes of control, the outside facility across the road should be considered *distant.* In the past, distant sites were inescapable; but now, escape is easy and cheap!

Sales Meetings That Work will help you in four main ways:

First, you will understand the needs and get the help needed via proved methods of control! The methods of meetings control contained in this book were the first comprehensive system in the meetings/ conventions industry. Having been imitated and reproduced, the original materials in this book have become The Source for knowledgeable, hands-on expertise for the entire meetings/conventions industry. Forms are easy to imitate—but we know the reasons that they were designed! And *Sales Meetings That Work* tells you those reasons. The several associations in the meetings field did not originate how-to materials. They did consolidate existing opinions that might or might not be qualified.

Second, this book will enable you better to control the hotels and other distant suppliers while you fulfill the future contracts that are likely in hand for hotel space. You might want to cancel. But if you must still meet at a distance in the near future, you can at least be better prepared by consulting The Source materials here for meetings control.

Third, when you have ceased to be site-dependent, you can ignore the book chapters devoted to distant site control and concentrate on those related to content—your company's message. The Source for control was also The Source for identifying that dichotomy of interests. In the entire industry, Audience and Training Profiles (among other guides) originated with us. Sites are usually not your reason for calling the meeting...unless you're selling sites.

Fourth, the brand new materials in this book deal very specifically with the approaches to video conferencing that still affect you more than 15 years after our early recommendations appeared. And new materials in the all-new Chapter 23 will help you to understand the distortions and outright disinformation already being practiced by what we call the Pollyanna Press of the meetings/conventions industry.

Those were the main points when this edition was prepared. Because of September 11, 2001, there's a whole new array of considerations; and among them are:

a) business must continue to communicate, whether or not in a central meeting room;

b) if air travel is no longer the joy it was in the days of the French Caravelle, then attendees will likely be frazzled before they begin the meeting: do you prefer extra days out-of-office routine in order to allow a calming down once there, or do you prefer them not be out of office routine at all?;

c) if the employee would rather not fly, what liability does your company incur if it insists and if something untoward should then happen? "Do you like your job?" is a holdover from KITA management days, and it's still destructive. Now you decide.

d) equipment available now will connect multiple locations for "live" interactive conferences or for computer-aided lessons...purchased for under $3,000 per connected site., plus the price of a phone call, on DSL or other broadband.

As a matter of simple fact, it's essential to recognize that an annual meeting is legally mandated to all industry associations by law. Large and showy exhibits help to draw members to the event, where business matters are often sparse in discussion. Election of officers and a light pass at key issues usually suffice. Does that describe your intent? If not, why practice their dictates?

The legal needs of any association are not yours in the sales or training room! The nearest that corporations can come to association legal needs is the annual meeting of stockholders—once each year. If your needs go beyond that specific event, then you have no "event" needs that can detract from the main message!

So rebel. Refuse to be dissuaded from concentrating on your message by persons and organizations whose interests are not compatible with yours. You will come to understand the thrust of the original slogan given to the industry by the title of this writer's previous book, *Achieving Objectives in Meetings*. When you have your purpose firmly in mind, you will be in control! Finally!

The author owes special thanks to Paul Zeissler and Becky Michael-Zeissler, a suburban Chicago team of writer/editor and fine-and commercial-artist, who were willing to shoehorn a Word Perfect 5.1 author into a contemporary software's real world.

Preface to the First Edition

If your responsibility for planning and managing meetings is less than a full-time assignment, this book is for you. It offers both the general theory and the specific practices you need to master any meeting-related problems you might encounter, from stating objectives to preparing agendas, from selecting facilities and media to actual production of the event.

Our step-by-step methodology will guide you to the right decisions whether you are a beginner or relatively experienced. The full-time corporate or association meeting planner will find a totally integrated system of meeting coordination which can yield near-perfect control. Although the references and examples are expressed in sales management terms, the practices are universal...applicable to any meeting of any size for any purpose.

Management control achieved through analysis and understanding of every element of the program is this book's unique viewpoint. It optimizes group communications by requiring a complete, clear message to be presented, together with all required tools, through media appropriate to both the message and the selected participants. Only that structure yields a *valid* meeting which has a right to succeed.

Only the achievement of objectives (objectively measured) constitutes success. Achieving instructional objectives and larger corporate goals through properly managed meetings was the concept/methodology which our *Achieving Objectives in Meetings* contributed to the industry. That book was widely credited with introducing the first integrated system for management control in the trade. Those who disagreed claimed that system was prefigured in some elements of a 1967 ringbinder text published by Dartnell over a JJK Company signature. Both groups are right: We created the pertinent materials in that aggregate ringbinder.

So the concepts and methods of the present book were developed in exact parallel to professionalism in the meetings and conventions trade. Five distinct phases can be traced:

First: As meetings and conventions became major events during the 1950s, member groups of the American Society of Association Executives struggled to bring manageability to meeting planning. Each association and each hotel had its own methods, and nothing was standard. Good meetings happened at great expense in time, temper, and hazard. Trial and error was the development mode.

Because third-party meeting production assistance was not then available, two leading groups, the Linen Supply Association of America and the Steel Service Center Institute, asked their producer of banquet entertainment, United Attractions of Chicago, to take on the job—to assist their respective staff convention managers. So in 1960 the convention coordination consulting function was born; and we (of sales development, not theatre, background) became a co-originator of these methods. They were developed by common sense and serendipity and were proved in action over the next half dozen years with an increasing number of adherent clients. These included the American Dairy Association, the American Gas Association, the American Meat Institute, the National Coal Association, and the Railway Progress Institute.

The technical precision of those programs became the ASAE standard; and a corporate client, Mobil Oil Company, was winning petroleum industry awards for the quality of its dealer conventions.

United Attractions' own sales pitch became: "The convention week is 2 percent of the participating executive's year—can it pay its way?" Cost-effective thinking is now new; it's simply a neglected idea whose time has come.

In entertainment for conventions, United Attractions originated the "themed" evening (with band, supporting acts, and appropriate stage backdrop at a flat fee, plus the clients' choice of star headliner at cost)—popular with buyers everywhere today.

Second: In 1966, Dartnell took a survey of its corporate subscribers, intending to market a composite ringbinder of tips and recommended methods from the field. We interpreted the questionnaire responses and evaluated respondents' "best meeting" entries. Although some individual meetings were quite good, the methods reported were so fragmented and rudimentary as to be virtually unusable. So many respondents' questions pertained to planning and participation that we wrote in the summary sent to respondents, "Not all meeting leaders are achieving satisfactory results by their present methods." Books already on the market were discursive and tips oriented; they offered few techniques beyond cosmetic seating diagrams.

Therefore, we provided basic *technical* controls for the 1967 ring binder as previously developed for the associations. Cautions offered in the ringbinder include, "Meetings need goals if they are to have a direction, and management needs tools by which to measure the results if management wants to control," and "The key element of every meeting is communication." By the early 1970s that terminology had swept the meetings trade; but only slowly were the words being converted to deeds, despite the fact that our guides (Balance Sheet, Master Requirement Summary, Countdown and Hotel Liaison Checklists, and Audience Interest Evaluator) were so widely imitated as to become generic.

Third: In 1970, at the height of the McLuhan era's "The medium is the message," we argued that the message is the message—and the medium can kill it. The first article appeared in Crain's new-defunct *Advertising & Sales Promotion* magazine and became a regular column, "Cavalier on Meetings"; a switch to *Sales & Marketing Management* magazine produced a total of over five years of columns arguing for professionalism in planning. That demanded precision in planning and production, fiscal responsibility, adult education techniques, plus standards and ethics—much to the consternation of industry suppliers.

The controversy provoked was perfectly timed to welcome (*a*) the birth of the meeting planner movement (the first convention conceived and produced by a one-time co-worker at United Attractions) and (*b*) publication of the ASAE's Hotel/Association Facility Contract (1972) which the convention press somehow overlooked.

Fourth: In that time of radical change, *Achieving Objectives in Meetings* was published (1973). Its methodology was augmented by the originator's rationale—in fresh text and reprinted columns: a why-to-do-it for the corporate meeting planner. The few ringbinder guides were augmented with a dozen others, all correlated to yield content/message control and protection. It included the industry's first PERT diagram to tie all the mechanics together. Because the ASAE permitted us to reprint its new contract, all the mechanics for total technical control were finally located in one book: a system!

What was new to the field in *Achieving Objectives in Meetings* was an effort to create the *message* context which the meeting format supports. That included group and mass communication techniques, adult education, sales training and sales promotion, humanist psychology and human resources manage-ment, and the deficiencies of the meeting suppliers. The context was presented by reference in a span of only 19 pages. It was not a book for beginners, and the introductory material said so. Reviewers in marketing publications praised the context and asked for more; the convention industry press suggested that it meant nothing. Our viewpoint was validated with Meeting Planners International adopted the book as a membership-drive premium and Denver's Metropolitan State College (the nation's first college credit course in meeting planning) bought multiple copies.

The book's concept itself went generic: the assigned title of a tenth anniversary MPI convention address delivered by the author in December, 1982, was "Achieving Objectives in Meetings."

Fifth: The present book is a direct response to the needs of the legion of sales managers and other marketing executives at all levels who occasionally plan and execute major meetings. Fewer than 2,000 companies have full-time meeting coordinators, although over 11,000 companies employ more than 1,000 persons each, and 70,000 more employ at least 100 persons. All these managers and supervisors need dependable assistance, and we believe this book provides it.

The proved methodology of Part II has been totally reorganized so as to present detailed how-to guidance even a neophyte can feel comfortable with; it provides a refresher course for the more advanced. Then, to provide a solid grounding in the relevant social sciences, the context and theory of Part I was expanded...fivefold! You can now understand how and why each decision is made and implemented as you construct a valid meeting. Now you are prepared to take charge of every function and to manage every contributor and risk, whether you alone or a company committee or outsider consultants are involved.

Because this book deals in concepts understood rather than in rote performance, you can adapt every practical program element to your exact and changing needs, now and in the future. Because of the recent entry into this field of directories published by the Bowker Corporation and Gale Research Company, you are freed from the fads and disinformation common in advertiser-dominated magazine directories of facilities and other suppliers.

Given theoretical grounding, practical mechanisms, and unbiased information sources, you can *control.* You can help your meeting participants and yourself to grow...to achieve your meetings' objectives and your corporation's goals...with humanity...every time! That's the mark of the professional; and the meetings industry needs professional, even among its part-time practitioners.

When you have succeeded in your meeting, we will have succeeded in our book.

A number of other will have contributed to those successes: Louis Haugh, then editor of A&SP, and Robert Albert, senior VP/Editor of *S&MM*—both for their courage in publishing views often contrary to the then conventional wisdom; former client and long-time executive VP of MPI, Marion Kershner, for quick and effective support of *Achieving Objectives in Meetings*; health care editor-writer Elizabeth McNulty Fromm, who assisted with reorganization; corporate librarian and information specialist Barbara Morton who assembled the index, and the Denver contingent, our sister, Bernadine Cavalier Irish, who assisted with library research, as did MPI librarian Ruth Ann Zook, who added gentle criticisms. Finally, Joyce O'Brien, who—looking beyond the controversy toward the idea—published *Achieving Objectives in Meetings* under the imprint of her own meeting planning company.

All the industry's events of the past two decades and all the known and unknown supporters have helped construct *Sales Meetings That Work.* To all who have helped: my thanks. To all who are willing to work to seek better ways to help others: my admiration.

Richard Cavalier

Contents

Part I

Part II

Part I

1

Building your foundations

Meetings are a communications tool. That's hardly a surprising statement. What is surprising is that the statement need be made.

For an indefensible number of years, meetings have seemed to be about meetings—that is, about the fact and count of the bodies present, the hotel decor, the dog-and-pony shows, the food service, the most spectacular new presentation devices available, and, yes, the applause. All that is supplier oriented.

The meetings and conventions industry with its captive press has for decades overlooked the proper focus of a meeting—its message—and has concentrated instead on its profitable facet—the production of goods, events, and services.

Considering industry attitudes, it would seem that your value to the meetings industry equals your budget. When your budget improves, so will your relative importance...as a spender.

We commented once that a lack of understanding must be the shortcoming which has delivered editors catering to the meetings industry into the hands of their advertisers—that editors were not knowingly working against the best interests of the Meeting Manager. We have since found strong evidence to the contrary. Some editors are, in fact, helping to move the industry in directions favorable to suppliers and unfavorable to you.

What's at stake? Besides your own effectiveness and reputation, there's a $4 billion market for goods, services, and hotel-related space and subsistence for the corporate segment alone; nearly $12 billion overall. Commercial transportation benefits directly.

Everybody is selling something. And by coincidence, editors find those goods and services and decors highly photogenic. It is difficult to photograph a message or a thought process; and so, rather than discuss complex ideas, the editors defer to their information suppliers.

This means, among other things, that the problems caused by poor quality or nonperformance or bait-and-switch and/or up-charging never seem to get into print. In his book, an insurance company training executive avoided calling some hotels dishonest. He merely observed that if you maintain an open bar and are paying per opened bottle, you'll be amazed at how many bottles are opened in the last half hour. Dishonesty is a problem throughout the industry. When you buy goods and services for your meetings today, you still buy according to the ancient hazard of *caveat emptor*—buyer beware.

Meetings are unavoidable in business. It's impossible to count the in-house meetings occurring hourly, but approximately 600,000 meetings and conventions are held off-premises annually.

So major an industry should be expected to exhibit standards of performance. It should institute a strict ethical code and discipline wayward practitioners. None of that is true. The meetings and conventions industry desperately wants to be considered professional. Since standards are at the root of professionalism, and since the industry has for years discussed but resisted setting standards, it must be viewed as unprofessional. Because the industry has refused to adopt a code of ethics, it can be seen as countenancing unethical business conduct. Can it therefore be considered an ethical trade?

Such conditions and circumstances affect you in a number of ways. First, if you have a substantial budget, you'll be hard put to get fair value for the money spent. And if you have an insignificant budget (or none at all), you'll get no direct help and mostly fragmented (sometimes conflicting) advice from publications and books in the field. The majority of publications encourage you to work with the status quo no matter how detrimental to your aims. Furthermore, by keeping issues out of print or out of focus in superficial stories, the press keeps you from learning about your rights and options while permitting the industry to avoid reform.

This is not to say that nothing good appears in print. There are some extremely good things. The problem is that until you have enough experience not to need them, you also don't have enough perspective to choose the things of real value to you. It's a double bind from which many sales managers at all levels have never escaped.

It's a matter of numbers, in a sense. While meetings are a reality of daily corporate life, the major group meeting is a relatively rare event in any given organization. So it could take a dozen years to oversee the dozen or so major meetings required to develop a sense of proportion and confidence. Because of the numbers, you might never make it.

That's the reason for this book. You can reduce your time-and-practice period significantly if you master the market conditions and methods of the field. This book is designed to help you do that. Not all the potential functions inherent in a major convention will apply to all (or even any) of your meetings, whatever their size, because every meeting—even of the same individuals within the same organization—is different. You must come to rely *not* on easy recommendations and checklists and other cotton candy solutions from the press but rather on your own understanding of your organization, your objectives, and your people.

Contrary to the blandishments of the industry, most of your choices can be made objectively. Some, in fact, dictate their own terms and solutions. For those few instances in which a subjective judgment can or must be made, you must learn to rely on your own gut instincts: if you've learned the basics, your instinct will serve you well. The last thing you should do is surrender yourself to the latest fads, which will be different next year anyhow. You don't construct meetings by flipping coins.

You do construct meetings by understanding every element you put into them. And each element contributes to the aims of the message or to your participants' ability to act on it. Because your message and participants are different in some degree every time, your program elements will be different too.

Therefore, your task in laying foundations is to understand the requisites of a valid meeting construct, to understand your choices in fulfilling those requisites, and to comprehend the theories which help you to make your choices unerringly. At that point, you're ready to learn the practical applications; you will not be misled because you will know *why* you are making each decision.

This book is presented in two parts. Part I is the theoretical basis for the work—the why to do it. Part II is practical how to do it. The remaining chapters of Part I will discuss the most significant concepts on which you must develop perspective and even expertise in order to make the most of the methods presented in Part II.

Here's what you'll be getting an understanding of:

Validity of meetings construct. This includes the prerequisites to the successful meeting of today and tomorrow, whether large or small, unfunded or expensive; appropriateness of response; findings in research by the U.S. Army; video conferencing. Score with values, not money!

Professionalism and ethics. You can't be led astray if you know the route you should be traveling. Your ability to fend for yourself and defend your company—and message—interests from distortion by suppliers will help you to guarantee the success of your efforts during the *event* your meeting becomes.

Medium versus message. The industry has never recovered from the damage done by Marshall McLuhan's dictum, "The medium is the message." Until you can separate the two (and understand their relationship to the *psychological surround),* you might buy expensive toys and wonder why your people can't perform better after your meeting.

People. Remember them? They're the reason you've called the meeting. Be prepared to deal with the most important thing in their real world: themselves! Your interest in them and your concern for how the message will affect them as human beings will convert them from audience to participants, from potential antagonists to enthusiastic assistants, from adversaries to assets.

Educational films and other prepackaged meeting components. So many prepackaged meeting components are available that you'd think no manager could be without usable meeting material. Well, think again! You have about as great a chance of finding really good industrial films and program components as a really good book or a really good TV program. Calling some of them *mediocre* would be complimentary.

Creating demonstrations and other visualizations. Of course an individual possessed of the five human senses learns from multisensual stimuli. Yet the things we *see, hear, feel, taste, and smell*—often simultaneously—conflict with each other as they compete for our attention. Pairing any two or more synergistically calls for more than accident. Even though audio-visual learning is normal, the "visual" portion need not be film...or how would civilization have survived over the 5,000 years of recorded history preceding invention of the lens media?

Getting a perspective on yourself. Your own prejudices, perspectives, and insecurities just might be getting in the way of the skills which won you a management position. From the day you begin to plan until the day the event takes place, you are a conduit for ideas. Unless and until you appraise your own attitudes and abilities as coldly as you would those of any other person you might appoint to take your place in the planning, you can't be sure your contributions are mostly positive. When you recognize your limitations, you have taken the first step toward minimizing or eliminating them.

What does all that mean in context?

It means that the meeting—however large or small—can be one of the most powerful and most dependable tools at your disposal. It is persuasive, engrossing, flexible, fair (because of feedback), and relatively inexpensive per participant once you make cost-effectiveness evaluations.

Once you harness that power, you can make meetings work for you in not only the traditional (and sometimes boring) ways in which we routinely exchange data and ideas but also in ways that extend your reach with distributors and dealers and direct customers. All middlemen whom you're selling through, and many of the corporate accounts you're selling to, have the same communications problems as you. Sometimes they need the same or similar information as you're planning for your internal staff, and they'll gladly take assistance.

The format or combination of formats you structure for your meetings will be codetermined by two key constraints: (1) the focus and size of your meetings (whether or not you have a choice); and (2) your general purpose, as distinct from the statement of message.

Focus and size are so interrelated as to be almost inseparable. The terms *large* and *small* have general meaning only in the context of focus, because all other uses are subjective and relative to the planner. That is, a group of 100 persons could be extremely large for a small company and negligibly small for a giant firm. Obviously each supplier would have a different viewpoint on that same hundred, depending on capabilities. As the industry uses numbers, the terms *large* and *small* are absolutely meaningless. Worse, they're confusing.

Here's how focus changes with size:

Small meetings (or classroom or workshop): All emphasis is on individuals and their needs; the individual is present at every sequence because *all* participants are always present in the meeting room in which the workshop sequences occur. The number who can participate in this way is about 30 maximum. (In psychology, the task-oriented *small group* numbers five to nine—a different concept.)

Large meetings (or assemblies): Emphasis is on the group, on generalities, on the "big picture" presentation, with details and practice sessions reserved for local small meetings after returning home. Workshops are either impossible or avoided.

Combination meetings (or assembly/breakouts): Both the general assembly and the classroom-30 workshop are used, with emphasis switching from group to individual as needed. All breakout groups must get all (but not necessarily identical) needed information, tools, and practice there and then.

Clearly, the structures you select will depend on whether you need workshops and whether your entire group can be accommodated in that workshop room.

The structure affects the speakers, too. Specifically, the expertise of the speaker is at issue. Whereas a speaker at an assembly meeting can present a written address on a topic on which he or she is not an authority, the small group would soon unmask the person. The authority who addresses the small group *must* be an expert—at least in relation to the knowledge level of the participants. Any "authority" who disproves his or her expertise will cause the participants both to turn off and to resent the attempted *con job.* That could have long-term negative effects for you and the company. Never risk your credibility. If no authority is available, say so; then explain how you (or your guest speaker) will compensate. If you'll all be learning together, say so. The participants will cooperate.

Logically, the workshop sequences presented in the small or combination or assembly meetings could be essentially the same. The crucial element is the *completeness* of the program scheduled. Any element can be scheduled for any location, obviously, but if it is needed for a valid construct, it must be scheduled. The single most common cause of the failure of large meetings is *incompleteness*—the failure to provide the tools the individual needs along with the practice to use them properly.

The problem of incompleteness is compounded in the normal circumstances of association and other organization meetings at which attendance and participation are voluntary. Most association delegates are top management of the member companies. As such, they would not themselves be overseeing the association's recommended program even if they understood it in every detail (which is generally impossible with one verbal presentation) and even if they wish to implement that program. The net result is that a lot of intelligent association-developed ideas get lost in the shuffle between assembly room and home office.

A *complete* program in that context would require a self-contained take-home package which the delegate could hand to the proper subordinate for implementation.

The association problem might not affect you directly today, but corporations are increasingly expecting their sales executives at all levels to become active in related associations and civic groups. Eventually you will help develop a program in that context.

So much for the theory of focus and size as co-determining constraints on format. We'll take up the practical control mechanisms for all types and sizes of meetings in Part II.

A second key constraint that co-determines your meeting format is your overall purpose. It's likely that marketing executives and their functions generate or sponsor more meetings than any other company department or function. We're treating sales and advertising as dimensions of marketing whether or not your own organizational chart reads that way. Much training is conducted there, too.

And there's the rub. Even though the direct sales department deals in hard figures of product or service units and specific gross sales volume, the indirect sellers, advertising and public relations, are not given to clean figures. Because the advertising and public relations managers can almost never pinpoint the exact result obtained from a particular effort or campaign, top management has learned not to expect too much from the imprecise communication arts.

Meetings have been lumped with the imprecise. That's a mistake. As a direct result of asking too little on a cost-effective basis, management gets far too little back from its meetings expenditures most of the time. Many trainers have *also* failed to measure results. Let's look at two of the most common reasons for calling unnecessary meetings:

First, spread the blame for impending disaster. If Mr. Slick can get a committee together to discuss the end of the world and if the committee (luckily) agrees on nothing, then Mr. Slick is blameless when disaster strikes. In defense, cheat! Refuse to take part once the stratagem is identified. Walk out, or don't attend in the first place. And make a written memo of your nonparticipation.

Second, supervise and develop salespeople. This is the task allegedly fulfilled by those horrendous Friday afternoon bull sessions that everyone pretends are tolerable business technique. Switching them to Monday mornings simply puts the downer on the workweek instead of on the weekend. In defense, cheat! Make your own meetings worthwhile.

Legitimate purposes for calling a meeting will fall into one (occasionally two) of the three categories below:

1. Problem identification: pinning down specifics after noticing a pattern of things that are not quite right.

2. Problem solving: once the problem is clearly identified, to define the solution and then develop a workable solution.
3. Solution delivering: with the problem and its solution known, to provide how-to instruction to the multitude.

Notice that the first two categories are information-seeking formats and the third an information-delivering format. On that distinction hinges the choice of establishing a "conference" format, which is advanced by and through the exchange of ideas as a process, or a training/workshop format, in which the direction and end product are known in advance.

Every meeting you ever conduct can be categorized in this way, and your thinking will be shaped by the requirements of the category or format. Guides to this thought process are provided in Part II.

You will find that information-seeking formats are used most often with peers, and information-delivering formats with subordinates, especially at the lower echelons. Executive policy conferences and strategy sessions only rarely depart from conference format—what each person thinks about information presented helps shape the final conclusions. Memos, phone calls, and edicts would not suffice in the creative process which underlies a true conference. That creative exchange is not to be confused with ordinary feedback or other after-the-fact opinions.

Brainstorming sessions, no matter at which level of the hierarchy, are intended to be solution-developing meetings; because judgment is suspended as a main rule of the game, however, brainstorming is not a complete problem-solving process. Later evaluations and decisions are needed before a real solution can be delivered via later meetings.

Here are some of the real-world purposes for which you call meetings. Notice how quickly you can now categorize them.

Field coaching. For the newly hired person or the one in a sales slump, this is an excellent supervisory technique. Even when you guide the person so as to use his or her own problem-solving power (called Socratic Direction), you are working from a position of superior information and probably even with a workable solution already in mind. This procedure is best in a one-on-one meeting. It's not a planned group communications technique and will not be discussed further as a format.

Field supervision and training. This is almost exclusively solution delivering, especially when headquarters sends outlines or packages. Field market surveys are the notable exception in information-seeking attempts.

Regional conference for managers. This is probably a combination of all three types, with one likely to predominate in one session and another in the next session. The "What can we do about __________?" type of meeting sounds like solution seeking, but it usually reflects a lack of definition of the root problem. Inadequately defined problems lead to efforts wasted on shallow, ineffective "solutions."

Regional meetings for salespersons. Because of diversity and size, these are almost exclusively solution delivering. Breakout groups can seek inputs both in conference format and by questionnaire; but by the time the meeting is held, its content has been determined.

Distributor/dealer meetings. Because the sponsor-customer expects you to have a good reason for calling his people together, this is usually a solution-delivering meeting. Don't neglect the opportunity to carry away valuable market information.

Distributor/dealer training. This is solution delivering. You have the goods in a package and are really conducting a practice session on the intended new direction using new tools.

Public interest meetings. Anyone involved in a business or other organization involved in a public issue or political dispute could be called upon to talk to the public. Whether you use an information gathering or an information-delivering technique (or both) depends on whether and how well the issues are already formulated by the time you enter. Generally, you follow the lead your public relations department sets. Good luck!

New product presentations. At this point, if you don't know what you should be telling them, you're really in trouble.

Incentive travel awards. Since the company or employee must pay tax on the value of the trip, there is no legal purpose for any meeting. The company is chiseling if it tries to get much work out of individuals who have already worked hard to win the trip.

Motivational trip/meetings. In this situation, if a genuine training or other bona fide meeting is held in a highly desirable location (major city or resort; domestic only, now) and if the participants have no choice regarding their attendance, the entire trip is tax deductible for the company. Work them hard! The glamour of the trip is worth the extra effort. Spouses might attend at their own expense, or the employee might win the spouse's trip as an adjunct incentive (taxable). If the basic budget is that of the annual or other scheduled sales/training meeting, then the company gets fantastic results in attitude and/or skill changes at extremely small increments in expenditures. (IRS restrictions are discussed in Chapter 19.)

Annual/central sales meeting. If this involves secrecy of topic or scarcity of product models as a prime factor, you might have no choice; but be aware that the large central meeting feeds on its own size, requiring expenditures substantially larger than several regional meetings would (details in Part II). If your main reason for holding it is tradition, consider canceling. While top managers always hope to get good ideas from the field, the group emphasis really requires that the formats be essentially solution delivering-even for breakouts.

Obviously, with solution-delivering demands appearing so often, a competent manager—you—must be prepared for each meeting. Old hands will tell you that program preparation requires one week's coordination time for each hour of program; for speaker rehearsals, about triple the actual speaking time.

Is there a shortcut? No.

Is it worthwhile? Yes!

Meticulous preparation of the elements demanded by a valid meeting construct will guarantee you the success of your program! During nearly four past decades as a professional developer/ writer/coordinator of corporate and association programs, we have never seen one of our programs fail! This is not to say that no hitches ever occurred—those are almost unavoidable. But no client has ever lost a message because of a mishap.

That sweeping statement covers everything from training for small groups to assembly sessions for crowds of 6,000; for simple manager-presented sessions with demonstrations and flip charts to multimedia presentations and closed-circuit television sequences from remote locations; from speaker-augmented outlines to completely self-contained packages, including audiovisuals and workbooks. Plus stagecraft for business purposes and stagecraft for entertainment.

We learned the techniques contained in this book by a fortuitous combination of common sense and serendipity. As to serendipity, we were confronted with common situations needing methodology while evolving the convention coordination function back in 1960. Our methods now are among standard practices. As to common sense, at times when we felt we had the luxury of trial and error, errors didn't occur if we had the common sense to approach the communications problem from the participants' viewpoint. Over these many years, we have distilled our experiences into the principles and methods presented here. Everything has been tested countless times, and everything works!

Moreover, we teach and encourage you to think your way through every meeting rather than use somebody else's notes and checklists. Only when you understand every element of your meeting and why it's actually there can you control the meeting and deal with any mishaps.

It's not that checklists are bad. They are extremely good for extremely narrow applications: namely, where exact sequence and time allowed for performance are critical. Pilots need checklists to prepare for takeoff in complex aircraft. Everything must be done in exactly the correct sequence every time within seconds; there's no time to think, no margin for error, no room for personal opinion.

Surely, though, that does not describe a meeting. It might describe a multimedia sequence within the meeting, and the operator uses a checklist he himself prepared for this presentation.

By preventing you from thinking through every element of your meeting, the borrowed checklist can actually damage your meeting, cheating you of both active, creative analysis and intellectual (rather than paper) control. Checklists can be lost; what's in your head won't be!

Can't you forget something? Sure, it can happen. But are you the only one who's aware? No backup? And can't you also forget to check the checklist? Things are *happening* as the event progresses: your intellectual computer must process data as it appears. There's more to controlling a meeting than reading your checklist!

If someone offers you all necessary checklists, watch out! You're about to buy some cotton candy, and no matter how big a mouthful you take, there's nothing to clamp your teeth on.

So go the difficult route: think. Think about all the elements of validity of construct. Think about your needs, your objectives, your participants and their needs and attitudes, your purposes, and your means of measuring the success you expect to enjoy. Think about the overall company goals that might require group action through meeting(s).

Then you'll be ready to start putting your meeting on paper as an explicit message. No matter what your suppliers tell you, you will make few arbitrary decisions. Your message will dictate most of them, and your gut feeling for your people will dictate the rest.

When you are prepared to assess every offer of goods or services in terms of what can be done to serve your message and your objectives, you are prepared to *manage* your meeting, to take charge, to protect your objectives from all self-interested outsiders. If you intend to plan and execute a productive meeting, nothing matters but the message, your participants, and their achievement of the measurable objectives you set.

Keep all these interrelated concepts in mind as you read the balance of Part I. You'll be surprised at how fast a lot of once confusing situations become clear.

And you'll be surprised at the insights you will develop on results—good and poor—of your past meetings. That new perspective represents growth. It will contribute directly to your ability to plan valid, more useful meetings.

When a meeting assignment overtakes you, don't look for easy answers. There aren't any. Instead, build your understanding. Comprehension of underlying principles is the bedrock in which valid, productive meetings are anchored. On the foundations of understanding you can build the simplest or most complex structures any message can demand. You'll build them knowledgeably and confidently because your footings are solid!

2

Validity of construct

The surrender of logic to technology has been disastrous in the group communications field of meetings and conventions. Major companies now commit thousands of hours and millions of dollars to support hazy objectives and unproved but glittering methods in a mindless celebration of mankind's gregarious nature. They're called meetings; but by squandering precious time and limited resources in poorly directed talkfests, they become a mouth trap, in which small companies are caught with the large.

The emphasis in meetings belongs on people, not technology. Meeting planning is complex because people are complex; and the intricacies of machines are irrelevant!

Once you shift viewpoint from machines to people, you can develop a program correctly and completely. Of course the precise effect of any given meeting cannot be calculated in advance, but that's no reason to discredit either the meetings or the cost-effectiveness calculations that prove their worth.

The many immeasurable effects of advertising and public relations have taught us to live with uncertainty with respect to the achievement of goals. Yet those channels are largely one of external communications, and little outside the organization is considered controllable even in theory. Uncertainty simply doesn't apply to meetings.

Meetings are internal. You can control all their essential details, even when outsiders participate. Meetings can be made far more cost effective once managers at all levels begin to account for all costs and benefits routinely.

All fuzzy thinking has to stop. Business has been clamoring for more effective meetings ever since the 50s, when meetings became big business. However, any meeting can be more effective than those preceding it while still remaining totally inadequate. More effective meetings is a meaningless concept. That phrase—and the lackadaisical attitudes which support it—need to be abandoned.

Each meeting must stand alone and achieve all its objectives. That's the sole criterion of success.

You'll hear talk about "perfection of little details" too. That's more cotton candy from the trade. It's not easy to create a meeting perfect in every detail; more to the point, perfection is not necessary even if it were attainable. Even the best meeting probably can be improved if it were repeated. Professional trainers who repeat some training sequences numerous times usually adjust and fine tune after each and every program. That does not mean the first program was poor; it does mean that we grow a little with every meeting we create.

Perfection aside, it is relatively easy to design a meeting which will accomplish stipulated things predictably, because results proceed in common-sense, causal relationships.

The real culprit of failed meetings is disorganization. Few people who call for meetings have first determined *(a)* what they want to accomplish, *(b)* through whom, and *(c)* by which methods. In short, management is often unprepared to direct or lead in the meeting room. Yet the blame for disappointments is pushed onto the quite blameless participants. That's both unfair and dishonest: a failed meeting is a management failure!

A properly constructed meeting must provide for the message, the audience, and the implementation techniques and tools, all in their proper relationship. Such a meeting can be said to be valid in its structure.

The validity of the meeting being planned is crucial. In logic or argumentation, the validity of a syllogism (consisting of major premise, minor premise, and conclusion) can be demonstrated visually by use of a Venn Diagram (see illustration). Those arguing may color in the diagrammatic "territory" claimed by all three elements of the syllogism. Only the least amount of territory claimed by each proposition can be colored in—that is, all, most, or some of the corresponding circle. Only the all premises enter the tri-sect proof area.

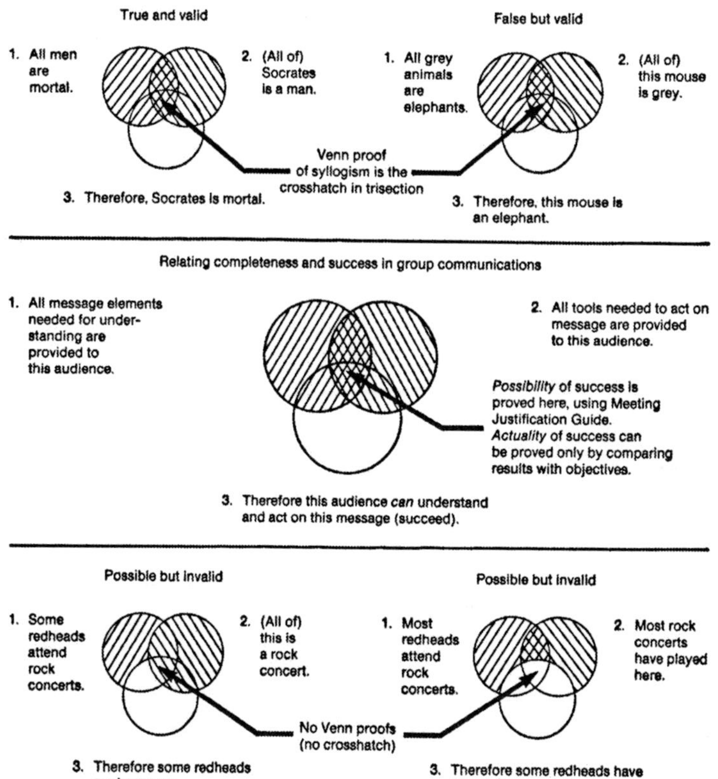

Rules of proof are strict. Only if both premises are all premises can an all conclusion be drawn; and no valid *some* conclusion can be drawn from two *some* premises. Possibility, likelihood, and truth of the propositions are concepts different from validity. A Venn proof of validity is a visual certification of the soundness of the logic presented.

Now, substituting our meeting elements of message, participants, and tools for the Venn elements of syllogism, we can see that *allness* or completeness is just as important to the meeting as to the logical argument. In our analogy, an incomplete or half-truth message is a *some* premise, as is an incomplete complement of required tools. As in a Venn Diagram, you cannot draw any valid conclusions (about meeting success) predicated on inadequate components. What you're really doing is gambling, and you have only a gambler's odds of success.

Clearly, unless we provide all the requirements of a comprehensive, lucid message delivered to a proper and prepared audience by means of the relevant techniques and necessary tools, we cannot logically expect to achieve objectives. Nor can we claim credit if an invalid meeting by accident accomplishes something of value.

In an era when capital conservation is an article of corporate religion and capital expenditure, a cardinal sin, the invalid meeting is an anachronism—a real goof! Furthermore, no organization's management can afford the discredit of failed meetings, even if money didn't matter. Meeting participants are judging management too.

Management can fail in any number of ways: by setting out an incomplete or unfair assignment or unlikely task before an unprepared, incapable, wrongly selected, or hostile audience, or by using inadequate tools or incorrect or inappropriate media, including those so impressive that they dominate and detract from the message.

Invalid meeting structures—incipient failures—should not be tolerated. They need not be tolerated because the elements of a valid meeting are programmable with reasonable effort. No, valid meetings are not *easy* to construct. You have to think! But when the three main elements are carefully thought out, the meeting structure will perform predictably and dependably: the meeting will accomplish the chosen ends. The achievement of objectives—and only that—is the measure of success!

What about applause?

We still hear about the supposed importance of applause in the meeting room. Applause proves nothing about the achievement of objectives. Applause is one among many methods of *response;* it is the best and entire response expected of the audience being entertained. Entertainment is the provision of present-moment satisfactions. By contrast, adult education requires the creation of present-moment dissatisfaction to promote change. Thoughtful silence could be the highest accolade!

Clearly, applause is no substitute for an appropriate, measurable response. And appropriate response is the basic measure of understanding in communication. Conversely, inappropriate response is a key signal of a problem.

By this process we return to simple educational principles: appropriate response will verify the student's comprehension, and an inappropriate response will call for corrective action. For that reason, we need to provide for *individual* reactions, for practice, and for testing. At some point during and/or following every meeting, you must provide for every educationally stipulated element of complete programming.

Besides being an imprecise measure, applause can be quite destructive to management's goals. It can seduce participants into believing they have accomplished something, only to expose them to failure and criticism later when they cannot fulfill new assignments.

Research in the social sciences long ago demonstrated that most employees are conscientious and want to do a good job; that they want a feeling of accomplishment; and that they perform at their best unless and until management destroys their initiative with poor policies and poor supervision. We will explore these ideas in another chapter.

From the common-sense standpoint, it's obvious that the fact of any meeting conveys a sense of expectation. You know before You go into any meeting that someone wants something from you, don't you? That produces anxiety in most people. And the fact that the participant is a part of a crowd does not necessarily reduce that person's anxieties. It could heighten them.

So if the meeting participant cannot understand what is expected of him (or does know what is expected but is not given the tools to do the job), then that person becomes frustrated, feels inadequate, and becomes resentful. That's why so many employees hate meetings.

Because it is possible to *enjoy* a presentation without *learning* from it, there's been controversy about the role of the maximedia format in meeting rooms. Let's define *maxi* as anything significantly in excess of that required to support the message. It does not refer only to multimedia but also to overly elaborate single-medium formats, too. *Excess* is the key because that in itself becomes a focal point and detracts from the message by splitting attention. We'll take these ideas up again in another chapter.

Historically, business and associations felt that the use of visual media was a cost difficult to justify. In the early 60s we convention coordinators had to bully clients into buying A/V support for key addresses. Although corporations had for years used live skits in new-product presentations, associations rarely used actors before 1960. And the first multimedia sequences (staff, actors, music, and visuals used simultaneously) were staged in 1960, by two of our client associations.

Obviously, there's nothing new on the meetings scene apart from video conferencing, newly affordable. The maximedia push is simply selling pressure supported and maintained by the industry press because spectaculars please advertisers and are photogenic.

The overemphasis on media occurred because of the coincidence of two events of the mid-60s: the New York

World's Fair and the publication of Marshall McLuhan's *Understanding Media,* both in 1964.

Eastman Kodak's hemispheric screen was in truth spectacular. Kodak's message was, "Ain't film grand?" and the fair audience agreed. But Kodak's message is not your message! Moreover, only the confusion of message (content) with medium (format) can support McLuhan's tautology. We'll return to that concept.

Proponents of maximedia claim that the excitement of the extravaganza enhances the meeting. That's conceivable only if outright entertainment is conceivably good for that program, as it was at the world's fair. But that's unlikely, because your audience is selected and your purposes are narrow. The value of maximedia in the meeting room has never been proved, but the disadvantages of attention splitting have been proved. We'll take up these ideas in a later chapter too.

Moreover, the idea of preparing written materials in such a way as to heighten the interpersonal communication in groups was taken up by Charles W. Dawe and Edward A. Dornan in *One to One: Resources for Conference-Centered Writing.* You might not need the full course that they've designed, but you might get the idea.

In 1970, at the height of the Marshall McLuhan era, we argued in print the fallacy of his dictum, "The medium is the message." In the lone-voice article which became a five-year column, we argued that not only is the medium not the message, but the medium can become the problem. And we called for a turn to adult education principles, as outlined therein.

That viewpoint was largely without support until in 1973, when portions of a 1971 study by the U.S. Army began to appear in print. Entitled "Comparison of Pictorial Techniques for Guiding Performance During Training, it was conducted by the Human Resources Research Organization (called HumRRO), of Alexandria, Virginia. To summarize more than 30 pages of text and data in a few lines is always dangerous, but we make a fair approximation of that and subsequent studies, in the view of

Joseph H. Kanner, Ph.D., of the Army Training and Development Institute at Fort Monroe, Virginia, with this:

> Complexity and expense of the medium have less bearing on learning results than does the skill with which the medium is used. A workbook which effectively employs the principles of reinforcement, strategic practice, visuals, and text which relate to each other can equal or outperform computers, films, videodiscs, or any other technology which does not employ these principles.

Such a finding is anathema to the maximedia crowd. And while the publications directed to trainers took up the study, the many publications of the meetings and conventions field ignored it.

Such clear abuses of reader confidence have led to charges against the press of selling out readers to advertisers. In this climate, half-truths, incompetence, and deceptive practices flourish. And for this reason, standards and ethics will be the prime issue of the 80s...or, rather, should have been. Looking back, we see that the problem of industry ethics was "solved" by industry publications' silence rather than by action.

As technology, including video conferencing, moves meeting structure even further outside the competence of many suppliers, some will fail and others will take advantage of uncertain customers to stay afloat. Because you will often be buying tangible components to support an intangible purpose, legal recourse is difficult unless the purpose and desired effect are stated in the contract.

It's a lot easier to be prepared before buying, because all recovery actions presuppose a failure. How many failures can your position tolerate? Changes will come ever faster, and the pressure to accept change *for the sake of change* will overwhelm the insecure meeting planner who can't differentiate between message and medium.

Changes will probably develop on a double track. First, the meetings industry will inevitably turn toward educational formats to optimize results; relatively small, interactive formats will predominate by count. That's within today's capabilities for all managers. Second, the assembly meetings of tomorrow will take increasingly to the air via video conferencing to save travel time and much money. Live action will be sacrificed to the extended reach and economics of the television medium. And only the problem of security of the broadcast signal is holding back this change.

We're talking about radical change. Such change requires a powerful catalyst. We have it now in video conferencing. For the first time companies are seriously questioning the *need* to travel.

Because of the dependability of satellite transmission and the virtually uninterruptible (short of tower destruction) nature of land-based micro-relay systems, the message instead of the people can be traveled. This can be done for any assembly-type meeting in which secrecy of message is not an overriding concern.

Because the technique is still new, receiver installations are still relatively few and somewhat expensive. Cost per participant will determine usage for a number of years; and that cost will tend to be lowest when the on-line stations are relatively few—as with regional meetings. Later, each city (or even each office) will be reached easily and economically. Computers can provide basics now; and even desktop videos and transmitted pictures and voice are available. Justify your travel!

Because of the acceptability of electronic linkage in human communications (even for meetings, via telephone-conferencing), videoconferencing will begin to affect program formats even when it is not used. That will happen because the medium lends itself admirably to inclusion of the best educational formats.

In order to accomplish all the business of the meeting within the reserved transmission/broadcast period, Meeting Managers will put new emphasis on structure and agenda. Because microwave transmission can be intercepted, sensitive material will be distributed in separate premeetings packages and used for breakout sessions. Because air time is costly, the workshop sequences and measures of performance will be conducted off the air in the various locales using self-contained postmeeting packages.

What will be broadcast is exactly that material which even today justifies the justifies the assembly meeting: the one-way presentation of identical information simultaneously to all interested parties.

By the end of the 80s, meetings will have become both more structured initially and more flexible intrinsically; more expensive overall and much cheaper per person; more confined in miles and virtually unbounded in electronic locale. The changes of the next half dozen years will be frustrating and exhilarating and demanding and rewarding—in combinations and degrees never before experienced. And they will affect you and your meetings.

The more predictable effects of video conferencing on meeting formats, budgets, locales, and results are staggering. Because of remote linkage, fewer people will travel shorter distances and stay fewer nights in hotels, whose existing meeting rooms will be less valuable without video conferencing equipment. Halls and theatres equipped now for satellite reception of sports events become new contenders as meeting sites.

If a facility does not have the necessary up-and-down *linkage* permanently installed, it can be installed temporarily. However, the availability of earth satellite trucks of AT&T and similar equipment owned by networks, including public television, or sold by manufacturers,means that if you must bring in temporary equipment you can have it anywhere—including your own office. The hotel dominance of meeting sites is ending.

There's an additional side effect. When staged maximedia extravaganzas are converted to video format and video projection screen size, their live quality will be lost and their questionable entertainment value will come sharply into focus. So the dog-and-pony show will finally be buried. It died in value long ago.

In place of live sequences will come pre-taped sequences designed along educationally valid lines. Some—but fewer—of those sequences will use actors. Tape's flexibility and error-erase capability will permit staff experts to take bigger parts in the presentations. That will also eliminate the professor hired to mouth a script in the hopes of converting it to an "educational" format.

All that is predictable. But the unpredictable results will be at least as fascinating and perhaps revolutionary. What will happen to interpersonal relationships when people begin addressing each other intelligently? What will happen to productivity when management learns to state its objectives clearly and in terms the labor force can relate to its own interests and welfare? What will happen when incompetent leadership is unmasked?

One sure answer among many: a revolution in the direction of the information flow. More information affecting corporate direction will originate at the bottom, and only management's jealously of its historical prerogative of arbitrary decision making is delaying the change. It will be a revolution which releases human potentials on a broad scale for the first time ever!

Obviously, it's time to grow again. Time to grow deeper and more sophisticated about the human element. However much supply-side economists might want to treat labor as a raw material or commodity, people will remain people. They will perform in proportion to their commitment to a direction and to a management they perceive as committed to them. To treat people other than as individuals performing out of personal motives is to short-circuit the communications process and short-change earnings.

Increasingly, people are being viewed as the prime asset of a viable organization. Increasingly, meetings are being viewed as an opportunity to provide learning experiences, because business people have already recognized that education will be the source of the next big jump in productivity.

The need to educate employees in the future is immense. We are accustomed to the displacement of skills in the factory as new capital equipment is introduced, but now electronic information gathering and processing are doing the same in the office. In a time when even the "skilled" secretary can become the "inadequate" word processor operator with the purchase of a minor machine, the numbers of valued employees requiring retraining become awesome. The count will surpass those huge numbers of unskilled and under-privileged for whom federal programs were designed in the 60s and 70s.

With huge numbers of people needing retraining, some conclusions are incontrovertible. First, there are not enough teachers or experts in any given topic to reeducate vast numbers of individuals on a one-to-one basis. Group communications is the only answer: meetings and training groups. Next, if the meeting room is to do its share to reeducate, then the meetings field must mature. If the supplier must become ethical and professional, so must the organization and its meetings managers become more competent.

Marginal suppliers have been able to prosper in the past because executives have for too long paid lip service to training and Meeting Managers. Both groups have historically been populated by persons just passing through those jobs on the management climb. They turned to the trade literature of the time, which was filled with the current events of the time. So fads swept the meeting rooms of the land. Wave after wave of fads, some innocuous, some harmful. All of them were wasteful of resources and potential. While fads flare and fade, the damage done to your individual programs can be total and long lasting.

Competent top management will soon be delegating power to the meetings and training managers in the same proportion as responsibility. Hierarchical rank and personal income will begin to define a career position. New personnel might need extensive formal training so as to avoid low-level experimentation at the market fad level. That opens a new career opportunity for training consultants.

Efficient management will require that the group communications functions be budgeted at a level which can guarantee that the valid construct of the meeting will be honored every time so the potential of the meetings format and the participants can be fully realized every time.

When meetings are made accountable, the return on investment will be visible. The accountability of meetings is an idea whose time has come. And the concept of *validity of construct* will help you to deliver in the meeting room as elsewhere on the job! Now!

Isn't it amazing how complex the "simple" meeting has become?

3

Fantasy, reality, and ethics

The meetings and conventions industry is beset by a greater degree of supplier control than any industry I know. Suppliers have been successful in discouraging magazines in the field from putting knowledgeable people on their staffs, so articles continue to be glib while missing the point.

The point is that when all the hoopla the magazines celebrate is ended, the reader has no understanding of what *was* accomplished versus what *might have been* accomplished, to say nothing of understanding what was *accomplished at the given price* versus the *value,* if any, of what was accomplished. Nor does the reader have an inkling of the ease or difficulty of the Meeting Manager's obtaining the (photographed) assistance versus the wisdom of the advice received or even his need for such assistance at all.

The industry doesn't talk about these things for several reasons. First, the industry wants to pretend that everything suppliers offer has importance and value to somebody, even if only to Pollyanna. Second, the industry refuses to notice that some of its suppliers are incompetent and even dishonest, even though the patterns of abuse abound. Because kickbacks are the norm, recommendations and advice are suspect until proved otherwise. Third, to suggest that some things are better than others is to suggest that an objective standard exists, and standards have been a threat against which the entire industry has closed ranks.

Do you like horror stories? Let me tell you a few:

If the industry were unaware of the existence of educational principles or were unaware that deceptive and illegal practices flourish, the industry could be considered simply nonprofessional. However, advertisers eschew forthright reporting and demand and get distorted press coverage of key issues. Such circumstances argue for the labels of "unprofessional" and even "unethical."

Do the facts support such charges? Well, examine them. A few are simple, and a few are quite involved.

We have already mentioned an insurance industry meetings manager who warns against the needless opening of bottles of liquor at parties being billed by the "bottles opened" method rather than by the drink ticket. That's simple dishonesty and quite widespread.

One major cosmetics company reports a doubleheader in the under-the-table business arena. Not only did its airline rebate the travel agent's commission to the cosmetics firm (illegal under CAB regulations), but competing hotels offered as much as $25,000 to the meeting planner personally to buy the corporate business. He was not surprised—he'd heard similar offers often. Hotels continue to make the offers because some corporate meeting planners are on the take. It costs the hotel nothing: it's added to the final charges!

Unfavorable—and therefore unwelcome—information usually doesn't see print in the meetings and conventions industry.

In 1958, Dr. Joseph Kanner, then working at the Pentagon, completed two studies which "found no significant differences in learning when comparing color versus black/white television." The Pentagon was pelted with complaint letters from television set manufacturers, who evidently felt the public had no right to know. Yet Dr. Kanner spoke on the subject and coauthored an article, "Television in Army Training: Color versus Black/White" *(Audiovisual Communication Review,* vol. 8, no. 6 [November/ December, 1960]).

Admittedly, television was not a significant production factor in the convention industry in the early 60s. However, because the images presented to the eye by TV and film are virtually identical, the findings apply equally to film formats. Yet that information has never appeared in the convention trade press, which continues to lionize maximedia. The maximedia blitz is all color and movement and gets its effect by overwhelming the senses—the antithesis of educational technique.

And, as previously mentioned, the meetings trade press ignored the 1971 HumRRO study, although the training press picked it up. Meetings industry magazines plead that the material is not germane to their readers' interests. One publisher printed excerpts in its training magazine but not in its sister meetings magazine, although its relevance to both is salient.

That dichotomizing of the industry has been a boon to suppliers. Although you conduct every meeting in the hope your participants will learn something and change their attitudes and/or habits (or, occasionally, reinforce existing modes), the meetings and conventions industry pretends you have no need or dependency on them for learning theory and learning-aids analyses.

In a sense that's a defensive stand: their staffs have little actual experience in constructing meetings, and most have no background whatsoever in the social sciences, including education. They know only what they see, and what they see best is spectaculars, which are easy to photograph and report.

Incompetence and advertiser interests go hand-in-glove in the meetings trade press. Would advertisers support competent and honest reporting?

When *Business Week* launched its very first "Meetings & Conferences" special advertising section in March 1977, it featured such direct "consumerist" aids as 11 essentials for a complete meeting plan, facility evaluation tips (including "bargain hard"), and commentary on the then-new Tax Reform Act of 1976, which limited meeting expense write-offs. *Business*

Week reported that the IRS had established limits because of abuse by vacationers. At the time, some foreign travel promoters bragged that they provided false agendas that groups could submit directly to the IRS to evade applicable taxes. If you wish to know what amounts of *per diem* that the US government considers fair in cities worldwide during the millennium's first year, you might want to check the Internet at http://www.state.gov/www/perdiems/index.html.

Not only did the meetings/training/conventions industries not flock to the support of *Business Week's* first attempt, but the second attempt a year later was shot down, too. *Business Week* has abandoned the general-information format even though its mailing list is so prized that trade interests still buy special advertising supplements promoting destinations. Unfortunately, that magazine had similar negative experience with its special advertising issues on video conferencing, which just happens to bypass the hotels and travel firms whose ads support the magazines in the narrow field. That can be seen as passive resistance. Is there evidence of active cooperation between advertisers and publications?

Consider the important trade issue of *breakage*—the advance guarantee by the meeting planner to the hotel of the minimum number of meals which will be paid for, whether or not served. That problem affects corporations less than associations, since attendance is voluntary at the latter; but weekend and long holiday weekend dates affect menu planning for both equally.

Meal function guarantees have traditionally been given about 24 hours before the function. In recent years, hotels have argued for the extension of that time to 48 hours as a rule. Buyers have resisted because breakage represents unnecessary expense to them; it represents extra profit to the hotels, which would be delighted with 72 hours' advance notice.

Now the issue: One meeting industry publication commissioned an article on meal guarantee policy. We found that respected major hotels across the nation still offer the traditional 24-hour advance period, extending it only for long weekends or unusually complex/expensive banquet menus. Those hotels which "preferred" the 48-hour advance indicated in every instance that they would compromise for repeat guests and in cases of legitimate problems. Not a single hotel would admit to a standard 72-hour advance policy, as the magazine implied was becoming "standard."

When these facts and quotes were presented to the editor by phone, he encouraged the writing of the article. When completed, the article was killed on the pretext that there was "no interest" in the topic. Not only did the article not appear in that publication, but the same publication actually printed a contrary story helpful to its advertisers, falsely labeling the 48-hour advance period the "industry standard."

Some months later, the membership newsletter of one of the largest associations of meeting planners verified and published our 24-hour findings. However, the newsletter did not relate the circumstances to members because of officers' fears that any embarrassment to the editor could affect the free publicity that the association felt it needed. In short, the association has participated in selling out its own membership to a sold-out press. That association has since changed its name, but its initials remain the same. If we'd done that, we'd change our name, too.

Two court cases of the mid-70s offer insights, too. Kickbacks to staff buyers at American Airlines were successfully prosecuted by the airline, which hoped to end a lamentable industry tradition. About the same time, 19 international airlines pleaded no contest in a case brought in Brooklyn Federal Court by a U.S. attorney, who noted that their conduct "has occurred in violation of criminal law" forbidding rebates and kickbacks. Deregulation was one government weapon against a practice so widespread as to be nearly impossible to police and harmful to customers paying full rates.

Although deregulation has ended the practice of kickbacks (in favor of open horse trading), no court directive can change the mental climate in which kickbacks flourish. *Caveat emptor!*

Perhaps the most serious side effect of the rebate problem is the growing practice of permitting third-party coordinators of programs to fund their service by taking "commissions" from suppliers. There are many objectionable features. First, since you will pay for the service in any case, it's best to pay up front and bind the coordinator to you. Second, if the coordinator is free to negotiate the best rebate possible, he might be working to your direct disadvantage by skinning the supplier so closely that he loses his incentive to serve you well. Third, the commission agent can actually sell your business to the highest bidder, who then feels little sense of obligation to you, the client. And fourth, the newly endorsed practice sets the industry back exactly a decade: it was on this point that one major group of meeting planners broke away from its founder's organization and declared independence.

There's only one way to assure the ethical independence of a consultant: pay the person for the information and remove the profit motive as a matter of contract. Further discussion in Part II.

If you don't get credible information and substance, what do you get? Fluff, hype, cotton candy, and pretty pictures.

You get miles and miles of checklists, which coincidentally border on acres and acres of ads. You get multiple-guest interviews which just happen to indicate that the diversity of opinion in the trade is too great ever to be standardized. You get studied attention to nonissues, such as complimentary rooms and liquor—all business gifts are intended to induce a feeling of obligation. You get the most imaginative room seating diagrams one could hope for, despite the fact that, if everyone can see and hear, the seating pattern is irrelevant. And you get ersatz technology, such as the crowded charts that tell you how large the type must be in your art to be seen from a given distance on a given size of screen—which completely overlooks the fact that the eye is a variable-focus lens which can eliminate all print measurements by duplicating viewing-distance ratios (art-is-to-eye as screen-is-to-viewer). You also get abundant coverage of the latest fads, which are the only topics not already consigned to boredom.

In short, you get the print version of television's *vast wasteland* in every issue of the meetings and conventions trade press. By controlled circulation. Free. If you control a budget.

Let's return to the idea of magazines' faking it by refusing to critique significant problems. That idea of delivering deserved criticism is not ours alone. Other publications in other fields practice it. Check our brand new Chapter 23 in this book for a more complete development of the topic.

What do you have a right to expect, budget or not?

When dealing with suppliers to the trade and their press, you have a right to expect a reasonable standard of knowledge from those interviewed and interviewing. You have a right to read intelligent interpretations of data, events, trends, and research—not just raw materials regurgitated from a reporter's typewriter.

So the case against the meetings industry and its press is not only that it is too superficial or unskilled or lacking in perspective and consistency (all of which are true) but also that the industry and press persist in disinformation and silence on fact and conditions advantageous to suppliers and disadvantageous and even harmful to you. Silence and a lack of standards both reduce competition, leaving buyers with the impression that the differences are essentially Tweedledum versus Tweedledee.

There was a time when industry contracts were full of fine print and were often ignored by the hotel. That time seems to have passed, partly because of the standardizing effect of the basic contract developed by the American Society of Association Executives and partly because of adverse publicity regarding nonperformance to contract in the days when consumerism was at its zenith and the associations of meeting planners were new and still independent.

Today, we recommend that you get everything in writing—every single point which could make a difference to your program. Don't accept assurances, which are a stock-in-trade in the industry; no one intends to fulfill most of the idle promises tossed around. Moreover, verbal agreements are routinely disavowed; and unless your point is in writing, you'll get little sympathy and no restitution.

As for restitution generally, damages can be paid only in money, and then only after a protracted battle in most cases. That money is little consolation if your program was damaged, with a subsequent loss of opportunity and your personal reputation.

Hotels are not the only offenders. Some producers of visual programs bid low with the intention to overrun your budget. Your safety lies in obtaining the sample slide, which shall be the prime reference about the complexity and detail expected in your slides (or movie/filmed slide presentation). Reference sample movie or video presentations by title as a guide to quality of studio sets, actors, lighting values, and so on. When held to a specific sample as the standard on which your contract is written, you have a better case to take to court, and a far better chance of avoiding problems.

Airlines are constant offenders. We've mentioned that 19 international airlines—including U.S. carriers—were named in *criminal court*. That management attitude which permitted widescale violation of written international/governmental agreements on pricing is the same attitude that is brought to your contract for special convention services, whether or not it still affects prices. Most airlines promise convention services but are capable of overseeing only the most rudimentary group arrangements, such as special ticket counters. These ersatz services are more valuable to the airline than to you because of the opportunity to lock competitors out of the ticketing procedure.

The best example of the problem is the type of advertising which states, "Meet Ms. Smith (of the smiling face). She's our staff meeting planner, and she's already planned seven meetings today." Since skilled meeting planners know it takes about one week's time to plan one hour's meeting, the ad is obviously the work of an ad agency which doesn't know the field, either. Buyer beware!

Don't be intimidated by this recitation of industry ills. Its purpose is to alert you to the problems you will surely encounter. But if you are prepared in advance to deal with them, you will be alert to the fast shuffle and will write intelligent contracts. That, in turn, will assure you that the mental picture you hold of your meeting can be realized in actuality. Or, conversely, if you cannot get anyone to guarantee your mental picture in writing at your budget figure, you know before contract that your mental picture needs adjusting.

Throughout your negotiations, remember that you are the customer. You do have a right to state your expectations. You have the right to honest information and first-quality goods and services. You have the right to minimum standards and an industry code of ethics by which to judge the presentations made to you.

Standards are the essence of professionalism. It is possible to claim professionalism as a fact of the nature of the employment; in that sense, shoe-shine boys have a profession. But in the larger sense of minimum capability proved—as with doctors and medical technologists and CPAs—only specific standards set and enforced can achieve and justify public trust.

When you call a meeting you are dealing not with slides and scripts and razzle-dazzle but rather with goals, motivations, career decisions, reputations, earning ratios, and performance factors for all participating individuals.

In that case, is it too much to ask that suppliers who deal with other people's jobs and lives have significant training and actual expertise in group and motivational psychology before attempting to structure motivation programs? At present, anyone with a warehouse can offer gewgaws and claim that some sort of contest qualification constitutes a motivation program.

Is it too much to ask that groups who inflict encounter-group training on unsuspecting employees have degrees in analytic theory so they can recognize the psychic damage which occurs in high percentages of those undergoing the training?

Is it too much to ask that suppliers of visual programs have some understanding of the basics of visual communication? Any sketch artist can offer "programs" today regardless of ability to interpret concepts visually—the salient skill.

Too much to ask that producers of stagecraft be proficient in the creation of skits/films which produce measurable results rather than simply applause? Too much to ask that a producer outline for you all the alternatives available in any given situation so you can choose? Too much to ask that the creators of training programs actually have substantial classroom or equivalent training experience behind them? Too much to ask that airline "convention services" be more than reservation desks and other trivial services of more value to them than to you? Too much to ask that hotels describe in detail their public rooms and services committed to you?

And is it not reasonable to ask that the purchasers of program components—yes, managers such as you—develop a common body of knowledge from which to learn and refine the craft as each raises his or her own level of performance to an art?

The "helpful hints" genre of information is passé. It is in fact destructive in an era when employee goodwill and cooperation are becoming valued beyond dollars. This is a time for proofs and principles, ethical commitments, and answers.

Why should a competent Meeting Manager *not* want to measure and prove? Why should his suppliers *not* want to assist him in that? Why should corporations continue to accept promises and assurances in place of pilot programs and industry-funded studies? And finally, why should an industry be permitted to bury the very information it so desperately needs to become truly *professional!*

Unless standards are set, suppliers of meeting components and their transportation and inn keeping adjuncts will continue to escalate costs for an increasingly irrelevant level of sophistication in media. And the failing supplier will continue to blame the meeting participant for not learning from the pretty program which had no real content from which to learn.

Change is on the way. Several colleges now offer degree courses in the basics of meeting production and the ancillary hospitality trades. The practice should be encouraged.

But the laboratory cannot be made to resemble the real-life constraints of business conditions or the vagaries of accidents during the production of a legitimate program. Yet we can hope that the students will learn that there is more to the production of a program than just show biz, and more to valid programming than subjective choice or the flip of a coin. Perhaps 5,000 graduates from now, these students might become a major force and factor in professionalizing the industry.

But that doesn't change the fact that today there is no standard for any element of meeting design, no public way to recognize competence or reward excellence. Where subjectivity is all, it is really nothing at all!

In summary, it is fair to say that the field of group communications is unusual—perhaps unique—in the degree to which its suppliers have been successful in preventing the adoption of a set of standards and/or a code of ethics. Therefore you as a manager of people and as a sometime manager of meetings must understand, so you can move independently and confidently in the meetings world.

For less theoretical ideas that are more easily practiced in the everyday business world, see Don Peppers' *Life's a Pitch*. Although we might differ with some specifics, nevertheless his book reflects life as lived in the fast lane of the advertising world. And he very specifically discusses the subject of ethics in his old boss' three principles: *Make money; have fun; be ethical.* Why should ethnics be an ordinary consideration for most business but seemingly anathema to the meetings and conventions crowds?

4

Separating medium from message

When the late Marshall McLuhan pronounced medium and message identical, his tautology launched one of the sorriest spectacles in the meetings business: the maximedia binge. Remember that *maxi* refers to *excess* regardless of the medium or format.

So persuasive was his slogan, "The medium is the message," and so pervasive its influence (because it coincided with supplier interests) that it survives today. It cannot be ignored.

That slogan became the rallying cry in the mid-1960s for anyone who had anything whatsoever to sell to the meeting planner. The entire television industry made McLuhan the darling of the vidiots with such marketing slogans as "As advertised on TV," implying added worth. The mass mind was being led to equate an advertising budget with special quality.

But it didn't stop there. Exhibitors were subjected to the same hype from exhibit manufacturers, who pushed bigger and flashier. Film makers pushed glamour and printers pushed four colors of ink.

Few questioned the slogan. Some newspaper reporters and book reviewers pronounced the McLuhan book brilliant. So there was never a pressure on suppliers to prove the claims.

Is the McLuhan dictum valid?

No. The slogan proceeds from a bit of thinking so sloppy and blatant that it's hard to believe that McLuhan could have propounded it other than facetiously. In *Understanding Media,*

McLuhan stated, "The content of any medium is always another medium. The content of writing is speech, just as the written word is the content of print, and print is the content of the telegraph."

Really, Marshall. Tongue-in-cheek is one thing, but foot-in-mouth is quite another. Formats can contain other formats. So what? The content of writing is ideas; the content of words is also ideas. The format of books is words, and the format of words is letters. Words are abstract symbols for concepts. Even when words are misspelled or poorly translated, the concepts behind them endure. Any given word and its spelling are only conventions.

In that basic confusion of content/message and format/medium lies the fallacy and the damage of the McLuhan thesis and slogan.

There could be some minor philosophical differences between the words *format* and *medium,* or *content* and *message.* But those distinctions would be in the nature of "treeness." That is, no single *tree* fulfills the *entire* abstract concept we condense into that four-letter symbol. Don't worry about the philosophy of it all.

Do be concerned that you get our message: "The message is the message." And don't you forget it!

The problem is with the medium you might choose to express that message. If you indulge in maxi media presentation, you will probably divert attention from the message to the medium. That is counterproductive, even if the audience enjoys the diversion.

Here, too, McLuhan launched confusions. He writes, "The electric light is pure Information. It is a medium without a message...unless used to spell out some verbal ad or name." A light bulb has no information to offer; it is purely potential for transmitting (as a medium) some given ad or name.

McLuhan makes several unremarkable points, such as, "For the message of any medium or technology is the change of scale or pace or pattern that it introduces into human affairs." True, and not particularly new or original or even insightful, especially when the standard textbook reference to Gutenberg's printing press follows. Moreover, that entire train of thought is in a wholly different plane of reference from the application of the slogan to television or from the medium/message dichotomy.

McLuhan's work was startling. It is so marvelously convoluted that the reader's attention is constantly drawn to the language itself and not to the paucity of thought. The criticism that the shock appeal of the book proceeds from McLuhan's need to create a substantial work on the subject, after having been funded by the U.S. Office of Education and the National Association of Educational Broadcasters, seems fair. We are left with a collection of essays which offer, instead of insight, mere argot and sophistry. A loss. Those grants could have bought research and understanding instead of verbal gymnastics and confusion. That work is yet to be done.

Yet we have a valuable lesson: the way in which the highly articulate author's language seduced the reader into ignoring the error in the ideas themselves demonstrates our thesis: that the medium can overpower the message—or hide the lack of it.

Even less to McLuhan's credit is the fact that the concept he was writing about was not original with him, even though he was credited with much originality by the pundits of the time. Credit for developing proof that TV was a powerful and effective advertising medium was the result of the investigative research of Thomas E. Coffin, once a professor of psychology at Hofstra University.

Coffin left Hofstra to become NBC's TV market research specialist in 1949. It appears that when McLuhan attempted to enter the discussion about 15 years later, only a far-fetched idea would get any attention from the media—and therefore from the public. In the 60's, people were both fascinated by TV and repulsed by the quiz show scandal. Strong action was needed, but the industry apparently opted for strong words instead.

Understanding media as he thought he did, McLuhan probably had a field day being far-fetched. But in our opinion he has done immeasurable damage to the legitimate needs of Meeting Managers who have a primary interest in their own message, rather than in his medium. If you want to succeed at the business of creating effective business meetings, then you'll have to begin to think for yourself, because the meetings industry is beset everywhere with private interests that do not necessarily coincide with your own. McLuhan is only a stunning example!

McLuhan's book is entertaining. It makes us feel quite satisfied with what we have "learned." We might applaud it. But on inspection, we find it facile, shallow, and often in error.

The same thing can happen in the meeting room. It is possible, by creating an enjoyable meeting, to hide the fact that the company has nothing to say—that is a purpose of some misguided executives. But that's the type of meetings people come away from asking, "What did he say?"

The question of medium versus message is not moot even in the television industry today. On May 1, 1982, Hodding Carter examined "The News on the Nets" during his "Inside Story" commentary. Several news commentators described their own and their networks' concerns about the roles assigned to not only the visual material presented, but also to the electronics tricks which embellish the visuals. According to Carter, the question appears particularly acute at ABC, which uses electronic gadgetry most frequently.

If both scholars and broadcast networks are concerned about the problem, how can the convention industry pretend it does not exist?

The media are flexible and powerful. They can help you to transmit knowledge. They can also entertain. They can entertain while you are hoping to teach. If that happens, you are creating present-moment satisfaction that interferes with your need, as a teacher, to create the present-moment dissatisfaction on which change will be predicated. Remember Malcolm Knowles!

It's important to remember that there is definitely a place within a total program (especially one lasting several days) for entertainment *as entertainment.* The need for psychological relief (change of pace, change of scene, and so on) is well documented in the books on education. Our argument is about the substitution of entertainment values or methods for teaching/learning values or methods within a given presentation, whether by error or naivete.

Serious repercussions can result. There is the resentment of the participant who later feels that he was used or shortchanged.

Because movies (filmed or video, equally) can convey and evoke emotions and emotional response to a degree other media cannot match, the movie can be used to manipulate participants. Emotional involvement makes people contribute money to a cause when they can't spare the money. It can make employees agree to things they will regret on sober reflection. Problems will follow.

How much more honest is the approach which acknowledges problem situations directly. To present the problem and its proofs and its potential solutions and its preferred solution to employees without falsification or emotional warping is good management. It is also good educational theory, because the new learning will withstand reflective thinking.

Whatever your meeting room problem, appeal to the reasons, the common sense, and the self-interest of the meeting participants. You can then expect and deserve to make a lasting impression and gain long-term commitments they will willingly carry off.

Not all communications occasions involve problems, of course. Some revolve around simple needs to transmit information. Often that is done by memo. Sometimes the memos are read by all for whom they are intended. Sometimes they are sent to supervisors who relay—and sometimes reinterpret—the content. In any case, the memos lack immediacy. They might be important, but too brief to require or justify a meeting.

Some organizations have solved that problem by using a brief TV address by top management on a particular topic. It can be a live or a prerecorded address, but it conveys the ideas directly from the mouth of the boss to the ears of subordinates. Everyone hears the same words, nothing is colored by middlemen. Yes, people often misunderstand spoken messages, but the televised address is then a matter of record and its content can be reviewed.

Much attention has been given to the fact of the television appearance. Television apparently exhibits, in these circumstances, the power of persuasion, immediacy, and authenticity. That is not a product of the medium; rather, it is the power of the appearance of top management in a forum which is essentially an assembly meeting, yet effaced because of the willingness of people to accept the mediation of electronics, as with telephones.

That is, the power is that of the boss and the message forthrightly presented; television is simply the more economically feasible alternative to the meeting: a subtle, critical distinction.

Notice that the video presentation replaces an *assembly* meeting; one-way video could not replace a small meeting or easily manage a breakout from the assembly. And two-way video fits the nature of video conferencing, different from the purpose and technique of the *management report* at issue.

In this context, television is not more effective than the assembly meeting it imitates and replaces, but it is far more cost effective. Because the assembly meeting and its video imitation is more effective than writing, the method's use will probably grow. And it will succeed unless it begins to suffer from imprecision. That is, speakers are often careless about the words they speak; they would be quite meticulous about those words if they were to be delivered in written form.

So we can conclude from all of this that the medium is certainly *not* the message, but it does affect the message. It can enhance or overpower. It can destroy. It cannot replace.

In all your meetings, the message is the message!

Having separated the function of the format/medium from the content/message, we can see why the choices among the various media available are as different and as important as those we take for granted when, for example, we select advertising media according to whether we intend to reach people in their homes, their cars, their stores, or their sports arenas.

Your choices, therefore, are largely objective. And the research conducted by HumRRO indicates that although the differences in cost between printed illustrations or photographs or slides or sound/slidefilm or movies on film or video might be great, the differences in results can be nonexistent.

With information such as that, you realize that the value of your next meeting is predicated *not* on your budget but on your skills as a communicator.

If you had a simple sales message, would you become confused by the differences which are unavoidable when you "translate" that message from broadcast to direct mail to billboards to displays to shelf extenders? Of course not. Each medium has understandable restrictions and desirable advantages. You use each to optimize a *needed* advantage to speak to the selected audience.

In essence, that's what happens when you select your support media for the meeting room. Your own conclusions about the effects on your message by your chosen media are crucial.

The presentation techniques you select must serve the learning process. Prominent educators and industrial trainers have made significant contributions toward the practical application of key teaching/ learning principles. We'll examine just a few of the most significant in capsule form.

On entertainment: "Entertainment has as it goals satisfaction and pleasure in the present moment; adult education's goal is dissatisfaction and change.... Entertainment establishes a relationship of oneway flow of communication from transmitter to receiver; adult education relies heavily on dynamic interaction among the learners and between learners and teachers," according to Malcolm Knowles, a prominent trainer.

On motivation: "Transmission of learning is made possible only if other elements such as past experience, present motivation, and affective state (largely attitudinal considerations) of the learner provide an appropriate ground to close the sign (symbol) circuit by which communication is effected," according to James W. Brown and James Thornton, Jr.

We have covered the first consideration at length in this chapter; we will cover motivation in another chapter in Part I. There remain considerations of mass communication techniques (which is a topic so vast it must be studied separately, if at all) and the psychological/physiological phenomena of learning, which will also be covered in more detail in another chapter.

What follows in the next chapter is a practical appraisal of training films intended by their producers to be elements of your meetings. There are substantial problems in that industry, and the *medium* versus *message* dichotomy is perhaps the greatest.

Computers, Disks, Internet, and Other Dot-com Stuff: Exactly this dichotomy between medium and message has come to the fore among corporate trainers. Their disenchantment with the electronic media as miracle worker is made evident in a June 1998 article by M. David Merrill (of Utah State University) in *Training* magazine.

Computers and their offspring have absolutely no intrinsic value as trainer or training content. As media, they are simply delivery mechanisms for a message that must be properly prepared. Whatever a teacher might deliver, the computer can be programmed to deliver. What the teacher does not know, the computer cannot know. But because (until recently) disks were expensive to press, they could not be used effectively where budget is small or ultimate audience is minor. These days, you can burn your own disks.

This is not a happy truth to the manufacturers of mechanisms. And they can afford to buy silence from the magazines through advertising. However, the genie is out of the bottle, and the future can now be dedicated to *educating* in the meeting room, rather than mistakenly entertaining.

In January 1999, a Mexican educator, Antonio Mesa Estrada, addressed world educators in San Antonio. He made the point that the wonder of television was permitting the Mexican Board of Education to reach anywhere, despite distance, terrain, or poverty. But he also made the point of being able now to deliver top quality instruction to every point equally. The computer does not write the texts...who will? He says the teacher's mission now is more important than ever before.

Although it is true that not every meeting can be considered a training session, it is equally true that if something new or different need not be covered, no meeting would be necessary. So there is and should be an *instructional aspect* to every purposeful gathering. Respect it!

Electronic wonders have occurred in the past few years. More are coming. Computer-assisted instruction barely existed outside college/corporate alliances when the first edition of this book was written. But computer and other electronic media rank with lens/light media when the chips are down. It's up to you to choose among all the options according to your needs and their individual advantages. It was never possible to choose wisely, yet blindly, any medium for its fine colors distinct from the message it should carry. Message and audience *dictate* media!

Your job as a Meeting Manager is to determine how best to deliver the message in your hands. Do you have it yet?

5

Looking at industrial AV

Which surgeon recently received the "Appendectomy of the Year" award? Which lawyer the "Settlement of the Century" award? Although professional associations of architects recognize design problems imaginatively transcended, they have also criticized savagely, as in one award for "That (Remodeling) Project which Most Desecrates." In the professions, awards are few and based on professional standards and principles.

That's not true in the industrial audiovisual market. Not only are there no nontechnical standards, but awards are given by the bushel for successes claimed but crowned with never a proof.

All the frantic talk about creativity and excitement in awards seems calculated to mask the fact that the lens media have never proved the value of such technical elements as costumes, camera angles, fast cutting, and so on, although the potential distraction caused by excesses in these elements has been identified.

Because none of the awards is given for the success with which the particular film has achieved the specific objectives of its sponsor.

We will use *film* as a generic term, embracing the video image, which is virtually identical to the eye despite technical differences, and the sound/slidefilm, sometimes committed to movie film and termed *semi-animation,* if lens motion is added. Emergence of computers shifts from lens to electronics but does nothing for meeting content. So you must.

The differences that affect you and your meeting participants are not the differences of technology so much as the purposes of the sponsor.

The term *sponsor* is not used in the trade, but we will use it in the advertising sense to indicate work done by others for *their* purposes and offered to you, on loan or rental.

There are, as a result, three separate categories of self-interest: first, the production studio creating a risk-venture film for distribution in hopes of profit; second, the corporation or special interest group making a film to convey a message or viewpoint on a specific issue or topic; and third, the film you might commission to fulfill particular needs of your meeting and/or organization. We will refer to the first two as sponsored, and the last, as commissioned.

The uses of the industrial film, whether sponsored or commissioned, include management and supervisory films; training and motivation films; sales and sales service how-to films; interpersonal communications and other group skills; general safety topics; and public policy information films, such as for EEO.

Given all these uses plus the three categories of self-interest, it's obvious that the films entered in any contest can be considered successful *(a)* on the most general, subjective bases, including entertainment value or *(b)* for specific achievement of pre-established goals. The latter has never been tried.

That's reasonable. In order to claim success based on objectives, audience effectiveness would have to be measured—a job that would fall to the distributor of the sponsored film or to the commissioning corporation, which might not, for instance, want to reveal points of market strategy that underlie the objectives. The lead time and complexity of assembling and interpreting data for the sponsored film would delay the award period until proofs were in hand—which conflicts with the purpose of obtaining attention (and sales) for new offerings.

Together, those difficulties suggest that success awards probably cannot be given and that the superficial, self-congratulatory awards should be abandoned. Jiggles, camera angles, and costumes do not add up to "creativity" in the meeting room sense.

With the recent introduction of festivals of new industrial films, it's now possible to expose the new offerings to a broad corporate and association audience without the hype and hoopla of an awards ceremony. Moreover, an audience that can view dozens of films in a brief period will come away with a better sense of what is available and what constitutes a quality film. That might be a mixed blessing for the industry.

As a judge of entries for a 1982 summer awards program, I viewed more than 20 films. My fellow judges and I agreed that of the group, two were superior films entitled to share first prize and three were excellent. The remainder were marginal to poor, with three so bad that they deserved to be given booby prizes. That's a ratio of 10 percent superior and only 25 percent to be recommended.

These ratios—and the clear gaps between quality groups—were confirmed by a film magazine editor who subsequently attended two festivals which presented several dozens of films each.

Face facts: you have one chance in four of finding a worthwhile film if you can review everything available. If you are operating on a hit-or-miss basis, booking a film sight unseen because you've heard its title (most titles are terrific!), you have a three-in-four chance of presenting a dud.

Never schedule a film you have not already viewed in its entirety at least once—unless ordered to do so in writing by a superior. Whenever possible, gather the opinions of your fellow managers and friends in other organizations regarding potential films for prevue. Be sure the reasons they think a film is good coincide with reasons you might have for showing it; that is, another person might be solving a problem you don't have.

What quality distinguishes the superior film? Absolute fidelity to the stated thesis: everything needed is there, and nothing irrelevant is included. In the visual arts, that's known as purity of theme. The result is an engrossing, informative film.

What lesser achievement marks the excellent film? Usually it's one that does a satisfactory job of presenting its thesis (you do learn something) but its organization or content or irrelevancies become noticeable deficiencies, although not of a severity that handicaps purpose or your usage.

Some of the others might be called better-than-nothing by users; but we feel nothing is usually better than marginal material.

Ours is an uncompromising position, surely. But endless compromise has brought the industry to its present state. And the converse of much that the compromised industry celebrates has been demonstrated by research.

We have previously mentioned the U.S. Army study of 1971, conducted by the Human Resources Research Organization (HumRRO) and its application to industrial uses. The army studies are valid because employees become soldiers become employees. If anything, dubious motivation is more a problem in the army, and methods that can work there can work anywhere in industry.

There are three embarrassing sets of facts:

First: As noted earlier, the 1958 Pentagon studies by Dr. Kanner demonstrated that there were "no significant differences in learning when comparing color versus black/white television." Although some trainers feel color is useful in clarifying intricate detail, that was not indicated by Dr. Kanner's study nor by any other known study since. TV and film images are identical to the eye.

Second: HumRRO tested demonstrations for both procedural and conceptual learning tasks, with interesting results.

In a procedural task test (assembling a firearm), HumRRO used 144 subjects under all 16 conditions created by 4 types of test pairings; all tests had control groups. HumRRO measured both time and assists required to produce one perfect performance and concluded that results obtained by the traditional motion picture format were no better than those using the control format, a printed illustrated workbook! Only when the original motion picture version was reduced to step-by-step procedure (presumably killing the editorially creative elements on which industry awards are based) did the film outperform the printed workbook (which was not also revised). Relativity of the revised film to the task was credited. Conclusion: Motion adds to cost but does not automatically add to training results.

Third: Psychologists long ago concluded that the highest form of creativity is problem solving. To *create* is to combine previously unrelated concepts into a new relationship that provides insights and new understanding. Instantly, the merely artistic or innovative (a new but minor change or variation) is seen as beside the point. Further, irrelevancies can distract, as we will see in another chapter.

When those three sets of facts are linked in practice, they push aside all the hype and emotionalism substituted for objective proofs of success. They prove the damage that has been done to management goals by misinformation and disinformation and silence. They reveal that a substantial number of producers and A/V practitioners are incompetent in the prime purpose for which they were consulted: to convey a message which can be acted upon by a viewer in a prescribed manner, such as new or varied job performance, attitude change or reinforcement, or even purchase.

The same facts also dictate the conclusion that whether the A/V presentation is used inside or outside corporate walls, for a captive audience or stipulated segments of the general public or the general public itself, the objective(s) must be stated and measuring methods and criteria must be established.

Inescapably, the distributor becomes a link in the proof of success of the broadly disseminated sponsored film—or the multimedia package becoming so popular. Given video as the equivalent of movie film, projected slides as the equivalent of printed illustrations, and sound/slide or slidefilm as the equivalent of semianimated movie film, we see that it is *function not format* that sorts out the best medium for the best cost-effective ratio for the given problem or message.

Talk cost effectiveness, and you're talking business!

The business of making an effective film was discussed in detail in the HumRRO report. A few of the more significant findings: First, training results apparently depend more on the skill with which any medium is prepared than on the sophistication of the particular medium. Second, results can vary according to the method of showing (interrupted, uninterrupted, and/or repeated showing of either type) but variations seem to depend on the skill level of the viewer as well as the complexity of the task. Third, step-by-step procedure does not necessarily aid conceptual learning—a blow to B. F. Skinner's programmed learning theories. Fourth, showing wrong-way methods (as the film trade insists on doing in its cliché wrong-way/right-way structures) degrades performance because some wrong-way learning takes place. Even the fairy tales told us: "Remember, children, while I'm gone don't put beans in your nose." Whereupon they did.

If you use or commission a significant number of films, you might wisely read the HumRRO report. It's available from the National Technical Information Service of the U.S. Department of Commerce as Document No. AD-730675, signed by E. E. Miller. Phone 703/605-6400. Credit cards accepted, for a cost of about $30 per copy.

Sponsorship of an industrial film for any purpose instantly removes it from the realm of entertainment and thrusts it into the realm of adult education. That's true whether the film is intended for restricted or public viewing.

Logically, one cannot expect to work a public audience as hard as a captive corporate audience; even so, the public relations film cannot escape the need to measure results. Again, because the public relations fraternity accepts the fact of untraceable effects of a single given release, PR people are less inclined to expect focused results from a PR film. But there's a great difference in the position of a newspaper reader who is anonymous and not beholden to anyone for a news release scanned and the same reader turned viewer of a borrowed film. The film viewer is identified and often encouraged to comment on a loaner; he is entitled and often eager to comment on a rental. Feedback is essential in filmed as well as live meeting segments. In addition to the quality control feedback exercises, many groups need the field research data the outside audience can provide at relatively low cost.

It is the responsibility of the lens media to bring business methods back to the business market. Dollar value or skill levels or other tangible objectives must be established on the quantitative side; and human relations, including personal growth and interpersonal relationships goals must be satisfied on the qualitative side.

Many strictures mark the competent sponsored film. It, like the commissioned film, must respect the dichotomies operating: both message versus medium and industrial usage versus public commercial features. The latter distinction is identical to the dichotomy between the Broadway stage and industrial theatre, which is covered at length in Part II.

Are you shopping for a producer to be commissioned?

If so, choose one who recognizes that the film you plan is only a single element of a larger program, larger objectives. Some commission producers care only for their assigned segment and resist efforts to meld the film into the program's frame. Ego problems are common and are destructive to the overall program as well as to the given film.

Be prepared to approach potential producers. For perfect understanding—and your own safety—state your objectives in writing for the initial interview; expand it to full Roman numeral outline before meeting with the chosen producer's creative staff. There can then be no question about intent or salient points.

At the point of outline, you will be divulging restricted and sometimes confidential information, and the producer must honor that confidence both in words and noncompetitive activity. An explicit statement should be included in the covering contract. If you are commissioning a film intended to be used as a loaner by others, then a paid, pre-contract market survey might be needed to confirm the existence of an audience which *can* and *will* heed your message. Costs are too high to permit you to *hope* someone out there will be waiting and watching.

And while we're remodeling the house malpractice built, keep the related concepts of creativity in practical focus: fuzzy notions about which shapes or color combinations or cutsie costumes or smashing camera angles constitute creativity can fuzz your results.

Fuzzy objectives and fuzzy guidelines help the incompetent to disguise ineptness. That, in turn, punishes the competent and talented, who consider the integral work, not its fragmented marks. That's how superficial awards injure even the industry distributing them.

This is not to say that none of the elements commonly thought of as germane to style and professionalism in fllmmaking are useful to sponsored or commissioned presentations. Those techniques which contribute to comfort in viewing or to ease in following the story line are needed and desirable. Those which call attention to themselves are generally undesirable and attention splitting.

In any case, don't be intimidated by technology. It is not itself a substitute for content or clarity or creativity as a problem solver. Avoid excess technology and you avoid maximedia.

Look to your problem! If you have a problem and if you solve it with the help of a film, then your solution was creative in the ultimate, quite apart from artistry of details. And if you have a problem and if your film does not help you solve it, then your film is neither creative or relevantly successful, even if the colors and camera angles are award winning.

Obviously, an award-winning film can be a failure for its owner—and many have been—simply because the award criteria are superficial and irrelevant.

With technology developed to so high a state, need the irrelevancies of industrial film technique be honored at all? After all, camera and directional techniques are taught in college these days and kept exercised in Hollywood; technique will not wither. The underlying problem is that many industry film workers would like to make credentials useful in Hollywood, and they'll gladly bend your budget to serve their own purposes.

Industrial A/V of all types will benefit when the producer's allegiance is given to the problem as the determiner of the technique. It's your right and your duty to yourself to protect your objectives with unswerving dedication to your own goals; you have the power of your opinions, your peer opinion network, and your budget to back you.

Be satisfied before you commit that these issues are settled:

To distinguish between content and format before selecting a medium,

To distinguish between entertaining elements and those that are educationally valid and intrinsically engrossing even to a layperson in the field.

To force selected technology to support the learning process even to the point of disappearing: great art conceals the artistry.

To discuss and commit to writing the ethical matters affecting your project: *(a)* the confidences and noncompetitive relationship; *(b)* standard guidelines for elements of treatments (a sample of recommended handling), variations of execution from treatment, variation from projected budget; *(c)* the disparity of quality from sample submitted and accepted by title; *(d)* the need for fresh thinking by avoiding clichés of teamwork and wrong-way/right-way—that is, easy ersatz solutions; and *(e)* written resumes of the applicable education/training backgrounds of the creative staff who will work on your project.

It's evident that problem-analysis and problem-solving techniques will become required reading for many who were never before aware of their existence. Basics will be reviewed for you in Part II.

Once that reformation is underway, film makers of sponsored messages can get on with the real studio services: to select the most cost-effective medium for the given problem and then to produce a competent filmatic execution of the message expressed to achieve the objectives stipulated.

Questions of cost effectiveness mean that color and motion could be questioned and must be justified. Then the producer and client can rediscover anew the quite marvelous properties of motion pictures properly used—the power to: convey appropriate emotional overtones (regarding child abuse but not firearms assembly); or manipulate time into new realities through slow-motion or time-lapse photography; or burst the strictures of place (the camera can take you anywhere); or defy the strictures of space (the camera can put anything before you); and, of course, the replication on demand of critical movements, both identical every time and tireless in repetition.

Unless at least one of those key properties of the motion picture is used legitimately, the medium is misused and the money is at least partly wasted. If the special properties of the motion picture are used only to record a live demonstration or natural event, then no "creative" service has been performed and a studio billing at creative rates is unjustified. Pay for the technical crews and processing at standard overhead rates.

To justify a billing for creative services, your producer must be able significantly to enhance your outline and your viewer's perception of the filmed event. He can do that only with skill and talent and knowledge of basic educational principles.

The most competent among them will *distinguish* between your overall programming and segment scripting; *recognize* that each project you bring is different from all other projects either of you has done before and needs to be rethought; *honor* your Roman numeral outline or challenge it directly and convince you objectively that changes are needed; and *require* the finished product to serve the dictates of your purpose.

This is not to say that the producer need be subservient. The competent producer has valuable skills which you are seeking. So he will coach, correct, and stand his ground when you're wrong. The producer will operate with a clear conscience because he is working in your best interests—demonstrably. If you don't perceive that, walk. But be sure you distinguish between an honest producer's legitimate "unables" and your personal pipe dreams, so you don't buy another producer's glib promises.

And be honest. Some clients have helped to make producers cynical about new business by overstating their needs (to get lower per-unit quotations) or by taking one producer's thinking to other producers for competitive bids. If you wish to do so—and it's a very effective way of assuring hard work—you *must buy* that initial work and provide in writing that the originator must compete to win the execution of the project.

Don't forget the measures. Measured achievement is fair, unemotional, and never arbitrary. If you don't begin work from the defensive posture that only unqualified praise represents success, then you can work with whatever results prove out, and improve if not the film in hand then certainly the next one. Improvement is part of the basic tool kit of every professional.

The filmmaking and distributing industry is broad and fragmented. Your best reference is *The AV Market Place* (AVMP) a guide published by the Bowker Corporation, publishers of *Books in Print* and other highly regarded directories. AVMP contains thousands of entries for producers, distributors, dealers, film processing labs, sound recording services, music scoring services, and various library services.

An important aspect of Bowker directories is their accuracy; computers keep revisions updated, and quick turnaround from data closing dates to publication tends to assure the accuracy of entries. Major libraries usually buy and shelve Bowker directories in the reference section.

We've covered a lot of details about principles and practices that can or should be based on known findings. There is a lot yet to be learned about the field of learning, and the industrial film industry could perform essential work if it would explore the key and poorly understood concepts of "illustration of text" versus the far more cogent "visual interpretation of concept."

Learning more about how we learn via audiovisual media would be a contribution to training theory which would lay a claim to the film and meeting trade's maturity, professionalism, and commitment to improving the understanding—and so the skills, attitudes, and maybe even the life—of the film viewer!

That would be film at its finest. Look to it!

6

Ear, eye, and A/V learning

What is the precise relationship of the auditory to the visual material in the learning process? Nobody knows. Publications in the meetings field regularly quote as fact a percentage-based ratio; but in all our readings in psychology and education, we have never seen such a ratio expressed in scientific papers.

Multi sensual learning is the human norm, of course. But researchers have found that the major source-sense in any learning process varies not only with the topic being learned but also among different learners of the same material.

The much-quoted percentage ratio originated in the 50s in an informal, internal estimate prepared by the Mobil Oil Company for the purpose of evaluating executive presentation methods. Mobil has never considered the studies either scientifically sound or valid. The ratios, heavily weighted toward visual learning, do help to sell slides and visual media.

The field is too complex for that easy answer. Much information is available on various aspects of learning. Studies differentiate between such spheres as knowledge, meaning, comprehension, and understanding; or cognition, information processing, and memory. Because these studies are distributed among the fields of psychology, psycho biology or psycho physiology (how the body functions to create the senses and produce the responses), and education, the results have not been correlated and collected into a handy reference book for meeting planners.

Moreover, because scientific evidence depends heavily for its validity on single-variable methodology with replication of results by other researchers, and because there are so many varieties of learnable topics and billions of persons as potential test subjects, audiovisual learning is not necessarily a first choice of subject for research.

The U.S. Army studies have shown that color and motion are not necessarily aids to comprehension and learning. Other work done on the subject of the interdependence of the two key senses has established that visual cues do indeed enhance the understanding of spoken material when those visual cues link poorly organized or disjointed information. That tends to explain the common-sense observation that good A/V presentations tend to outperform verbal-only presentations.

Split-brain studies have demonstrated that the left hemisphere of the brain specializes in sequential processing (as in language) and the right hemisphere in conceptual processing. Although the ears have a bias toward the left side, the eyes feed equally to the left and right hemispheres. Presumably, then, the eye has the capacity to link or translate the two modes of learning—an original conclusion—if the material is prepared so as to facilitate that translation.

In this chapter we will attempt to codify some of the relevant principles so that we can improve the effectiveness of A/V presentations as learning aids. So that those few principles are removed from the area of pure speculation, we will summarize the most significant findings in the several fields of research. You will then understand the reasons for particular methods and choose more securely in borderline cases.

Can we compare the two senses?

Probably not. Visual cues seem to impact on more cells of the brain than does something spoken, which might account for some discrepancy in what is retained. On the other hand, the eyes fatigue or cloy much sooner than the ears do; so for an extended program, the ear presents advantages.

Until the 19th Century there was no "science" of communication, and until this century there were few educational theories. Adult education became a phenomenon after World War II because of both the mass of GIs returning to school and the abundant new learning that had taken place in various fields as psychology. These are a result of government experiments in mass-persuasion techniques for training and propaganda purposes.

A landmark book, *Experiment on Mass Communication,* by Carl Hovland, Arthur Lumsdaine, and Fred Sheffield, was part of the explosion of information.

Next up was role playing (King and Janis; Jansen and Stulurow; Corsini, Shaw, and Blake); the development of training programs (Rose); attitude change (Cohen; Sherif and Sherif;P.Weick); and media (Rossi and Biddle/Knowles; Brown and Thornton). All the areas were very new, and little was directly useable by the meeting planner. (See the Bibliography for specifics.)

In England, D. E. Broadbent *(Perception and Communication,* Oxford: Pergamon, 1958) attacked the problem of concentration and distraction in learning. That seminal work provided insights into attention spans and information overloads.

Recognizing that the brain cannot process large numbers of simultaneously received stimuli equally and instantly, Broadbent introduced a "filter" theory. He hypothesized that to avoid bottlenecks, the brain filters and sequences material and selects the most pressing (our word) for immediate processing. Overload is put into short-term storage until handled and transferred to long-term storage. Broadbent's filter biases accepted as pressing the novel or intense over the familiar; acoustic over visual signals; sounds of high over low frequency; and signals of biological importance. Work by other researchers bore out many of his theses, including loss of information during short-term storage—a key finding.

Subsequently, Melton demonstrated the presence of both short-term and long-term memory but disagreed with Broadbent regarding sequencing delay and loss of information. Melton states that long-term memory is characterized by *(a)* presence of learning and *(b)* effects of the established phenomenon of forgetting through interference of new stimuli/learning.

Soon after that, Waugh and Norman contributed the terms *primary* and *secondary memory* to clear up confusions of terminology in various writings and to consolidate compatible theories regarding memory storage. They argue that a primary memory receives everything and that thinking about or rehearsing it will transfer some material to secondary (permanent) memory. The balance will be forgotten, some of it within seconds or minutes.

Working at about the same time, in the mid-1960s, Hernandez-Peon confirmed a filter process but disagreed with Broadbent about the permanence of filter biases. He finds actual neurophysiological blocking of certain *classes* of inputs when attention is distracted.

We can fairly summarize findings in the field of stimuli filtering to demonstrate that an overload of stimuli results in the loss of much material presented; that distractions cause further blocking; and that lack of opportunity to rethink or rehearse causes still more loss of potential learning. All these counterproductive circumstances are present in the maximedia blitz, which depends on overstimulation for its “excitement.”

Even more important to the relationship of the auditory to the visual portions are findings reported in *The Psychology of Perception,* by William Dember and Joel Warm (New York: Holt Rinehart & Winston, 1979). They believe that vigilance is essential to learning and comprehension; that is, the sustained attention leading to alertness and consequently to peak performance over an extended period of time.

Dember and Warm find that performance efficiency in sustained attention tasks involving auditory signals tends to be superior to that in tasks involving visual eye signals. Related experiments reveal rather low correlations between people’s ability to sustain attention in different sensory channels simultaneously.

That suggests that "distractions," in the sense of the findings previously summarized, can include the opposite half of the audiovisual combination. And new evidence indicates that auditoryvisual correlations can be increased by closely equating the types of discriminations required in the two types of tasks. Clearly, the learning purpose is not served by the willy-nilly pairing of words and pictures.

The legitimacy of all those findings was enhanced in the late 60s when Roger Sperry and Michael Gazzaniga carried the then current research on hemispheric specialization of the brain into new areas. They experimented with patients whose left and right cerebral hemispheres had been surgically separated to eliminate severe epileptic seizures. Separation was achieved by severing the *corpus callosum,* a bundle of nerve fibers connecting left and right hemispheres in the normal brain.

It was already known that the left hemisphere tends to control motor responses of the right side of the body, and vice versa, and that the eyes feed information to both hemispheres. But the hemispheres cooperate, and with the corpus callosum intact information flows where it is needed.

With the corpus callosum cut, Sperry and Gazzaniga demonstrated, the patient was stymied. The person could recognize in the visual left field/right hemisphere a word in the abstract sense (that is, find its identical letter picture in a list of different words), but could no longer say that word because the language ability in the other hemisphere was estranged. Many related experiments by these and other researchers show that the left side of the brain is specialized to process language, mathematics, and general analytic tasks which process information serially or sequentially. The right hemisphere seems specialized to process abstracts and spatial tasks; artistic creativity is its province, and information is processed in a simultaneous/wholistic/conceptual manner.

Even these findings are not neat and clean. In aural tests, normal persons seem to process music differently depending on whether or not they have previous musical training. Most of us tend to hear melody as a right-hemispheric creative whole—the melodic picture. However, trained musicians process in both hemispheres: they hear the "grammar" of the music in the left side (tonal relationships, time values, and so on) simultaneously with the melody. This would seem to suggest that writers would hear poetry differently from persons with lesser language skills because language and technique would be distinct from the "story."

We could conclude that all creators of learning aids should first determine whether the material to be conveyed is sequential or conceptual in nature and then favor ear or eye, respectively. Workshops must convert sequential information into gestalt understanding.

That sounds simple. However, some learning tasks are in the cognitive domain (knowledge, such as arithmetic) and others in the affective domain (attitudes). Still others involve sensory-motor skills in which practice is at least as important as knowledge or attitudes. Has anyone ever learned to ride a bicycle simply by reading about it or *wanting* to ride?

Obviously, even a well-prepared visual presentation could fail to produce desired results if the expectations are unrealistic; that is, if the film shows bikes being ridden but the program does not provide breakout sessions to practice riding. And some sales tasks—especially those involving product demonstrations—must provide practice sessions simply to be *complete.*

We already know that we learn differently with eye and ear, and even that one can interfere with the other. But what is learning? It's a complex process of converting sensory stimuli into memory-preferably long-term memory. There are many related concepts to be mastered.

One of the best texts in this area is *Cognition and the Symbolic Processes,* edited by Walter Weimer and David Palermo (Hillsdale, N.J.: Lawrence Erlbaum & Associates,

1974). In the chapter "Toward Understanding Understanding," Jeffery J. Franks sets out the following terminology:

> Understanding: a cover term for all aspects of cognition, including memory, meaning, language, perception, etc.
>
> Tacit knowledge: a reference to knowledge of which we are not (and possibly cannot be) directly aware.
>
> Knowledge: a reference to static, semi-permanent, long-term memory relationships.
>
> Meaning: a reference to relationships activated or generated as a function of some knowledge relationship within the present environmental context.
>
> Comprehension: a function of the extent to which adequate (coherent, complete) meanings have been generated in a particular context.
>
> Pattern recognition: classifying a particular input into its appropriate perceptual/conceptual class.

According to Franks, "The structure of meanings is determined by (systemic) knowledge just as the structure of sentences is determined by grammar...Overt manifestations of meaning (imagery; overt and covert speech; and responses) are analogous to surface structure in sentences. Tacit meanings are like the underlying structure of sentences."

Psychologists hold conflicting theories about whether long-term memory (knowledge) is a generative conceptual system or a storehouse of specific memories of past experiences. Although tradition favors the latter, Franks argues that both are valid at different times and in different contexts.

In short, Franks' research and theories demonstrate that in even the most simple of verbal communications (written or spoken) the language and the abstract conditioning of the individual person regarding the individual words will color the communication. He is in accord with another seminal writer,

Arthur L. Blumenthal *(Language and Psychology: Historical Aspects of Psycholinguistics;* New York; John Wiley & Sons, 1970), as well as with his colleagues John Bransford and Nancy McCarrell whose paper appears with Franks' own under the chapter title "A Sketch of a Cognitive Approach to Comprehension." All three honor the highly regarded findings of Karl Buehler about the need for any two conversing parties to share the same "field" of reference or abstract meaning.

Bransford and McCarrell conclude that people do make cognitive contributions while comprehending; that such contributions are prerequisites for achieving a "click of comprehension"; that knowledge of underlying abstracts helps determine the individuals' contributions; and that meanings derived as the result of such contributions is best viewed as something created rather than retrieved from storage.

Bransford and McCarrell further demonstrate that test subjects make assumptions (and falsely "remember") data that might be implied but was never stated. They conclude that "comprehension occurs only when the comprehender has sufficient alinguistic information to use the linguistic cues specifically in linguistic input to create some semantic content that allows him to understand." Prior knowledge alone is not sufficient to assure comprehension; knowledge must be activated.

That concept was presented by Wundt (quoted by Blumenthal, 1970) as "the mind of the hearer is just as active in transforming and creating as the mind of the speaker."

Briefly, there is scientific data to back up the commonplace observation that different people hear different things in the same words; or that people tend to hear what they prefer to hear in a spoken message. And they prefer to hear whatever will avoid psychic dissonance—that is, they tune out new material at odds with what they already know or believe.

You must support your controversial concepts with concrete examples if you hope to persuade. Hovland (1953) demonstrates that high credibility of speakers increases the amount of opinion change; low credibility reduces opinion change (and can negate prior acceptance).

One of the great values of any appeal to the eye, therefore, is the identicalness of material presented to every person; even more, the visual can be held before the eye longer than a word can be held in the ear. This serves the rethink/rehearsal sequence believed necessary to convert the information into long-term memory. The fact that a physicist will get different information from a "picture" of an equation than will a layperson is a different concept: a matter of "field" rather than "time."

We must conclude that a prime responsibility of the visual is to narrow the interpretive focus by limiting potential (mis-) interpretations of the spoken word.

In this aspect, the visual portion of the A/V presentation is admirably suited to serve the auditory portion: the eye can present to the right hemisphere (conceptual processing) the "big picture" of the material under discussion. The eye can then fixate repeatedly on different portions of the image to study details. By contrast, the ear hears and processes details that do not finally make sense (or deliver a big picture) until the last word of the sentence has been spoken.

Can the eye truly guide the ear to comprehension?

Definitely, according to findings of Bransford and McCarrell. The team devised an unlikely picture accompanied (not described or explained) by a written paragraph intended to be read aloud to viewers of the picture. The paragraph was so disjointed that no clear idea or progression was apparent—it was the grammatical equivalent of nonsense syllables. Several variables of presentation were tried.

Recall of the spoken words was predictably poor if the subjects heard only the paragraph, with no visuals. Recall was not appreciably improved even if they saw the picture after having heard the entire paragraph. But their recall was quite good if they saw the picture for 30 seconds *before* the passage was read to them. Moreover, most subjects felt that the disjointed paragraph was acceptably organized if they had seen the picture first.

In a related, second type of test, a similarly disjointed paragraph read without a title was poorly recalled; but hearing a title in advance gave enough context so that recall was improved.

In a third type of test, a paragraph was ambiguously designed to reflect either a common or an exotic experience. The either/or decision varied according to the title attached, but recall of specific test items was better on an element most "coached" by the title.

We can conclude that not only is the eye able to present concepts to the right hemisphere while the spoken material goes to the left hemisphere by way of the ear, but the eye can present "roadmaps" that tell the ear where the material is headed.

Is that necessary? Probably. The response to auditory signals in language is extremely complex. We have already seen that the listener must make a cognitive contribution to his or her own comprehension using knowledge already in storage.

But the listener makes an additional effort-that of making units of sounds intelligible.

George Miller laid a cornerstone in the foundations for the study of language comprehension in his *The Psychology of Communication* (New York: Basic Books, 1967). Miller establishes six distinct functions essential to comprehension: (1) The listener must *hear* the utterance as an auditory stimulus; (2) *match it* as a phonemic pattern in terms of his own phonologic skills; (3) *analyze* and *accept* the utterance as a sentence in grammatical terms; (4) *interpret* the utterance as meaningful in semantics or field; (5) *understand* the utterance's meaning; and (6) *believe the validity* (and the speaker's intent to deliver that meaning with those sounds. We can understand without believing, of course).

With that explanation of process, we can appreciate the miracle of human speech. And we can accept more easily the inability of the listener to understand and comprehend every detail of a complicated thought after a single hearing.

Miller also established the concept of *Magic Seven.* Apparently, seven items is the outer limit of "chunks" of information the mind can retain without forgetting in short-term processing. To complicate matters, the seven items need not be bits of information—such as a series of single-digit numbers—but can be up to seven internally related concepts, each containing more than one bit: phrases.

No one is recommending that all information be delivered in sets of sevens, but that finding of the "chunking" faculty does argue for think periods, practice, and avoidance of the blitz techniques of maximedia.

We needn't even be overly concerned that we present only the "proper" type of information to either half of the brain because the normal brain is quite capable of shifting information around—over a period of time. It also creates the creative "aha" experience for itself—that is, a sudden insight which correlates previous detailed (presumably left-hemisphere) learning.

But it does matter (on the basis of noninterference and rethink-rehearse and the filter biases) that we make an effort not to overload the circuits or present incompatible material to the ear and eye simultaneously or challenge cherished beliefs or prerogatives without allowing time both for the learner to understand the message and comprehend the ramifications. If we meet the physiological strictures of the brain half way, we will get more work out with less input. That's efficiency.

To present the scientific bases for our own argument, we have read the original papers summarized here. Encapsulating a paper or book into a single brief quote is unfair to the authors as well as to their ideas; however, tracing, reading, and interpreting that technical material can be time consuming beyond its immediate value.

Therefore, if you are interested in reading more deeply, we recommend your starting with an excellent college text that puts the pieces together: *Cognition: Mental Structures and Processes,* by David Dodd and Raymond White, Jr. (Newton, Mass.: Allyn

& Bacon, 1980.) The extensive bibliography will steer you to other significant work in the field.

We can put the heavy stuff aside and get on with the practical application of the evidence the laboratory has put at our disposal.

Whatever information is presented in a meeting must ultimately be useful to company and meeting participants. That usually requires a conversion process from the *data* state to *meanings* state, which could involve cognitive and/or dexterity usage. That conversion process is called either education or training, depending on whether the learning is *(a)* general preparation for approaching unknown problems in the future or *(b)* carefully selected to bring the best available knowledge and techniques to bear on the problem immediately at hand.

There have been attempts to define *learning* as something done voluntarily or in schools and to define *training* as something required, usually by the company. Those definitions are shamefully narrow, meaningless, and useless.

Various researchers in the education/training disciplines have attempted to argue that *liking* and *learning* are closely interlinked; but one author acknowledged that in reading about 800 papers in preparing his own monograph, he could argue his thesis in terms of trends but could provide "no conclusive evidence, pro or con." His readings include the papers of Zimbardo and Ebbesen, who deal in the affective domain (attitude).

In the 1960s Edgar Dale developed what he called the Cone of Learning for Cognitive and Affective Learning. A pyramid rising from the most concrete experiences, his base, to the most abstract, his apex, Dale's all-circumstances/all-media assessment reads: Direct, purposeful experiences; contrived experiences; dramatized experiences; demonstrations; study trips; exhibits; educational TV/motion pictures; still pictures; radio and recordings; visual symbols; verbal symbols.

Researchers building on Dale's thesis have hypothesized that differences in response to concrete/abstract media vary by age of learner. To establish attitudes in adults or change attitudes in young people, use abstracts. To change attitudes in adults or establish attitudes in young people, use the concrete. These postulates, too, are inconclusive.

The inconclusiveness of the research makes perfect sense when we consider the variables: the topic, the individual learners, the concreteness or abstraction of media, and the cognitive or attitudinal or dexterity nature of the new behavior.

Changed (occasionally, reinforced) behavior is, after all, the end point of all the information passed around in meetings. And behavior springs not only from the animal drives that are so important in the theories of such behaviorists as John B. Watson and B. F. Skinner but from nonissue motives based on values and interests. Values and interests can cause—or motivate—an individual to act against animal nature, and so hopelessly confound the strict behaviorists. Because of the cognitive contribution the listener must make to the material spoken, he or she must maintain an active interest throughout the presentation if they are to comprehend. Motivating the listener is your job too.

But motivation is different in every individual and the priorities of each of us change with circumstances and often over time as well. So in Chapter 7 we will deal with motivation in the context of other human relations theories, and in Chapter 8 we will check the substantial differences between *incentive* and *motivation.*

In the balance of this chapter, we will deal with the practical aspects of visualizing for the meeting room.

The message presents management's request/directive to the meeting participant, who on understanding and comprehending might agree to cooperate. If so, he must be provided with the tools with which to do the job requested or directed.

Those tools, which are tangible or otherwise sensate implements, make possible a direct action by the learner upon a material or a concept, such as a problem. Tools, therefore, have an intrinsic value in relation to the message. They might tell the learner how to do something or describe size or shape or usage, or verbalize or demonstrate a product's features, advantages, and benefits, which are not always obvious, tangible, or sensate.

The tools you might create to support your message could be slotted into Dale's cone of learning. One problem is that he has listed learning sources which cannot necessarily be accommodated in the meeting room—such as field trips. Differentiate between the overall convention and the basic agenda-directed meeting. Another problem is that the hierarchy tends to imply some sort of superiority from one medium to another, as some interpret it.

In March 1970 issue of *Advertising & Sales Promotion* magazine we presented an assessment of practical meeting room tools (yes, they can be called media) evaluated for their degree of credibility/manipulability/accessibility from the learner's viewpoint. Unlike Dale's cone, the tools are not ranked because their practical value depends on the specific circumstances of usage each time.

Briefly, the categories we favor include these: (1) Products and real objects: highest credibility; but size can be a problem and benefits can be insensate. (2) Charts drawings, chalkboards: lend immediacy and flexibility when generated but are difficult to view by crowds and take valuable time to draw. If prepared in advance, they are static images, in the sense of photographs. (3) Photographs: substitutes for the genuine article when cost or size is too impractical to permit distribution. Static exhibits are 3-D photos, both less credible than reality. (4) Books, booklets, outlines, tape recordings: orderly presentations of selected factual information and opinions delivered complete; but such presentation lacks immediacy and is impossible to control if printed matter is distributed in a large audience. (5) Demonstrations and sociodramas, plus exhibits that contain one of these: highly convincing when performed live as a form of vicarious practice; but need generous lead time and subject to human error; (6) Role playing: unmatched for creating participant insight into other people's behavior, but must be supervised by a *trained* leader; explosive, unpredictable, powerful. (7) Projected images of any of the above (except role playing) on a screen: excellent for magnifying detail, conveying emotion, and changing time relationships in movie form; otherwise one step removed from the conviction level of the tool for which it is a substitute.

Notice that by eschewing rank order of any type we are free to choose that medium that best serves the dictates of the given message in the context of the particular product and meeting room. There is no other way to choose responsibly.

All of the foregoing lend themselves to audiovisual form of presentation. When used that way, they are subject to the same types of strictures we've established for the traditional film/video A/V presentation, based on the psychological studies previously discussed.

Here are a few of our own premises for the optimum use of audiovisual materials:

Premise 1: All visuals should present basic concepts when it's possible to do so and roadmaps for the auditory portion when concepts cannot be visualized.

Premise 2: Visuals should interpret spoken material, not merely repeat it. Words should appear on screen if the word is strange or part of a series; but the printed word appeals to the left hemisphere (duplicating the spoken word) while doing absolutely nothing for the conceptualization of the right hemisphere.

Premise 3: Avoid illustrating a script in a mistaken bid to conceptualize. If you are discussing wine making, the use of grapes, vineyards, and bottles does nothing to aid the understanding of fermentation, the chemical process at issue.

Premise 4: Simplify the visuals. In photos of complex subject matter, reference the exact information needed by masking or highlighting specific areas. Overly complex visuals tend to overload the learner's circuit and split his concentration.

Premise 5: When conceptual slides are available, open the related commentary with a conceptual statement which agrees with the slide's content. Then go back and fill in details for the ear as the eyes studies selected areas.

Premise 6: Keep the auditory and visual portions wholly compatible so they can function synergistically—each aiding the other for heightened clarity and viewer understanding of intended meanings.

Premise 7: If you can add elements of theme or style without violating any of the other premises, and if you can afford the possible additional cost, add them. But do not overpower your message!

That's it. These simple rules will assure you an audio-visual presentation which has every right to succeed in conveying your message effectively and efficiently.

It all comes down to judgment. Perspective. Understanding of your needs, your people, and your alternatives. While the ads say your program needs gee-whiz media and intimidating hotel decor, the truth is that your people really need honest information about your ideas, your intentions, and your view of how it affects them. The more simply and completely you can state your case, the more likely they are to cooperate.

Now, given the research we've reviewed and the seven rules we've advanced to aid the A/V processing, can you "buy" the pitch that your meeting can't survive without the hype, the glitz, and the blitz of maximedia?

If you can't buy the pitch, why buy the media?

7

Art versus science in human relations

Identifying or creating a need that can be filled at a profit is what business is about. Sometimes the pull of the need is so great that the customer will stand in line to be served, enduring poor service and minimal quality until he discovers that a choice exists. That's called competition.

When the national economy was agrarian and labor was mostly unskilled and certainly less sophisticated than now, employers had little competition in the labor market. They could state terms on a take-it-or-leave-it basis. Labor was considered a raw material to be used or discarded like any other. Times have changed.

Despite the Reagan recession, the reservoir of skilled labor is restricted. Employers now see superior employees not only as worth conserving but as worth further investment to train and develop. Although upper management was first to enjoy the new "fringes," employee education and training soon ceased to be seen as a fringe benefit. It became policy in many firms and began to trickle so far down the hierarchy that in some firms any employee who chose to attend night school would be assisted financially.

For many years, corporations have competed to recruit the top performers in college graduating classes. Money and perks made all the difference in the early years; then a trend toward personal growth began to replace money and corporate prestige as employees' prime consideration. Today the training and personal-growth enducements provide the determining factors not only where money offers are equal, but also where training is better and money is less. That cancelled treasured theories of money motivation.

From now on, human considerations and the corresponding ideas. of corporate responsibility will shape corporation direction to a degree which could not have been conceived of only two decades ago. Co-determination as practiced in Europe will no longer be locked out by Neanderthal managers. Rigid consensus as practiced in Japan should be rejected. But one thing is certain: change is inevitable and the current rounds of wage concessions by labor in exchange for security and profit sharing is the cutting edge which will pare the *labor-as-raw-material* concept from corporate policy.

Before he became the Secretary of Labor, Robert Reich took a body of ethics philosophers to task for not challenging questionable business practices and asked whether conflict-of-interest with potential grants might be the reason. The group were stung, but they congratulated him profoundly after the presentation. We witnessed it.

A more aware, more inner-directed population is opting for a voice in its own destiny. One fallout of the layoffs of the 90s was the understanding given to employees that they might be loyal to the company, but the company will not necessarily be loyal to them. The short term greed that dominated company actions will have long term consequences in employee relations.

Human relations programs already in effect in major corporations—including flex-time and sabbaticals—have produced results exceeding those of the sweatshop. People are dependable, responsible, and cooperative when given what they perceive to be a fair shake. That some managements are surprised or even unaware says little for their capability. In our experience, there are relatively more poor managements than poor employees. The next great leap in productivity and so profitability will come when business demands professionalism of its managers, when dog-eat-dog politics is replaced by healthy competition, when employees are permitted to achieve beyond the skill level of the insecure supervisor.

The personnel problems of a company cannot be solved by the Meeting Manager alone; yet by conscientious and judicious application of people-methods in meetings, that person can help acclimate the company to the potential of its prime asset—the intelligent employee. That employee is listening. And thinking. And judging.

Even the most technically perfect meeting will fail its purpose if it has nothing to say about the human situation in which the audience/participants/learners find themselves. *People* are what meetings are about, in the last analysis. You cannot affect people unless you can communicate with them; you cannot affect them even with substantial innovations and compensations unless you can first communicate honestly with them on an adult level; you cannot affect their basic motivations without first affecting their value systems—their ways of thinking and living. And since it is neither desirable nor even possible for management to get inside the head of each and every employee, the employee must be encouraged to respond voluntarily.

That means you must understand people (distinct from each individual) in order to program meetings that achieve. Some managers have an accurate gut reaction to the people they work among; others are less involved personally but are well versed in the psychological and behavioral theories governing adult education and motivation. Both methods seem to work, although only the latter types can articulate the reasons.

That doesn't mean you need a college degree in psychology or sociology before you can program meetings confidently. In fact, the only relatively certain theories in the field deal with observed group behavior and psycho neurology (how the living organism's brain tissues are structured and function to produce senses). Here, scientific data can be considered reliable, and often conclusive.

That's not true of motivation, which is value based rather than tissue based. Because motivation is a reflection of what the individual is (in the nebulous sense of mind or spirit), work in the motivation field is now and might always remain an art rather than a science. But part of the art is recognizing and accommodating the scientific data that affect your plan. That was the thrust of the entire preceding chapter. It is also the thrust of what follows in this chapter.

As a compensating factor in the *schooling* versus *gut-feel* department, the gut-workers sometimes can call the shots on sensitive issues far better than the theorists simply because people outwardly conform despite inner reservations. People also act in some situations differently from the dictates of their values. That phenomenon is known as *alienation;* if prolonged it can produce neurosis and trips to the psychoanalyst—the "shrink." It usually produces guilt and anxiety rooted in *psychic dissonance.*

By contrast, *psychic consonance* (or harmony between actions and values) is the mark of the integrated personality—the person of integrity. To complicate matters, a person can have consonance without being right about his values—enter the concept of *ethics.*

As Aristotle stated it more than 2,000 years ago, the rule of ethical behavior is simple: *to do the more admirable deed when there is a choice.* Notice that there are no hard-and-fast dictates (as with religion-based morality) and full understanding of the difficult situation. Ethical dilemmas can occur when none of the alternatives is intrinsically desirable or clearly admirable.

But most individuals never face such situations. When the man of little integrity says he has *no choice* but to injure his neighbor or competitor, what he means is that the admirable choice is less profitable or otherwise less beneficial to him. Greed, not dilemma, is his problem; the corporate veil conveys no mitigating circumstance. On society's failure to recognize that fact are many private fortunes and regressive company policies based.

It's obvious that ethics, management policy, labor relations, and meetings management are all aspects of the same broad concept: interpersonal relations/human relations.

Both the art and the science of human relations are complex. Then should gut reaction or theory prevail? A logical conclusion is that each group should have a fair competency in the methods of the other, although we must admit that some managers are already so alienated from themselves as to be estranged from others and incapable of sensitivity without much rethinking and restructuring of their own value systems. One gets to know people by earning their respect and trust. That can be a long and slow process for some, quick and enjoyable for others.

Fortunately, there's a dependable shortcut to the command of theory because of the writings of such innovators as A. H. Maslow, Dr. Mehmet Beqiraj, and Dr. Viktor Frankl—all artists in motivation—and Dr. Frederick Herzberg, a behavioral scientist.

Those who don't understand human motivation usually pay lip service to motivational research and then careen into clichés about contests, incentives, and awards.

Motivation and *incentive* are totally distinct concepts. As we have seen, motivation is value based, intensely personal, and inner sourced. By contrast, an incentive is a carrot, an external-sourced activator that reflects what the corporation wants. Incentives justify for the recipient the expenditure of somewhat more energy; but by appealing to superficial reasons or human foibles and failings—such as acquisitiveness, pride (not self-esteem), envy, or greed—incentives can create a compensation nightmare, an unreasoned demand for more of whatever was offered.

However symbolic or valuable, incentives do not necessarily motivate an employee and almost surely cannot motivate a stable, intelligent individual. Although the incentive might cause the individual to do the required work, the extra effort is usually seen as a bargain or a bribe—the extra effort to be discontinued after the required period or after the object is obtained.

Besides attempting to motivate or bribe, the company can attempt to bully. People can indeed be bullied into energizing for limited periods before they turn off.The old saw is "Winners get to keep their jobs." Bullied employees resent new programs of this type and are predictably hostile. Research has shown that bullied or otherwise resentful employees invest their main interest and energies in pursuits other than the job.

People are often bribed into working harder in order for a company to avoid a permanent hike in pay scales. Merchandise is the preferred reward because it cannot be confused with income and never looks "deducted," as cash-award taxes do. Merchandise is also promoted by incentive award companies, most of which originated as merchandise warehouses looking for new markets. Most incentive-house salespersons talk of motivation, but few understand it and most confuse it with incentives.

People can be motivated—or, more accurately, they will motivate themselves—when they are approached on a value basis. And for most people values center on home and family; not on new ashtrays for the house, mind you, but on security and love relationships, including friendship. Only at their lowest growth level are people motivated solely by security/money drives. Money alone can't buy a mentally healthy person, to whom the subjective reward of the job—the psychic income—is more important than salary. These are dedicated, inner-directed people often found in social-service positions at lower-than-market pay scales.

Inner-directed individuals deal with the quality of life apart from the standard of living. They put themselves into their jobs if permitted and encouraged; if stymied, they return what they consider to be a fair effort under the circumstances. Nothing short of either improved compensation/situation or a new understanding of existing compensation/situation will move them. It's a defensive posture, and it cannot safely be ignored.

Anyone who knows people has seen it. What is surprising, then, is that for nearly two decades industry has applied only selected theories and sometimes irresponsible interpretations of the basic research that attempted to codify value-based behavior.

A pioneer, A. H. Maslow, established five categories of basic human needs on an ascending scale. Lowest and most fundamental are physiological needs (food, shelter, sex); then safety (the security of those needs); belonging and love; esteem (self-respect and prestige); and self-actualization.

It was Maslow who demonstrated that if basic job security is threatened the employee reduces his job effort and seeks satisfaction in other directions. Although his early theories suggested that an individual progressed from completed step through the next higher step, Maslow later revised his theories to indicate that the three higher levels are inverted at will by individuals according to their own values and changing priorities. But he confirmed his beliefs that the healthy growth of personality creates self-actualizing tendencies which can be realized either in occasional episodes (with the duration of years or projects) or in total dedication to a cause or an art. "What a man can be, he must be," Mr. Maslow asserts. The Greeks of antiquity heard Socrates' saying, "Know thyself," and today's young people say, "Do your own thing." That little has the nature of mankind changed in millennia.

Until the 60s, most psychological theory advanced the idea of "homeostasis" as the source of drives; that is, the seeking of balance largely through avoiding pain and seeking pleasure. "Getting" materially could be rewarding in that view.

Maslow and others criticized modern economics as "the skilled, exact, technological application of a totally false theory of human needs and values, a theory that recognizes only the existence of lower needs or material needs."

The disillusionment of the young, according to Maslow, must be expected when they can "get" the material and animal gratifications and still not be *happy.* Maslow's early theories posited the ability to seek "peak experiences" and happiness directly.

His colleague and loyal critic, Dr. Viktor Frankl, challenged the *pursuit of happiness* principle endemic to American life. Ultimately, in a long and famed philosophical correspondence,

Frankl persuaded Maslow that peak experiences and happiness itself were by-products of fulfillment from other directions, namely the commitment to a valued goal. Frankl's "will to meaning" is compatible with Charlotte Buhler's "living with intentionality"; he concludes that self-actualization is an effect of meaning fulfillment. That, in turn, hinges on decision making which, in turn, hinges on personal values including love and giving relationships.

We can conclude that whether you subscribe to the homeostasis theory or the value-rooted theories of human motivation, you can appreciate that individuals are not inclined to work against their own good—even in the meeting room—and so the fairness and reasonableness of the meeting message are crucial elements of success.

However, application of the homeostatic principles have produced understanding of the job environment too. Dr. Frederick Herzberg identifies 10 motivation-hygiene (maintenance or dissatisfying) job factors. Predominantly satisfying (in descending order of frequency) are achievement; recognition (propounded by the incentives industry); the work itself; responsibility; and advancement. Always heavily dissatisfying were the control quintet: company policy and its administration; the quality of supervision; salary; interpersonal relations, especially with supervisors; and working conditions.

Dr. Herzberg validates the word *type* when applied to various job fields. Certain characteristics are common to employees with like jobs, although whether in chicken or egg relationship is not specified. Yet the Meeting Manager must approach accountants differently from salespersons and differently from line workers.

The message—when the findings of Maslow, Frankl, and Herzberg are combined—is that people will find their own interests in their jobs if the organization makes it possible. And the entire concept of *job enrichment* of today proceeds along those lines, essentially undoing the job minimizing effects of the *efficiency experts* of the past.

In recent years, a tendency to denigrate the work of Maslow has surfaced among trendy trainers and even social scientists themselves, presumably because humanists are still being shot at by behaviorists, who have computers on their side.

The computer can do incredible things with precise data, of course, but the value-neutral computer also gave us the Edsel car and the Viet Nam war.

Yes, the value-based humanists can prove little, which does not prove they are on the wrong track. Leonardo's helicopter was not aerodynamically practical; Louis Pasteur couldn't cure syphilis; Marie Curie didn't devise or foresee an atomic bomb; and even Albert Einstein miscalculated the shape of the universe. The works of I. S. Bach were orchestrated by pedants of little note. Apparently it is the task of genius to create insights the academicians can embellish.

Even if Maslow and Frankl and others should be proved "wrong" in significant detail, that in itself would be a further benefit because even *that* proof will require a greater understanding of the nature of man. Even that *proof* will advance the humanist cause because the objective is to understand and therefore release individual potentialities.

To appreciate the humane approach of Frankl and Maslow, it is necessary only to read the work of B. F. Skinner. There one sees the sterility of numbers, the crushing superficiality of an impeccably scientific pedantry. Skinner has examined human response to motivational stimuli in such a way as to open us wider to manipulation and close us further to understanding. Skinner and his predecessor, John Watson, cannot appreciate value-based theories because they cannot appreciate the *dignity of man*—the existence of which can never be proved.

On a more scientific basis, M. Brewster Smith dismisses Skinner's man as the *vacuum self* and criticizes Skinner's inability to deal with experiences of inferred processes in Skinner's "black box" (of intellect) behind observable behavior.

Brian MacKenzie says of behaviorism that, "both the attempt and the movement were ultimately failures...because it never managed to produce a significant body of lasting scientific knowledge."

People are complex. The functioning human being is made different by each event experienced, by every emotional crisis faced, by each new person with whom one has more than passing contact. So the given person is both different and identical, simultaneously and perpetually. It is the same type of problem as that of time and place, on which Einstein formulated his Third Dimension theory.

Far more than computers, laboratory validity, and job policies are at stake. Dr. Mehmet Beqiraj has related the unrest under the socialistic and communistic systems to the turmoil of other peasant societies throughout history—including our own. His "peasant" is a social type who lacks the comprehension of environment needed to control his own destiny. Peasant societies are coercive and repress internal dissent; lacking true satisfiers to distribute as rewards for labor, the peasant society dispenses status and substitutive satisfiers, such as fiestas, which offer temporary relief from stress but no solution to basic problems. With cars and television sets seen as substitutive satisfiers, the Western world and especially the United States are seen as societies of "technologized peasants" by Beqiraj. Future stability of the system and society will depend on provision of true satisfiers for self-realization.

The ramifications of these theories are stunning, and their corollaries are fascinating. Even among the status-quo types, a mentally healthy individual cannot escape the need to develop and express himself/herself; so an active mind cannot limit itself to narrow company routines, or even problems, for a lifetime. By minimizing or opposing their innate needs, industry will further alienate people.

Man's progression from satisfaction of animal needs through self-realization to giving is adequately documented; yet none of these esteemed theories claims or even suggests that the lowest levels cannot be satisfied by vicarious experience. The concept of all civilization argues for vicarious progress. It is, therefore, impossible to dismiss the youth culture's dissatisfaction with the status quo as simple, unfounded rebellion. They have, instead, been much maligned by their shaken elders.

Having never known the basic insecurities treated by Maslow, young adults are probably proceeding directly into the upper phases of personality development. If so, they are ahead of their elders, neck-and-neck with advanced social theory, and seeking without precedent. An honest society needn't fear them.

Science is only now coming to understand the human condition. Discovering the range and depth of human needs and their legitimate expressions is industry's immediate problem. Diehard traditionalists in both industry and the social sciences are apprehensive, because the methods of both will be outmoded if the events of recent years are accepted as legitimate behavior.

Current research at the millennium is learning more about which areas of the brain are involved in specific activities, but not learning exactly how learning is produced. Scientists are finding (by injecting chemicals into animals) that excitement can work to enhance learning; but two problems still result: a) different people are excited by different things, and b) the brain is not a tape recorder, and so different people will fail to learn the same things or everything. The latter is where the world has been for a long time...simply not previously proved scientifically. This writer has chosen to say "never proved": Don't expect miracles of learning from dog and pony shows or multimedia extravaganzas!

That legitimacy is difficult to deny. People are aware of things which affect them; they are better educated and far more sophisticated today than they were in the late 40s and in the 50s, when efficiency experts and motivation specialists came onto the business scene. It seems that some of the people who are selling corporate response to human response have failed to keep up with people.

Employees know that the company cannot bend to each and every one of them on each and every issue which might confront any party at any time. They'll compromise at a fair point—one determined by their values and their perceptions of the company's forthrightness. History is a factor.

But whereas the family and friendship network generally involves chosen values, the organization's demands (and incentives) involve imposed values. People are naturally predisposed to put their own value structures ahead of the organization's. Only when you demonstrate that a given new direction will enhance some aspect of the employee's business and/or personal life will you have his undivided attention, undivided loyalties, and unstinting effort.

If you cannot prove the fairness of your direction, then don't resent the employee's reservations. Expect occasional resistance; if rational, it's healthy. Set your goals accordingly. Begin to deal with the real world of human motivation and human response-it's been ignored too long by the meetings and conventions trades.

There are no easy answers or all-purpose solutions. Listen to your gut reactions when problems develop. What would you do in an employee's position? Let that guide you until the books have more answers.

Further studies are required. Possibly no behavioral variant can be dismissed before it is invalidated by objective research. That will be slow and sometimes expensive, although the human relations programs which result will be less a cost than a savings when contrasted to the hidden costs of noncommunication and the possible disintegration of entire companies.

Stockholders will have to adjust to the knowledge that there is no alternate labor supply. Assuming that a given corporation might become inoperable by a foreseeable date, then the total assets of that firm, divided by the estimated number of operable years still remaining yields an "annual labor depletion allowance." How much of that ALDA is the corporation willing to invest annually in benefits and employee education and self-realization programs to extend the profitable life of the firm?

In this context, superficial incentives (seen as bribes) and multimedia extravaganzas can be seen as self-defeating substitutive satisfiers. People want to be themselves, and they want that self to matter to their employers. Whether that requires modest variations or a complete change of policy depends on each company's history. In any case, it will call for a fundamental honesty on management's part regarding every future problem.

Whenever a period of uncertainty or experimentation develops —and we are in one regarding both human relations and communications media—the opportunists have a field day. They compound and prolong the uncertainty for their own purposes, as the convention industry can testify.

Although only indirectly related to the meetings field, the types of human relations programs known as sensitivity training, T groups, encounter groups, or confrontation exercises are a hasty and harmful response to the need of people to know people. Whether programmed by licensed professionals or by self-styled experts, sensitivity training is quack medicine.

In its simplest sense, industrial sensitivity training is a group exercise calculated to bring people face-to-face with themselves through confrontational interaction with others, whatever the risks to their mental well-being, for the real or imaginary benefits any added self-knowledge can offer the company. Encounter groups are long on promise and short on performance and intrinsic value. None has been proved to offer a predictable and consistent, measurable benefit. Yet their faults are legion.

Professional psychologists who favor this money-making parlay on psychoanalysis argue that the incidence of psychosis produced or uncovered by sensitivity groups is "only" one half of one percent. The "only" person in your group to be destroyed could be you or another decent human being. Yet even those programs designed by professionals are in the minority. Slick package merchants neither recognize nor report the breakdown of a human psyche. So the real rate of destruction of human beings proceeds at a rate of up to 10 percent, according to studies conducted and observed at Stanford University.

In advancing the "right" of business to destroy a person sooner in a laboratory exercise rather than later in an actual (hypothetically projected) job crisis, industry exhibits a moral poverty not paralleled since the early years of unions, when some now-respected business organizations shot striking workers who "threatened to occupy" facilities.

Personnel relations have been made infinitely more difficult by the merger/layoff period of the 80s and 90s. Employees learned that loyalty might not be rewarded. Employers are now paying for their labor "cost savings" with employees who don't care and will jump ship for minor reasons, mostly money and training. Training is portable and relatively permanent just in case the company is not dependable or fair.

Moreover, *US News* (on November 22, 99) wrote that 98% of all college students surveyed admit to cheating in high school. How's that for a new-employee prospect? And the Y2K crisis-promoters forgot to mention that the year 1972 was identical in day and date to 2000 and could have been substituted briefly and cheaply on computers, if necessary, with hand corrections of any consequent calendar calculations made on specific correspondence. At merger time, ABC-TV and CBS-TV apparently both pulled early stories on nicotine that the NY *Times* and others published. The reasons for all were varied, but mostly they back-fired. Greed will not prove itself to be a profit-maker in the long run. If American business is so much into rip-off and opportunism, why blame the employees for trying to protect themselves? Why not try fairness instead?

Guerrilla warfare is gone as labor policy, but the subtle version evident in encounter groups persists. Because encounter group problems and confrontations are artificially created, the company loses the non-complicity it would have were the exercise situation a true job-related crisis. A person can escape from a psyche-cracking problem by resignation, if no other way. The employee is further victimized by such programs because they cheat the individual of supportive mechanisms—family, friends, concerned business associates—from whom she or he might have sought assistance.

By professional standards, the encounter program is indefensible in even its basic structure—quick start/stop in an environmental vacuum. In psychiatric theory, analysts not only interview the patient over a long period to build trust and understanding but also counsel the family and others who have contact with and bearing on the mental stability of the patient. Encounter-group patients—even if they should reach new awareness—usually return to the identical environment they left. That new awareness can cause new problems among co-workers, and even families, whose lives and perceptions haven't changed during the same period. To deny that sensitivity training and similar programs are a form of therapy is fraud, as is the process.

A basic tenet of sensitivity groups states that (absolute) stranger groups are superior in effectiveness to "cousin" groups (same company, little direct contact) and that both are superior to "family" groups (frequent or daily job contacts) in recognition that candor requires anonymity preferably but surely safety from reprisal. Another tenet states that the company benefits most from the team effect enhanced if the more threatening family group situation unites rather than explodes. So by its own tenets, the encounter group theory serves the company best when it puts the "sensitized" person at a potentially permanent disadvantage, either among unchanged peers or opposite a hostile superior.

However well the format is programmed, human response is unpredictable. Mental well-being is often a fine balance struck between anxieties and defenses. Unprogrammed—possibly violent —responses are easily triggered by superficially innocent encounters. Regressions, traumatic experiences lived or relived in session, and paranoid flare-ups are permanent dangers established by case histories. These dangers are inherent and unavoidable. And that's why sensitivity programs are criminal in all but law.

Increasingly, critics who are themselves psychologists and analysts are finding their way into print. Maybe their reservations will dissuade that occasional trainer or industrial relations supervisor who sees in these fad programs a way to garner praise in the company. In no instance should you, as a meeting planner, schedule an encounter session as an *interesting* event. You have no ethical right to experiment with your charges' mental well-being.

None of these arguments denies that many people are indeed ill adapted to their particular life forms. For some, the combined pressures of social and office conformity leave little energy, will, or sense of direction to encourage self-discovery or substantial change. Some are content with that.

Those who might want or need psychiatric help require personalized, competent attention. Sources of help are available if they seek it; and many companies cover analysts as well as medics in group health policies. But bargain rates for groups are scant justification for assembly-line psychiatry. Therapy doesn't work that way because people don't.

Business does have a right to teach better methods by job-related techniques which do not jeopardize the employee's welfare either by demanding psychic involvement or by inducing artificial conflict. Both management development (MD) and organizational development (OD) have been advanced as broad industrial responses. To the extent that OD programs might include confrontation/ encounter/sensitivity situations, we hold them suspect and objectionable.

Crises occur somewhere in the business community each day. Generally, psyche-damaging crises are the result of poor general management or faulty individual decisions come home to roost. In crises of causal relationships, mental stress develops in the individuals who cannot escape blame, or in the scapegoats for those who can pass the buck. Crises caused by natural or uncontrollable events do not produce traumatic reactions. Exhaustion, maybe; guilt, no.

Treatment of the frictional symptoms through encounter groups is too little, too late, an exploitation that makes the innocent and submissive at the bottom pay for the mistakes made at the top.

There is no valid objective of business which is not more adequately and more humanely served by small group methods—rspecially the leaderless group discussion (LGD), which separates the men from the boys under the shock-absorbing ego-buffer of task orientation. After a series of low-cost LGD tasks have been accomplished over a period of time, both individuals and company will have a fair and valid reading of the natural pecking order among workers, based on demonstrated strengths and weaknesses. That's really what the hocus-pocus of encounter group/sensitivity training is doing so badly at such high cost in dollars and mental health. The inescapable conclusion is that sensitivity training occurs in inverse ratio to the quality of company management.

The interrelationships of the concepts we've developed in this chapter are as complex as the concepts themselves. All must be integrated into not only the basic human relations program but also into the meeting which invariably will herald it

As an analogy, the world's melodic heritage is too vast ever to be fully cataloged; yet every known theme can be reproduced on the piano using only 12 tones and several variations of the 12 in different combinations. The 12 tones are the common denominator—they are not the music. Music is the result of programming original thematic ideas for instrumental media using those 12 tones in stipulated musicological formats: staff clef, bar, note, and tempo. And the same 12 tones whether expressing rock or classical.

You can't catalog people, either, but some of the prime tones of human motivation have been identified by Maslow, Frankl, Beqiraj, Herzberg, and others, including people at the Menninger Clinic and Michigan State University. Themes and ideas must be communicated via adult education formats established by Hovland, Lumsdaine, Sheffield, Knowles, Sherif, Cohen, Miller, Franks, Bransford and McCarrell, and others whose work extends and deepens the understanding we have of ourselves.

(More in Chapter 10.) But the resulting message-music is entirely your own doing —pops, flops, or classics!

So get back to fundamentals: people. If you want an employee behavior changed for the company's good, talk common sense and what's-in-it-for-me. If you choose to offer incentives, select those with true motivational appeal. For the practical aspects of this topic, see the next chapter.

So far we have discussed the direct verbal and visual methods of communication. Sights and sounds are accepted as the basic tool of an exchange of complex ideas. But there are other ways to communicate, and in interpersonal relationships the other ways might be of greater consequence: one-to-one is still the predominant ratio in the field sales call.

During the typical sales call, the first line of the opener will almost invariably follow a period of banter with which the prospect and sales person establish a personal contact.

When ready, the prospect signals and the sales presentation begins. The prospect's signal is not necessarily a bright semaphore. It can be a shift of posture, a change in tone of the voice, a frown or smile. Maybe a "Whaddya got?" is added, but by that time, some think, the course of the call is already charted. Can it be recharted? If so, is the expected course recharted before the opener is delivered, or is it altered bit by bit as the presentation proceeds? And how is any of it maneuvered in the typical eight-minute time grant of an initial call? There's a problem for the behavioral scientists.

The banter is cover for the gutsy nonverbal communication (NVC) which is taking place. Nonverbal communication is effective. It is potent and accurate. Over-40s say, "I think he's trying to tell me something," and the young call it "vibes." Good or bad, vibes and NVC are there, real, and fast.

British studies have demonstrated that within moments of private confrontation any two persons will agree on the assignment of the dominant/submissive roles, often by instant recognition, and with a phenomenal accuracy as measured by other dominant/submissive rating methods already validated.

In American studies of leaderless small groups, the self-proclaimed leader is often successfully challenged; the vanquished concedes; and the group ratifies. All without verbal support of the contest as such.

Nonverbal communication has never disappeared; but as a non-quantified concept in a scientific age, it was discussed in lower tones than was a proposition within earshot of Queen Victoria. But NVC is respectable again. Rehabilitation began with the recognition that people declare themselves with signs, symbols, possessions, gestures, postures, facial expressions, and touch more consistently and more accurately in these ways than with words.

The adage that the janitor and board chairman are indistinguishable in the sauna provides the value link between custom-cut clothing and the funky garb of today's young. With perfect 20/20 hindsight we can understand that crowns, uniforms, and ceremonies were developed to bolster the NVC-quotient of people whose personal stature fell short of their appointed rank. Spectacle could dominate from a (safe!) distance: Hail to the Chief, and all that.

What does it mean in the meeting room? Any number of things. First, what you and other speakers say will be augmented with the participants' own conscious or unconscious evaluations of the speakers and the surround. There's not much point in trying to fake it. Next, the standard syllabus of sales skills and cognitive training sessions must make a place for the people-related skills—eventually. Then, salespersons must be coached in reading, and in adapting themselves and their presentations to, the psychic needs of the people who might not buy (reacting to and manipulation of the prospect are two different actions). Last, the company must evaluate the signals its sends to its employees via managers and to customers via typical field attitudes.

Everyone knows the archetypal dynamite salesperson-the one who climbs to top managerial positions. But we've been amazed at the number of quota busters who are mild, self-effacing individuals. They neither push nor threaten; yet they sell. Does the dynamite expert know how to mask strength, or does that person sell to people who are willing to be intimidated? It matters only because there are so many more salespersons than sales managers in the world.

Some motivation specialists aren't sold on NVC. They contend both that human relations techniques are too complex for the amateur to learn in the training room (in a few hours, probably true) and that it's all a matter of personal attitude. We don't find the two concepts to be mutually exclusive. Rather, they might be symbiotic. You and your counterpart are sending signals. How you both react—and require each other to counteract—just might be up to you and the people you help train in meetings.

Science or art? It really doesn't matter which stance you adopt as long as it's the right one for you. Then make an effort to become versed in the other. Competence can be learned; and confidence will come when that competence produces the results you seek. Every time.

A lot of unqualified or prejudiced persons are trying to make you overlook video conferencing as a valid meetings tool (they grant Ford and universities the right), but the Massachusetts Institute of Technology has recently take a bold step: References and other outlines, and other course materials (not the courses *per se*)will now be available free on-line so that educational establishments all over the world can borrow core materials and create their own syllabi. This is an effaced meeting re: teaching.So why can't it work for you? Why can't effaced meetings regarding gidgits work? And who said so? Oh, yes—the travel and hotel industries, who have a vested interest in killing that idea.

Interesting, this meetings industry, isn't it?

8

Motivation and the incentive Business

Once you recognize that *motivation* is a simple word symbol for complex inner forces and *incentive* is the symbol for external forces working, respectively, within and on any individual it is relatively easy to sort out the practical effects.

As we saw in the preceding chapter, the incentive is a carrot Most employees are willing to work harder in exchange for the specific reward offered, assuming they see it as valuable; but they often see it was a trade-off, too. Fall-off of the extra effort is the common result of incentive programs which do not appeal to underlying motivations.

Is there a legitimate use for non-motivating awards/ gifts/prizes? Sure, but that usage is far more restricted than the incentives merchants would have you believe.

Incentives are great when only superficial habits are at stake. Gas station premiums and gifts given by banks for a new account are examples of incentives properly used: minor one-time actions promptly rewarded in kind. Any long-term benefits accrue to sponsors through human nature: it's easier for the recipient to continue the new habit (stopping in at the sponsoring station or bank) than to revert to the old—the last, also now a change. No big decisions or value judgments are involved.

Even these superficial programs can fail if the customer perceives the gift as a bribe and decides cleverness will yield more than a proper share. So the gas stations gave sets of things, requiring many visits; the banks establish a cash-purchase penalty for early closing of new gift-bearing accounts; and most discount packaging in supermarkets today offers coupons good on your *next* purchase of the same item.

How do incentives work in the company/employee context? What do you think time-and-a-half pay is all about? Or why do you suppose employees grumble about working on holidays but volunteer to work holidays in exchange for two extra vacation days? That's working a deal to everyone's satisfaction, and you don't have to go through a merchant to succeed at it. For minor or one-time actions, incentives will often work where a simple request fails.

But for long-term changes, especially of prerogatives or attitudes, minor incentives generally fail. That's because you're dealing in the areas of personal motivations, personal value systems, personal relationships. Don't be surprised if members of your staff won't trade their lifestyle for some ashtrays. Would you? If your problem lies with a single individual, you can have private conversations and check out the complaints; surely there are a few if the person's not cooperating. But if you want to motivate an entire group, send around a questionnaire and let it guide you toward creation of a motivation program.

Firms recognize flex-time and sabbaticals as two highly successful motivators. Company participation in individually selected charities is another. Is there a company that has failed to find interest in a youth scholarship program within minutes of announcement?

When you want to communicate with people, don't talk merchandise—talk sense, talk purposes, talk values.

Even though they constitute the biggest single value center in our society, families have been largely ignored except for using the wife's acquisitiveness as a goad to her husband (curiously, women's lib hasn't turned that equation around). But here are some of the many human considerations on which motivation programs can turn, followed by logical types of awards:

Family security (beyond immediate income): extra life insurance; mortgage insurance; non-gimmick, guaranteed retirement trust fund.

Children's education: summer camp; domestic trips; scholarships; trust funds; art or music lessons.

Accomplishment: responsibility; promotions; job enlargement; job enrichment; special training; general education.

Need to grow: education; foreign travel.

Need to share: charity and social action groups; youth programs; adopt-a-grandparent; retirement home visitations.

Escape mechanism: a cabin at a lake; company-owned apartotel complex in a resort area loaned to high achievers.

Self-realization: ask the individual!

Maybe nobody will be turned on by all those suggestions, but probably nobody will be closed to all of them, either.

Probably more important, given barely half of those incentives through a motivation program, a company can become a great place to work: psychic income!

Notice how inappropriate merchandise is in the context of motivations—things that matter. Notice, also, how many different ways education and the enlargement of experience can generate benefits for both the employee and the company.

That's the context in which so many firms have found overwhelming response to incentive travel. Travel has a lot of things going for it: glamour, education, growth, novelty, and memories. Yet because travel is expensive, it tends to rank in priorities behind the children's education and even braces for their teeth. So travel is that dream for the future for the majority of people; most never achieve it on an international basis.

If the company can help provide something with such powerful appeal to so deep a set of motivations, why doesn't every company offer travel? That's easy. Incentives companies, having grown out of warehousing operations for merchandise, have relegated travel to the top 10 percent of all awards given. So if you don't agree to take ashtrays and TV sets, many won't talk to you about a few trips. Responsive firms sell 50 percent travel.

There's no reason everyone in a given category can't go, whether that's departmental performance, individual contribution, or perfect attendance records being recognized. Don't let the prejudices of the merchandisers determine your response: any travel agent can help you with the basics and write your tickets.

Incentive travel can be added to the company's existing motivational list very easily and inexpensively. For the general employee (both factory staff and line plus sales and sales service office support personnel), the company can charter aircraft and offer the savings back to employees as low-cost tours. Your travel agent can offer complete tours, see to details, and provide a package arrangement. The agent will be paid either by a percentage mark-up as your fiduciary or at unlimited mark-up for creating" the tour offered. That can mean a substantial difference in price for identical tours; so don't hesitate to ask or take bids, if you know what you want.

Don't overlook the general employees. They resent seeing others win major appliances and trips to which they have no access. Jealousy, greed, and acquisitiveness are closely related personality defects, and they can damage a program.

Neither can it be said that major firms that have long bought major appliances and travel as part of their incentives program are convinced that motivation is being served.

The nation's first incentive travel conference was held in New York City in February 1974, sponsored by New York University's School of Continuing Education, Division of Business and Management. We chaired that meeting.

Although announced for medium and smaller firms, and featuring user companies of modest size, the conference attracted mostly large companies, including the giants. For the record, the giants professed to be satisfied with their current suppliers but interested in *what's new in the field.*

But the conversations centered on motivational factors other than the peer-group belongingness so often emphasized and so little studied. The potential destructiveness of the contests and limited-win situations which serve the purposes of the incentives *suppliers* was also noted.

And it became apparent that the status quo in the industry's methods served the incentives business first and motivation second. That disenchantment was reflected in a subsequent survey taken by *Sales and Marketing Management* magazine; and in an anticipatory (1977) reference to the published report, the publisher noted, "Many managements simply are not convinced..."

Doesn't that show good sense?

For the sales staff, especially those sent to meetings in distant cities, great increments in motivational appeal can be achieved for insignificant increments in cost. Because our domestic airfares are so variable these days—high short-haul rates to all but the most competitive destinations—you can often go abroad for about the same price as you'd pay for a non-metropolitan domestic location. If you bought Spain for the price of Cupcake, Idaho, what would that do for morale? Or even if it cost 10 percent more? And what if you told the employee that the spouse could go along, too, *if...*? In this instance, both the classic motivational and traditional incentive appeals operate together. That's a superior combination which can't fail!

All right, we'll admit to being prejudiced. Having been through hundreds of cities in about 50 countries in all parts of the world, we're ready to go at the drop of a ticket. Our friends and associates usually approach the travel topic with, "I really wish...." And they really yearn.

According to the U.S. Passport Office, only about 10 percent of the population holds a passport, and that number includes the military dependents abroad. Moreover, of the civilian groups making up the balance, many travelers are former immigrants making a pilgrimage home; many more are retirees on a once-in-a-lifetime outing. Very few are employed, middle-income family types.

Which means a tremendous opportunity for your company. Your company's industrial relations goals and your own meetings goals will be admirably served when the company becomes the broker in the fulfillment of lifelong ambitions, whatever they might be.

What do you really want out of life? Probably your subordinates want similar things. Can your company help you and them to achieve/obtain those wants? If so, what can you offer in exchange for the company's assistance? What's in it for the company? Yes, morale and increased productivity count. And if you have a workable idea in mind, why don't you suggest it?

Your prime obligation as a motivator, therefore, is not to probe into the recesses of your business associates' minds. It's not even to buy merchandise or operate trips. Your key obligation is to help them determine worthwhile goals they and the company can work toward together for mutual benefit.

Do you *need* contests? No. Should you *sponsor* contests? That depends on whether you're trying to limit the wins. If you're sending all the employees, courtesy the established sales meeting budget, and inviting spouses, you want everybody. So the person-versus-self (that is, sales increase as the criterion) is the right situation. If you can send only a few dozen among thousands, a contest is almost inevitable. Even then, provide for both team and individual contributions.

And be honest. Statistics for sales events show 19 percent as a common sales increase level. All cost increases total about 5 percent, which includes 4 percent for premiums; so the employees are being cheated. Numbers and percentages change rapidly. The company should commit most or at least half of all increased earnings to all programs; and in the first couple of years all increased earnings should be plowed back into the program.

And be fair. Announce all contest rules up front, in writing. Determine in advance how ties or near-wins will be handled. If a hitch develops through the company's oversight or fault, work it out in favor of the employees. Otherwise you might spend years trying to recover the credibility destroyed in a struggle to retain a thousand dollars in the treasury.

Given integrity of approach, the company can develop its motivational program and incentive travel packages into the most potent management tool at its disposal.

So remember, don't say, "Hey, Buddy, I've got a deal. Work your butt off, and you'll get a ticket to Rome." Instead say, "My friend, if you care about us, we care about you. And here's how I can prove it." Now, *that's* a motivating offer!

9

Perspective on self and company

A Meeting Manager's position in the company hierarchy is not as important in itself as is an understanding of *(a)* the person's own real strengths and weaknesses in constructing meetings; *(b)* company personnel; *(c)* company policy and precedents in meetings and training programs; and *(d)* company politics.

That's true because the Meeting Manager serves in part as a conduit for the ideas and messages of others; in part as an originator of messages; and in part as a teacher/trainer for standard information and skills being imparted to participants.

You have undoubted served in all three of those functions—it's part of being a manager. But you will find yourself being all three simultaneously if you are augmenting a basic program prepared at headquarters with field offices providing local market information and methods. In a regional or centralized meeting, you might find yourself responsible for only a portion of one or more of these three functions. Change is normal and flexibility is your friend.

Throughout this book, we address the *Meeting Manager* as the person who controls each of the three key elements of the meeting: its message and authorities; its participants/audience; and its support tools, materials, and media.

Such a person might not exist. Few individuals are required (or permitted) to perform all those key functions without counsel. Yet the person ultimately responsible for the results of the meeting must be sure that every element which bears on meeting content is adequately provided for. Someone, then, either from personal background or from counsel taken from various other sources, must provide the expertise required to make every decision valid, authoritative, and intelligent.

That person becomes a coordinator of the work of others, in many instances. He might make a presentation during the meeting event, or he might work exclusively behind the scenes.

In any case, the *Meeting Manager/coordinator* is a pivotal figure who needs authority commensurate with responsibility. The coordinator of a symphony orchestra is called the conductor; and that person gets the credit or blame for the music even though he is the only one on stage who never makes a sound!

Unfortunately, the meeting planner doesn't have the conductor's visibility, prestige, or power. But that does not mean that a committee can or should make all the decisions. It does mean that no subjective judgments should be made by the Meeting Manager, or any assistant, until after an accurate appraisal of all pertinent information.

For a first meeting or a new manager that seems complex, but much of the personal preparation becomes routine after a meeting or two. The message and the audience reaction to it become the only significant variables. Once you determine where you fit in relation to the overall task, you become a constant. The *given* audience becomes a constant, as does the place.

Except for radical changes in top management (as sometime occurs after mergers), the company tends to remain a constant over any span of several years—policies tend not to change precipitously without visible cause.

Therefore, the two key considerations confronting the Meeting Manager are the *message* and *himself/herself.* There are many methods for determining and protecting the message, as you will discover in Part II. Help is abundant and outside resources are many.

But you don't fit a template. No set of forms will describe you. So the first step in planning the meeting that achieves is to assess your own experience and the aptitudes you bring to the assigned task. Do you feel comfortable with the human relations theories and psychological findings that were covered in earlier chapters? How much of the general theory is new to you? Familiar? Previously tested and mastered? How confident do you feel as a leader who must guide thinking and practice of others? How can you put your experience at their disposal? How can you encourage them to *use* the available tools and information?

Those questions might be a roundabout way of asking, "who are you?" Don't answer with a recitation of name, rank, and serial number but, rather, by a statement of self-perception.

If you were to list six or eight elements you value most in life, what would be included? If you're not sure, it might be wise to find out now.

You in the human context. Before reading on, close this book and make a list of whatever you value most. Do not reopen the book until you have finished—about six or eight entries. Do that now.

Ready with the list? Now critique it yourself.

How many of the entries are based on the tissue-level needs (food, shelter, sex) as described by Maslow? How many of your entries reflect purchasable things or conditions—anything fairly termed *security oriented* or *status-oriented?*

If the majority of your entries fit into either of these two categories, you're operating—according to Maslow—at the bottom of the developmental hierarchy, at what psychologists sometimes call the animal/acquisitive stage. If so, you might find yourself out of sync with the younger people and even with the more inner directed of the older people you supervise. You might find yourself on the flip side of value-oriented disagreements.

On the other hand, if you find that most of the entries reflect love and belonging relationships, achievement, and giving, you are operating in the upper levels of Maslow's hierarchy. Your emphasis is on what you *are* rather than on what you *have;* so you probably possess more than average empathy. You can more easily identify with people and see problems from *their* perspective, too. If so, you can succeed admirably in leading and motivating people via meetings.

As we pointed out in Chapter 2, the meeting has become complex because of people, not technology. We can speak of crowds, but you, yourself, as the Meeting Manager might be most important of all.

You in the company context. It's common to talk of *employees* and *company,* but even when we say "company" we still mean people. After all, the corporation is only an inanimate, artificial person, as lifeless as the paper which proves its existence. The ideas of its top officers become the ideas of the company; but are those ideas open to discussion and change?

The ethics of the executive body becomes the ethics of the company, sometimes collectively and sometimes at odds with written policy or past direction. *Corporate responsibility* is an ethical concept advanced in the 70s but accepted only recently; yet it affects you: your personal ethics are at stake when you implement policies you don't believe equitable. That can be an uncomfortable position at times.

Since it's impossible to discuss "the company" as a clear-cut entity with clear-cut direction, some of the interpretation of policy and its best application in your territory and in your meetings will fall to you. In general, do you feel comfortable with policy? If not, discuss discrepancies with your immediate supervisor; go as high up with the questions as necessary until the discrepancies are resolved. You cannot do your best work if you are not convinced of the intrinsic validity of that work.

You in the group context. Your job is easy or difficult to some degree in proportion to your familiarity with the group of participants as individuals and/or as familiar crowd. There is a crowd psychology and it does operate in larger meetings at most times and even in small meetings from time to time.

When you are meeting with your immediate subordinates, you can all feel comfortable; on the negative side you can try to fake it, thereby making an inadequate presentation. If you are meeting with your peers, you know the kind of problems under discussion and can get specifics by telephone when planning. If you are meeting with larger groups and don't know a considerable number of participants at several levels by name, then you are a stranger and need to ask for substantial amounts of input at all stages of the program's development. (See Part II.)

The majority of all company meetings are probably sales oriented; and salespersons and dealers or distributors make up the bulk of the crowd on the receiving end. If you sense that the composite management view of those personnel is based more on stereotype and prejudice than on personal contact, act. Give yourself a chance to succeed: make direct contact with a full cross section of the intended audience and convey that cross-representational viewpoint upward.

The time and money spent in learning exactly who is participating and how they think and what they value will be repaid many times over with objectives achieved—cost effectively.

It's wise to take phone surveys whenever you're not *sure* of attitudes toward the intended message. It's not impractical—and probably desirable—to take a formal survey whenever a meeting message is of particular consequence.

And when you finally address them as a group, speak the same language you used with them as individuals: their language and that of their customers. Take no chances with company jargon!

You in the precedents context. Precedent and tradition cannot safely be ignored—but need not be obeyed. The trick is to isolate the objectionable features and explain your stand. When problems crop up, it's usually because policy and precedent—more than the dictates of the message—are shaping meetings. Some companies have unrealistic budgets that waste more than they use wisely, either because too little is appropriated (and all is lost) or because budgets have been pegged too high (to hide the fact that someone was once sold a bill of goods). It's easy to spend money on meetings but it's difficult to get your money's worth without shrewd value analysis.

Besides money issues related to such things as the hierarchical position of the attendees (which affects the cost of the hotel and duration permitted off the job), tradition often tangles the lines of good communication. It's been a tradition to hear from some people who shouldn't be heard from because they have nothing to say. That bruises egos. Which leads into another sensitive area.

You in the politics context. If you believe a given policy is wrong, try to change it. If you can't change it, try to dissociate yourself from those whose influence can defeat you. It's conceivable that you have full authority in your role of Meeting Manager/coordinator; most likely, you don't. Yet someone will bear the ultimate responsibility for the success or failure of the meeting: you or the V.P. Sales or someone in between. If you're not that person, find him! Level with the person on all matters of discrepancy, whatever their origin.

Out of a sense of self-preservation, if not concern for the message, the responsible party must take up your cause. If he has been on the winning team for most of the internal battles, he will probably make a new effort to get you an exemption from policy, if not an outright change. If he is among the losers in the current power lineup, now is the time to find out. Then go to the real source of power and play your hand. Far better to know exactly where you stand before you make wrong commitments, while paper changes are easy and time is on your side.

You in the transition context. Any communications process must be seen as a transition process because of the power of new learning. As a Meeting Manager/coordinator, you are overseeing and hurrying the transition process.

If any of the ideas presented so far in Part I have made you uncomfortable, you've got to face the problem and work it through. Maybe you should redefine your own goals and expectations. Or reevaluate your assumptions; rethink your priorities; re-balance your education/ training mix; restructure your internal personnel development and support mechanisms. Or simply reorient yourself in the purposes of people and group communications. Be prepared to reeducate some of your suppliers along with your personnel. Be prepared to distinguish between essentials and embellishments, needs and wants, and message and format

This book will guide you toward the proper learning areas and decisions, but you must be willing to decide and act The book can help prepare you to design and execute intelligent programs, but you must be sure the intelligent product is appropriate for the given participants and valid as outlined in Chapter 2. Things will be different in the future because of your choices today. You are working with the ultimate tool: people.

In general, management has not yet begun to tap the creative potential of the workforce, especially those white-collar workers who regard meetings as pointless and burdensome. Yet those of us who have seen valid meetings open minds, evaporate misunderstandings, generate enthusiasm, and change lives can already appreciate the potential of the smaller-yet-enlarged meetings of tomorrow.

In order to communicate best with the workforce, management will have to surrender the ancient royal tradition of distance: aren't you and other managers yourselves only employees of the organization? Rejoin the group psychologically. Help and instruct. Give whenever you can. Show more than tell. You're a prime instrument of change in the transition process.

You in the world labor context. Co-determination of company direction is seeping into American firms from Europe and Japan. Those who see themselves as different because of different skills or experience—rank—have defective eyesight. If the executive predilection toward psychological distancing can be overcome, then the management/labor adversary entrenchments can be filled in.

To their acute embarrassment, some American multinational companies fought the issue of codetermination in their European plants years ago, were proved fossilized of intellect, and now provide the best argument in favor of the new humanistic trends in management. In Europe, labor sits with executives on the management board. In Japan, consensus is enforced with a fervor approaching fanaticism; it's unnatural and suspect. But both modes exist. So wherever your company policy stands in relation to global trends, look to the big picture.

Any management/labor rapprochement enhances the working relationships and advances the objectives of all parties without direct cost. Any channel for facilitating that rapprochement must be utilized.

If a meeting is the proper channel in a given instance, then meetings can help, because only meetings among all other internal communications formats provide for immediate interchange and feedback as part of their integral structure.

Intelligent employees are the means to new ends in business; and binding them to the cause is management's task. The *common* cause is the one which will succeed first. And even at field sales office level, significant changes can be worked.

Once the organization's upper and lower levels of the traditional hierarchy begin to communicate with each other, they can form (or possibly rediscover) a synergistic relationship that has a chance of fulfilling goals.

Valid meetings can contribute substantially to the financial health of the organization and to a gentle warming of its emotional climate. That gain will be reflected in morale and performance levels.

There's a lot of work involved in competent communications and job enrichment, and much of it will be done by the training manager and you. It won't be easy.

Has there ever been an age of easy answers? Probably not. The big difference between our time and past ages is that a greater proportion of the people are relieved of the grind of subsistence-level existence; so a greater proportion of the people can turn themselves to values and provocative issues. They can think and grow and share.

And you can help. Get on with the job!

Helping people to find new potential and new rewards in their work helps them to find new potential in the organization and in their own lives. You will probably discover that helping them to grow delivers more satisfaction to you than all the perks of distance and unsullied rank ever can. If you do discover that, you will have grown, too.

Without the growth that reeducation can provide to you and through you, there will be no way to manage and control the changes looming in every aspect of social behavior and business.

Quality of management is critical in the meeting room too. Give it everything you've got!

PART II

10

Relating message and meanings

"What do you mean by that?" How many times have you heard that phrase—or used it? It's the everyday acknowledgment of researchers' findings (Chapter 6) that for many complex reasons different people often draw different meanings from the same words.

Sometimes the words used are themselves ambiguous; but more often, meeting participants are assaulted with bushels of facts which have not been properly correlated. Therefore, the meanings are not clear and confusion is inevitable.

Carelessness accounts for part of the problem, especially if a valid meaning has been obscured. But sometimes the meaning of particular facts is not readily apparent-or can be read in several ways. Then an official *interpretation* must be adopted and that interpretation will color all related material.

Facts, if accurate, are concrete; meanings are relative. You've seen facts mistaken for meanings in something as common as the personnel interview. During an interview, you have surely been asked (and might have asked others) what the current annual sales figure is for your current employer. This question is intended to test the applicant's interest in the firm. But that quickie test is specious because someone's parroting a published dollar sum in no way indicates an understanding of the *meaning* of the sum. For instance, does the sum reflect a rising or falling sales volume for the preceding year? The trend for several years? The industry's yearly volume and trend for the same period? Naturally, sales volume is rarely related directly to the profit realized because efficiency, depreciation, capital costs, and even losses for the introduction of new products are independent variables. A person content to know only the sales figure is, at best, a shallow thinker.

One of the problems with complicated material is that management often attempts to dramatize the facts rather than meanings. Lining up facts and then trying to make the facts interesting via visuals, actors, songs, or any other production method is self-defeating: the meanings or interpretations intended must still be stated, or each person will interpret for himself/herself. That can create chaos.

Curiously, the interpretations can be right or wrong (according to the "facts"), just as validity is differentiated from the truth of a syllogism in logic. So the spoken message and the workshop/training sessions which follow must offer predigested facts expressed as meanings and methods or by other techniques. Any intelligent message presents its meanings so as to communicate—to evoke a response. Whether a response is favorable or unfavorable is possibly of less consequence than the fact that response has indeed occurred. After all, selling is the art of persuading despite an unfavorable initial response, isn't it? Otherwise, it's just order taking.

Occasionally you will be blessed with a message which is popular and greeted with applause; more often the message will state an obvious need, which might result in some grumbling but will be accepted and acted upon. So far so good.

But what about the tough ones—those with unpopular messages or debatable interpretations?

If you expect debate or opposition, be prepared to accommodate it. Choking off an expression of contrary opinions—especially on an emotional issue—will force the problem below the surface, where it will fester.

Every point of contention will have at least two sides: the company's and the employees'. The latter will of course be fragmented into individual opinions and attitudes. As we noted earlier, you can't deal separately with every person's own value structure, but you can deal effectively with general motivations and attitudes.

To do that, calculate the impact of the key points of discrepancy in advance of the meeting; answer those discrepancies fully. Gauge the anticipated attitudes and resentments and mention those so they know you understand. If there's a "loss" for them, acknowledge it; then tell them what they can gain. If it's flatly bad news, don't try to disguise the fact; do let them object—after the meeting, if necessary.

When you accurately peg the most likely reaction(s) to the given problem message, you can benefit in three ways.

First, you can reduce or minimize any nonessential elements of the original plan, especially those which will forfeit more by antagonizing people than can be gained. Management is not always realistic in its expectations, so sales managers are doing the company a favor when they spot potential problems in advance of the meeting.

Second, you can concentrate on any side benefits the new activity or methods might hold for the individual. Appeal to fundamental interests which coincide with the anticipated gain the company is seeking. And if there is no clear benefit to the company, why should the program be implemented?

Third, if the unpopular changes will be of major economic benefit, share some of those benefits via an incentive program paid for by a percentage of the gain. Don't be greedy: incentive specialists recommend giving the bulk—even 100 percent—of the first year's gains back to the employees. Later, half is fair.

Meeting controversy head on is not an easy task, especially because the final result must be generated by a feeling of trust, not warfare. There's no magic formula for that, but there is help.

Much of the work of measuring and changing opinions has been done on a rather shallow basis by or for commercial enterprise. Careless borrowing of terminology and hypotheses from one to another has marred the early work of even such an otherwise dependable source as the Opinion Research Corporation.

Several researchers have criticized their colleagues' work. In *Attitude, Ego Involvement, and Change* Karl Weick concludes that overall the work has been hasty and shallow. In *Attitude Change and Social Influence*, Arthur Cohn points out that some measures were based on ivory tower situations, not real life.

As a result of all that criticism, the opinion and persuasion people dug in and refined their methods. We are swayed by the end product, now used extensively by politicians.

But the deeper aspects of persuasion and conflict resolution are those of most value to you, although they are so complex that there are no pat formulas. But there are many insights contained in the mono-graphs of prominent scientists. These findings jibe with good sense as well as with academic statistical methods and so are worth summarizing here. In regard to:

1. One-sided versus two-sided presentations: "No advantage for one program over the other for the audience as a whole is revealed. While two-sided arguments are favored by better-educated men, they also shake the confidence of the less well-educated men." — C. Hovland, A. Lumsdaine, F. Sheffield, *Experiment on Mass Communication* (Princeton: Princeton University Press, 1949.)
2. Opinions and attitudes: "There is a tendency for people to believe in ways which will maintain an internally consistent belief system.". —Rosenberg, C. Hovland, W. McGuire, R. Abelson, J. Brehm, *Attitude Organization and Change* (New Haven: Yale University Press, 1960.)

   "People like to have someone admit he is slightly wrong so they may be slightly right. Such an admission is generally followed by an emotion of understanding, tolerance, and acceptance of subsequent positive statements." —H. Cantrill, *The Human Dimension: Experience in Policy Research* (New Brunswick, N.J.: Rutgers University Press, 1967.)

"An attack on an individual's conviction is likely to be interpreted as one directed against him personally.... Criticisms can boomerang by giving additional currency to the very viewpoints which are being criticized." —L. Doob, *Public Opinion and Propaganda* (Archon, 1966.)

3. Personal involvement: "The magnitude of reactance is a direct function of the proportion and importance of the behaviors threatened and the magnitude of that threat." —J. Brehm, *Theory of Psychological Reactance* (New York: Academic Press, 1966.)

Slot your problem according to the pertinent advice. Until sociologists agree on definitions of opinion and attitude they won't agree on how either affects behavior, and you won't get a handbook of simple rules. But you can get a feel for it now.

To Hovland opinion is a simple synthesis among statements perceived to be true, while to Wiebe this synthesis develops into convictions, or attitudes, which govern behavior of an individual. (G. Wiebe, "Some Implications of Separating Opinions from Attitudes," Public Opinion Quarterly no.17 (1953).

One thing is sure: the company cannot wait until all the definitions are in before dealing with employee objections, as the incident at the Lordstown, Ohio General Motors assembly plant some years back indicated. Assembly-line workers had evolved a system by which relay teams formed out of the basic crew alternated periods of heightened activity and rest. Although quality went up, both the union and the company objected because of bruised egos. The relay concept was killed. So was cooperation.

Until there's an officially validated overview provided by the sociologists, you might want to use this. It is fully consistent with the sources quoted above:

When presenting a controversial argument to a general audience which initially disagrees with the communicator's position or is likely to hold or to be

> *exposed to a contrary position, acknowledge but do not argue the contrary side; then state your strongest positive point.*

That means you'll have to put real thought into the best formulation of the message you express. Initially this thinking through could be time consuming, but once you've proved to yourself that you really know your people, your response will become almost automatic. From then on, simple keep-in-touch activities will help you maintain an updated viewpoint adequate for all but the most sensitive of issues. For those, get fresh opinions from the people to be affected, and do it in advance!

The crux of this entire issue of facts versus meanings is that for the most part you don't need to dramatize meanings. For intelligent individuals, meanings are of themselves important and interesting. Meanings are much cheaper to express because they are already related to the individual and invite personal involvement both in understanding the message and later in acting in accordance with it. Don't overspend; don't entertain!

If you understand and respect your people, and if you earn their respect, you will discover that there's no issue too tough or too complex to handle in meetings.

If you've absorbed the ideas presented in Part I, and if you think a meeting is the best format for presenting the given message, it's time to begin roughing out your control materials.

Control is as essential to the management of meetings as to any other function. Without control mechanisms built into your procedures, all plans are at hazard and success can occur only by accident.

The forms and charts which follow in this chapter and in the balance of Part II are intended to guide your thinking about problems and issues and considerations which must be resolved before you can have the integrated plan which deserves success. Do not assume that any of our forms are necessarily complete and adequate for your needs. As you use them let the sense of the material lead you to explore related areas determined by the unique conditions of the given meeting.

At this point, you're ready to work with the Message Profile and the Audience Profile. These concepts are a pair and the guides should be developed both in the same session.

Think through these concepts now, and make notes on all of our and your own questions. No glib answers...think!

Controlling the risk of failure. If you have properly assessed the meeting situation via the Message Profile and the Audience Profile, then you are relatively safe from failure caused by sheer stupidity.

Yet failure could still come from either of two main causes: first, as we have already discussed, the failure to support the message with the tools required to perform as requested; and second, a technical failure.

Technical failures are those in which the message cannot be delivered because *(a)* it gets lost in the theatrical/media trappings or *(b)* it is totally lost because of a mechanical failure, such as a burnt-out bulb.

Although no producer can prevent a burn-out (or any other mechanical failure) the producer is responsible for any failure to deliver that message because the producer is responsible for the technical sufficiency of the program. Any properly constructed and technically competent production plan provides fail-safe protection for the message. Back-up equipment is only part of the answer.

A good "Plan B" simply provides *in advance* a (choice of) workable alternative(s) to the planned presentation/production *techniques* that could—by nature of the medium—fail in the meeting room. Either backup equipment or acceptable delay or backup authorities could provide your fail-safe "Plan B."

Creating a "Plan B" for a meeting takes only a small extra effort but that's not the problem. The problem lies in recognizing the faulty production scheme that's smothering the message, or the one that's so complicated (with huge casts and/or computer-controlled banks of equipment) that fail-safe is impossible.

Sales Meetings That Work
MESSAGE PROFILE
(Use a separate form for each message)

1. Key concept of message:

   Who is the authority/expert for this message?

2. Ramifications — effects on present policies and methods:

   Conflicts:

   Changes needed:

3. Changes required in materials and tools as a result of Items (1) and (2) above:

   Tool: Change:

4. Who is responsible for implementing those changes?

   At corporate level:

   On staff level:

   On the line:

   In the field:

   Other:

5. What are the best techniques for implementing those changes (consider new tools and training structures; see Chapters 6 and 13, respectively):
6. Is a meeting the proper and required format? (Yes) (No).
7. If required, can or should meetings be conducted in various focales, given proper construction? (Yes) (No). Reasons:
8. Does the rationale of item (7) agree with the combined restrictive of items (3), (4), and (5)? (Yes) (No). Discrepancies:
9. Resolution of discrepancies above:
10. Effective date of all changes for policies, methods, tools, etc.:

    ______________.

    Planning time available:

    All components needed by:

11. Preliminary announcement of message needed by

    ______________.

    Probable text:

12. Are all considerations of message compatible with all considerations and potential objections of the audience (see Audience profile, following)? (Yes) (No). Discrepancies:

13. Resolution of discrepancies above:
14. If a meeting is the most practicable communications format, can the dollar benefits justify the dollar cost (see Work Sheet, next chapter)? (Yes) (No). Discrepancies:
15. Other value factors and determinative purposes, if dollar measures are not appropriate:
16. Is there clear justification within Items (14) and/or (15) above for conducting this meeting? If not, rethink the purposes of the benefits; consider canceling the meeting.

If you cannot obtain fail-safe protection at low cost, you are gambling on media.

Sensitivity to the needs of the message and the will to protect it require a firm resistance to the supersales personship of theatrical producers and other suppliers of media.

Slide, movie, and video producers are all selling their production devices and services; the message rides free, plucked from your files at a relatively low cost by a production writer. Unless producers sell you consulting time, they must sell you things. The big profit is in *things*.

With alarming predictability, the *recommendations* of the producers as a group have reflected the kinds of things they are best prepared to do. That is, the film studio rarely will recommend live performances; the stagecraft people recommend live actors, short film sequences, and elaborate stage settings; the slide producers rarely recommend other formats.

In other words, what is called a recommendation in the production business tends to be a shove toward whatever the bidder does best. Few are either willing or prepared to assess your program and then create the support mechanisms which the program itself demands.

SALES MEETINGS THAT WORK

Audience Profile

(Use a separate form for each message if effects differ)

Regarding Message; subject:

____

1. How is the audience affected by this message?

   Corporate:

   Staff:

   Line:

   Field:

   Other:

2. Is the immediate reaction of those affected likely to be one of (enthusiasm), (passive acceptance), (objection)? Why?

3. Does that reaction argue (for) (against) the meeting format? Why?

4. After the message is stated and objectives and methods are outlined, the training/education function is essentially:

   a. The improvement/reinforcement of existing skills or methods;

   b. Slight modification of existing skills or methods;

   c. Substantial change to previously used skills or methods;

   d. New complementary skills or methods to be learned.

   Describe each applicable function:

5. Is the training/education function compatible both with the applicable functions of item (4) above and with the tools previously selected (on the Message Profile) as best for supporting this message? (Yes) (No). Discrepancies:

6. Resolution of discrepancies or confirmation of compatibility:

7. Will the proposed new methods/skills/tools return a measurable dollar benefit (see "Work Sheet," next chapter)? (Yes) (No). Probable rate of return on investment: _______%

8. Are the authorities/experts for this message (on the Message Profile) recognized as such by the audience? (Yes) (No). If not, how can their acceptance be assured?

9. Given the time available between announcement of message and first measurement of results, are the selected formats practical, however valid in theory? (Yes) (No). Possible problems:

   Given the time available between now and target meeting date, is the meeting format itself practical, however valid? (Yes) (No). Best alternative:

10. From the viewpoint of the audience, is the message pertinent to their problems? (Yes) (Maybe) (No).

    If yes, state main appeal:

    If maybe, what inducements might be necessary?

11. If no, can the message be "sold" to a group? Consider canceling!

12. Given the combined effects of items (2) and (11) above, can the audience reactions be heightened or lessened (as applicable) by offering motivating incentives? (Yes) (No). Reasons

13. Given all considerations above, including methods/tools/skills, and authority/expert acceptance:

    a. Can the authority be committed to print, videotape, or film for multiple exposure? (Yes) (No).

    b. Can the local supervisors conduct the balance of the meeting if live or "packaged" authority is provided? In theory: (Yes) (No). In practice (Yes) (No).

    c. Are multiple meetings with traveling/"packaged" authorities the most workable solution? (Yes) (No).

    d. Is one central meeting the most workable solution? (Yes) (No).

14. Resolution of any remaining discrepancies (Items 9, 10, and 13):

15. Final decision on viability of the meeting from audience viewpoint:

While on the surface it might seem that the clients have preselected carefully, it is more often true that the client has no idea which of many program formats is best for communicating his message. Too many clients don't know what their message is before they go shopping, and some of them never find out, even though they pay handsomely to make a stab at it during the meeting.

If you shop for a producer before you know at least the rudiments of your message and the support tools it requires, you are probably wasting your time. Selecting the best producer for the job requires that you know what the job really is.

Although it's conceivable that you will stumble upon the ideal producer, it's far more likely that you will be led into a premature commitment—one that will bend your meeting to fit the producer's own limitations.

If you want to keep control of your meeting, it's necessary to be able to say, "This is my message, this is who my people are, and this is what I can afford. Now, what format do you recommend and what production techniques to execute it?" That's the only way you will establish your control over the project.

At this point, you are generally ready to take competitive bids. Plan to take three, and to tell each producer that he is bidding. The amount of time he puts into the bid is his choice; he is entitled to know the circumstances. If you attempt to cheat producers early in the relationship, they will have abundant opportunity to return the favor.

When you ask for an opinion, and if you hope to have any legally enforceable right to unbiased advice, you must pay for it.

Consultants, advice, and bias. When you don't know the answers, you must buy advice. You willingly pay for advice from doctors and lawyers—even from major consulting firms when multimillion dollar projects are at stake. Yet most meeting planners naively expect to get something for nothing when they need professional production advice and even something so basic as programming expertise.

Unless you pay for an opinion with the stipulation that it be unbiased and that the written recommendation belongs to you, your advisor is legally entitled to exercise his own biases.

Conversely, when you do not pay for an opinion, you are not entitled to take producer A's opinion and offer that work to producer B. Clients who cheat help perpetuate the industry's lack of ethics.

Your best stance in taking bids is to get a professional opinion in advance of preparing your bid specifications; then prepare the specifications in writing and submit identical copies to each bidder. The bidding producers are then entitled to rethink the conditions without extra fee, if they choose to do so. And their re-commendations will reflect the program needs you outline much more accurately than if general ideas were thrown out for starters.

When basic information is sensitive and you are unwilling to put it in writing, you might call a single conference of competing producers. You can deliver all information verbally one time, all bidders will have the same understanding, and no one will have a complete set of data. It's not as polite as the written specifications sheet, but it's safer.

There are three categories of assistance open to you: *(a)* paid advice on a consulting basis; *(b)* "free" advice from any supplier, directly or indirectly; and *(c)* supplier/advisor on a consultative-selling basis. Here's how they differ:

Paid advice. For a true consulting relationship to be operating, all three of the following strictures must be in effect simultaneously:

> **First**, the consultant must have a legitimate claim to expertise in the area in which he offers service. This expertise can be any combination of training and experience acceptable to you. For practical purposes, it should exceed your own expertise substantially. Marginally qualified consultants will write marginally acceptable recommendations and produce marginal results. To examine and compare the credentials of prospective consultants is your right and obligation.
>
> **Second**, for a fee the consultant *should* agree to evaluate—from your viewpoint and absolutely free of conflicting prior commitment—your problem and objectives and to investigate and evaluate all reasonable courses of action that could yield a solution to the problem. He reports in writing on the relative merits of the most significant approaches and probably recommends one. The consultant cannot guarantee the success of any recommendation—it's really only *professional opinion.* Yet several of the most

respected general consulting firms in the nation refuse, in defense of their reputations, to undertake a controversial consulting assignment unless the client agrees in advance to put their consulting recommendation into practice intact for a stipulated period following the report. Freedom from conflict of interest—not the fact of a fee alone—is at issue.

Third, by taking an ethical stance of freedom from conflict, the consultant guarantees the client both freedom from bias and freedom from profit-based motives; and guarantees both in writing. Should the consultant breach either of those provisions, he has breached both professional ethics and the contract, and the offender is liable under the law. You can and should expect strict compliance; and the reputable consultants and firms would consider nothing else.

Free advice. The second point above (freedom from conflict of interest) is implicit in the noncompetitive accounts structure used by both advertising and broad-scope sales promotion agencies, distinct from one-component suppliers. Yet it is in exactly your waiver of the third point (profit-making on goods or services supplied or purchased) that otherwise qualified advisors become supplier-advisors rather than the "consultants" they might claim to be. In exchange for your waiver on the profit restriction, you agree to accept "free" market and media evaluation service. Whereas your interests are somewhat protected by the standard advertising commission structure of 15 percent, no such protection exists in the conventions world.

Therefore, if you hire a "consultant" or "coordinator" who agrees to be paid in full or in large part by commission from your hotels and other suppliers, you are inviting a conflict between your interest in the best service/facility out there and his interest in the highest commission out there. You can be set up for disaster by your own doing. Some meeting planners are so insecure that they would rather hire an assistant in this way than admit to management that they need the help; such people should not be in charge of a meeting.

Similarly, members of the something-for-nothing crowd try to convince you that they are helping you when they turn you over to suppliers of related services. Of late there have been growing ties between theatrical producers and airlines or hotels. If what you are getting "free" from the one supplier is simply a visit with another you have gained nothing. Indeed that could be the start of a deceptive practice against you because either or both participants are free to profit mightily from their own advice. Many suppliers with vested interests have subverted the problems and needs of trusting clients and have made windfall profits. Legal—yes. Ethical—whatever happened to ethics?

Supplier-advisors. In purely practical terms, we must recognize that in some esoteric fields there are few nonsupplier advisors—that is, true consultants. Convention coordination is one of the fields in which practitioners augment their fee incomes by taking commissions or by up-charging. So there will be times when you feel you must deal with an advisor who will supply some elements. That does not make him a consultant any more than is a shoe salesperson who gives you the correct size of the shoe style you think you want, or talks you into another in-stock style.

Any supplier could function as a supplier-advisor IF he can be divorced from (or admits) the profit motive for such a program as yours. In any event, be certain *(a)* that the person truly possesses expertise in the meetings field; *(b)* that she or he will agree to take a specific ethical stance on the portion of services covered by your service fee; and *(c)* that you will have final choice among several types and prices of each type of goods or service purchased for you. At no time should you buy blindly or allow the person to "take care of everything."

If you feel you must go that route, include in your written contract these provisions: *(a)* you will own the advisor's advice and recommendations and reserve the right not to proceed; *(b)* all possible solutions, not only his services and products, will be examined and commented on; and *(c)* you will have the right to proceed, if you proceed, by furnishing the written report to several competitive bidders, of which he might be one. For all practical purposes, he should bid, having a better understanding than all others using his data. Always permit other bidders to rethink (without extra fee) the problem and solution; they might have better ideas. Keep in mind that unintentional bias can enter the recommendations of any supplier-advisor because it's human nature to favor that which we can do well. When buying, *beware*.

Consultative selling is a cousin to the supplier-advisor relationship. Generally the manufacturer of the complex goods or services can offer everything you need, but the specific components to be sold/purchased cannot be selected without a thorough study of your company and situation. That's true, for instance, of computers, which are offered in a range of capacities and costs. A consultative sales person owns his opinion; you are not entitled to take bids upon it. On the other hand, the person is not predisposed to sell you the wrong thing, especially because you have long-term claims, in most instances, for warranty and future service. That safety feature is missing from the meetings and conventions field: the event happens and is gone forever. Traceless.

Your conscientious application of these bias-neutralizing techniques will help to insulate you from routine supplier abuses. At the same time, by separating the supplier-advisor's professional opinions from his purchasing recommendations on commission, you can both feel more comfortable in a sticky relationship. That comfort might grow into trust over the period of a few programs, and that can lead to a long-term client/supplier relationship which he will not want to jeopardize for a few quick bucks.

When shopping, keep your eyes open: the con artists are out in force. Suspect any supplier-advisor who, in the paid-recommendation portion of the service fails to investigate all the alternatives you feel exist-in fact, don't pay for the opinion at all. Simply reject it with a terse explanation that it is not complete and therefore of no value to you; never go back to that source. Another warning flag should go up if the solutions in practice appear to be significantly different from those theorized in the paid portion of the opinion or if the person later wants to eliminate components postulated to competitors. That could indicate some change of direction on your part; but more likely it indicates an intentional distortion (or rigging) of the bid process.

These are demanding procedures, granted, but the ethical crisis in the conventions industry is so acute that nothing short of healthy suspicion will get you through.

The relationship of those three categories to each other and to your problem of obtaining trusted advice should be clear: the introduction of a legally enforceable ethical or fiduciary stance into every contract.

In his humorous book *Up the Organization*, Robert C. Townsend wrote: "Consultants borrow your watch to tell you the time and then keep the watch." What Mr. Townsend really said was: Top management is sometimes so narrow that it will not accept directly from subordinates the kind of solutions to internal problems that a consultant will arrive at after talking with those same subordinates.

If the consultant's prestige and disinterest are all that's needed to validate and implement a good solution, then the consultant has earned the fee. When management learns to listen to internal opinions with an open mind, it will often save the consultant's fee.

All answers must proceed from the problem itself. No one can bring magic solutions from outside; consultants can bring a fresh viewpoint, a freedom from the conventional wisdom of the firm, which so often strangles clear thinkers inside.

If you understand your message and your audience/ participants, you know the type of approach which will best serve your needs. What you are buying outside is the detailed information on methods and technology which will serve that approach best. If you keep that in mind at all times, you'll be surprised at how much sense the production process can make—even your first time in charge!

If you feel you need assistance in clarifying your message or in creating the proper support tools and media, think your way through the adjacent Consultant Evaluator and Something-for-Nothing Evaluator guides.

Sales Meetings That Work
Consultant Evaluator

Consulting firm name:_______________Phone: ____________

Address: ______________________________City: ______________

Contact's name: ______________________Title: _____________

Recommended by: ____

(If recommended by another supplier, also complete the "Something-for-Nothing Evaluator," following.)

Re: Message/problem:_____________________________________

Target start date: _________Latest delivery date: _________

Prior to first interview with proposed consultant, determine:

1. In relation to the specific message/problem, is this consultant being considered for:
   a. Specific knowledge of that problem area; describe:
   b. General reputation in related areas; specify:
   c. General reputation in non-related areas.
   d. Considering applicable points above, an apparently (acceptable) (good) (superior) prospect.

During the interview, determine:

2. If answer includes Item 1-a above, list applicable experience and references in detail; include their client contacts:
3. Name of consultant to be assigned: _________________________

Consultant's personal qualifications and credits in this problem area:

4. If answer includes Item 1-b above, list related credentials and explain their relevance in detail:
   a. Are those credentials really related to our message/problem? (Yes) (No)
   b. Name of qualified consultant already on staff:
   c. If none, how will that firm handle our account?
   d. If they will hire a new man to handle it (any man "now on vacation" probably has not yet been hired), can we hire a man for our staff instead? (Yes) (No).
   e. If yes, probable cost (salary, fringes, secretary, etc.): $______________annually.
   f. If hired, could that man pay his way in other areas after completion of this project? (Yes) (No). Explain:

5. Consultant's standard billing structure:
    a. per hour: $_________
    b. per day, open rate $_____________
    c. per day, short-term contract: $_____________
    d. long-term contracts: $__________ per week/month in blocks of ________weeks/months.
    e. Tangible-unit basis: $__________per unit (without regard to time); a "unit" described as:
    f. Additional costs, fees, options, etc:
6. Consultant's estimate of time required for this message/problem:
    a. Is cost estimate fairly firm or just ballparked?
    b. If closed quote is not offered, will the consultant guarantee an upper cost limit? (Yes) (No). If not, why not?
7. In justifying the paid-out cost:
    a. Will this problem recur in the future? (Yes) (Maybe) (No).
    b. If they must hire to accommodate us, can we hire the same type of person at a comparable cost for the first year/project (See Item 4-d, e, f)? (Yes) (No).
    c. Would the new staff man spend additional funds for related services in any case? (Yes) (No). If yes, why?
    d. Comparing costs, is a new-hire a better investment than the consulting contract?
    e. Is the cost actually cheaper for the time needed if purchased through the consultant? (Yes) (No). Justify (re: Items 4, 5, and 6, above): $ ____________ if paid to consultant vs. $ ______________ staff plus $____________ paid out.
    f. Is the problem area so atypical and the expertise so unrelated to our anticipated subsequent needs that consulting (at whatever cost) is the wisest solution?
8. Is this "consultant" a supplier of nay of the goods or services he could possibly recommend in solution of the problem? (Yes) (No). If yes, reread material on consultant/supplier-advisor in this chapter.
    a. Is there a potential conflict of interest?
    b. If recommendations and applications are properly separated by contract provisions, could he become an acceptable supplier-advisor?
    c. If yes, will he guarantee an unbiased written report (paid) and free us in writing from obligation to buy? (Yes) (No). Reservations:

   d. If yes, will he agree in writing that we will own the (paid) advisory opinion/recommendation and take competitive bids? (Yes) (No). Conditions:

   e. If no, does this "consultant" have a working relationship with any supplier which could indicate fee-splitting or other mutually beneficial arrangement? (Yes) (No). If yes, reevaluate via points a, b, and c above and consider eliminating him from consideration. Resolution of discrepancies:

9. All points considered, is this consultant apparently right for us? (Yes) (No). Why?

10. If we contract with this consultant:

    a. When can he begin?

    b. Can he meet the deadline? (Definite) (Probable).

    c. What are the chances of overtime/overrun or other extra costs? (None) (Possible): to __________ % maximum.

11. Final decision in comparing this consultant to other prospective consultants or supplier-advisors equally highly regarded and qualified:

Sales Meetings That Work
Something-for-Nothing Evaluator

Re: Message/problem:____

Prior to first interview with the supplier of the proposed "free" service, specify:

1. Our understanding of the nature of the proposed service is:
2. Amount of time to be spent discussing our problem: _____ hours.
3. How closely is the proposed service related to our problem or known needs? Specify areas of help:
4. By whom was this "free" service recommended:
    a. Referring party's relationship to supplier:
    b. Referring party's relationship to us:
    c. Is this referral standard procedure within referring party's contract with us?
    d. If yes, are we really paying a hidden fee?
5. Does the "free" service have a definite commercial value? (Yes) (No). Value: $_________ for hours delivered in first visit. Subsequent project cost/value: $_____________
    a. Is the service provided absolutely free to us because of our contract with the referring party? Absolutely no strings attached? (Yes) (No).
    b. If yes, has the referring party himself paid for it? (Yes) (No).
    c. If no, how does the supplier expect to be compensated?
    d. Would our anticipated purchases entitle us to equal time and service even without the referral? (Yes) (No). Why?
    e. Is it possible that the "free" service is a gimmick for which we will ultimately pay the supplier's entire normal cost plus hidden commission to the referring party? (Yes) (No).
6. On the surface it appears that we should (accept) (suspect) the legitimacy of the arrangement. If "suspect" is indicated, consider terminating consideration and refuse to see supplier.

When making appointment, confirm:

7. In the supplier's own words:
    a. How much time will be spent on his sales pitch?
    b. How much time will be spent talking about our problems: _____hours without fee.

c. What is the market value of that discussion? $____________

d. Is this "free" discussion part of this supplier's regular sales service? (Yes) (No).

e. Has the referring party paid cash for that service? Why?

f. How do the two suppliers' services mesh?

g. Will we receive a written report on results of this first "free" conference?

h. Is the service rendered with absolutely no cost and no obligation on our part to their supplier? (Yes) (No). Hooker:

During the interview, determine:

8. Are we permitted to use this supplier's information in taking competitive bids on the types of goods or services he might recommend we buy? Conditions:

   a. If yes, who has purchased the service previously?

   b. Okay to contact them? Name(s):__________________________

   c. If no, do we qualify for the service solely because of our contractual relationship with the referring party? Elaborate:

   d. Is this "free" service necessary to the other contractor's proper performance of the contracted job? Why?

   e. Is the service therefore indispensable and legitimate? (Yes) (No).

9. As the discussion progresses, does this supplier:

   a. Concentrate on what we need (analysis and service)?

   b. Push his wares (hard sell)?

10. Based on the answers given above, the "free" service is:

    Positive:

    a. Necessary to completion of referring party's contract.

    b. Possessed of true market value.

    c. A bonafide gift form the referring party with no strings attached —a "something extra."

    d. Offered in a tangible form which can be acted upon.

    Negative:

    e. Obtainable by any prospect/buyer who calls him.

    f. Essentially a supplier sales presentation, determining the same information needed by this supplier to create a presentation and quote for any prospect.

g. More binding than serving; hold suspect.

If one or more of items 10-e, f, and g) above is true, terminate the discussion now!

11. If items (10-e, f, and g) above apply, is misrepresentation by either the supplier or the referring party a possible factor? (Yes) (No). Why?
    a. How does the discrepancy affect our confidence in the referring party?
    b. Can we refuse this supplier and obtain a price adjustment to buy from our own source (or not buy at all)?
    c. Can the referring party's own service be rendered by a competitor? (Yes) (No).
    d. Is the offense serious enough to consider canceling our agreement with the referring party? (Yes) (No). Why?
12. If items (10-a, b, c and d) above apply and dif the service is valued or essential, are the supplier's credentials acceptable to us? (Yes) (No). If no, is there another source?

If the information given by us or reported to us is in the nature of consulting recommendations or supplier-advisory service, and if the importance of the problem and/or attendant costs warrant, complete a Consultant Evaluator from to determine possibility of, or extent of, profit-motivated bias or conflict of interest.

11

Money matters

Money matters can be a real drag on program planning: you can't let your imagination and your media suppliers run wild. On the other hand, when you comprehend that money *really* matters as a measure of cost effectiveness, you're better prepared to assess the effects and value of the program planned.

In some instances the value of the given program will be readily understood and no advance cost justifications for the meeting need be prepared. This is true of new product introductions, for instance, with-out which the product cannot be launched. Here, buying what's necessary at optimum cost is the trick—but the need to purchase or to hold the meeting is not questioned.

The same is true of the sales meeting in which the group will be prepared to sell better and raise net sales by a stated percentage point over a given period. The return on the time and dollars invested is clear, assuming success of the meeting.

Two questions immediately arise: First, is it necessary to measure results in clear-cut cases of need? And second, how does one handle the cases where need is not so easily established?

Yes, it's necessary to measure—always. Even with new products there will be some variation in sales results from the quota established. Whether you're producing above or below quota could reflect changed market conditions, error in quota, or success or error in training.

Because top management tends to suspect the sales people first, measures which establish that the given person has indeed mastered everything expected of him in meetings/workshops will refocus management and protect the innocent.

Even in cases of clear need, follow these steps toward defensible meetings:

1. Set one or more short-term goals with an eye toward achieving long-term objectives. Examples include teaching the sales people the new sales technique in this week's workshop; then to increase sales by 10 percent over last quarter within six months; then to gain an additional 3 percent of the market within one year.
2. Establish suitable measurements for each category of goal or objective. Consider exams, role playing, games for learning, and individual and team comparisons for net sales. Provide market analyses from outside sources to establish market share.
3. Select formats carefully. Is the meeting to be held in a central or regional location, or in field offices? Will it be taught by a trainer, the sales manager, tec people, or a combination? Will it be information delivering only or information seeking as well. How well does each alternative lend itself to measurements contemplated in the preceding paragraph?
4. Develop specific program elements which will fulfill both the training need and the measurement criteria. That will require tests and workshops and quotas, of course, but probably new sales presentation materials with practice periods as well. Clear training objectives (see next chapter) will dictate needs.
5. After the meeting, follow up on the measurements for each goal as it is achieved. Be sure to report to the individuals on the results, whether favorable or unfavorable.

If this last effort fell short, analyze it. Was there a goof in judgment of internal and controllable factors? Or were insufficient allowances made for external and uncontrollable factors?

Hard-headed analysis of every successful and disappointing facet will help you develop rules and skills that will permit you to conduct the near-perfect meeting every time—proved by quantified criteria.

A meeting has succeeded when you can say something like: "A full 87 percent of the people mastered 90 percent or more of the workshop material and are selling at or above quota; 11 percent of the people made marginally acceptable workshop responses and are being retrained and coached; 2 percent were found to be unsuitable and were transferred or terminated." With quantified results, it really doesn't matter who whistled and shouted: the group is performing!

That leaves the type of meeting for which the benefit is more difficult to measure. Among those are the situations in which attitudes and motivation are at issue. Keep in mind that poor attitudes *manifest* themselves somehow; if they didn't you wouldn't have a problem. These could show themselves as absenteeism, quality control slippage, job turnover, or work slowdowns. All of those have a cost; correction therefore has a dollar benefit

Dollar advantages lie in many unsuspected areas and can be brought into the support base of the meeting. Following are just a few examples from among our clients:

Problem: A manufacturer of radiation equipment found field service/warranty expenses so far off projections that the adequacy of the training program was suspect; salespersons were taking flack for situations outside their control. By calling for an audit of the related training program, we were able to establish *(a)* that the training program was excellent and not at fault; *(b)* that the "loaded cost" of a service call (salary, office overhead, truck amortization, and so on) far exceeded the cost or billable charge of minor repairs made necessary by owner staff carelessness; and *(c)* that design changes to answer the most frequent problems could produce a cost savings to the company of over $100,000 projected over three years. The computer was reprogrammed to flag above-normal instances, and the training department was alerted to send warning/quick fix instructions pending design change and permanent change of procedures.

Problem: A manufacturer of two-way radios was experiencing delays in 20 percent of applications submitted to the Federal Communications Commission on behalf of customers. Complexity was the culprit—several volumes of rules and interpretations governed the 20-item application form, and rules were numbered differently from the form items they governed. By creating a checking kit of interpretive instructions, item by item, with an overlay of key cautions, we reduced rejects from 20 to 2 percent within weeks of the meeting. Twenty percent of the client's Washington liaison office cost? Money!

Problem: A high-technology company was having problems digesting a smaller high-tec company it had swallowed because Wall Street analysts did not recognize the efficacy of the act. We were able to create a layperson's version of the smaller company's position in the field, elaborate on its competitive pluses, and thump for related electronics products in a way that convinced financial analysts, visitors to the plants of both organizations, and new-hires for both sales and office positions. One staff member commented, "Oh, *that's* what we do!" Even existing and potential customers reacted favorably to the common-sense approach: a runaway victory for plain talk. Higher stock prices or lower bond interest rates? Money!

It's obvious by now that even though the hotels and airfares are expensive these days in real dollars, those same expenses can be said to be high or low only in relation to the value of the problem they help solve. That relativity is precisely what is involved in cost-effective analysis.

So not only is it necessary to assess costs and benefits each time, but it's necessary to assess costs for *each* of the site alternatives.

SALES MEETINGS THAT WORK
Locations Comparison Sheet

		One central meeting	Four regional meetings City ___ count:	City ___ count:	City ___ count:	City ___ count:	District meetings count*
1.	Meeting room expense:						
	Room rental, if any	$____	____	____	____	____	$____
	Sales aids, catalogs, etc.	____	____	____	____	____	____
	Other support materials	____	____	____	____	____	____
	A/V presentations (one/copies)	____	____	____	____	____	____
	Stage: sets, lights, sound, unions	____	____	____	____	____	____
	Production assistance	____	____	____	____	____	____
	Crating/shipping	____	____	____	____	____	____
	Subtotals:	$____	____	____	____	____	$____
2.	Staff time expense; ___hours:						
	Salesmen, count:	$____	____	____	____	____	$____
	____x ____ hours						
	District managers, count:	____	____	____	____	____	____
	____x ____ hours						
	Regional managers: count:	____	____	____	____	____	____
	____x ____ hours						
	Top management: count:	____	____	____	____	____	____
	____x ____ hours						
	Presentation team: count:	____	____	____	____	____	____
	____x ____ hours						
	Preliminary trips: count:	____	____	____	____	____	____
	____x ____ hours						
	Subtotals:	$____	____	____	____	____	$____

3.	Facilities:						
	Central: __men x __nights	$____	____	____	____	____	$____
	Meals: __men x __nights	____	____	____	____	____	____
	Regional: _men x _nights	____	____	____	____	____	____
	Meals: __men x __nights	____	____	____	____	____	____
	District: __men x __nights	____	____	____	____	____	____
	Meals: __men x __nights	____	____	____	____	____	____
	Subtotals:	$____	____	____	____	____	$____
		One central meeting	**Four regional meetings** City ___ count:	City ___ count:	City ___ count:	City ___ count:	District meetings count*
4.	Transportation:						
	Car mileage, district +	$____	____	____	____	____	$____
	Airfare within district	____	____	____	____	____	____
	Airfares, district to region	____	____	____	____	____	____
	Airfares, district to central	____	____	____	____	____	____
	Destination taxi/bus, district	____	____	____	____	____	____
	Destination taxi/bus, regional	____	____	____	____	____	____
	Destination taxi/bus, central	____	____	____	____	____	____
	Preliminary trips	____	____	____	____	____	____
	Subtotals:	$____	____	____	____	____	$____
5.	Other expenses:						
	____________	$____	____	____	____	____	$____
	____________	____	____	____	____	____	____
	____________	____	____	____	____	____	____
	Subtotals:	$____	____	____	____	____	$____
	Grand totals:	$____		Regionals:	$____		$____

Based on specific destinations compared, the most economical meeting plan would be:__________

Note: For specifics on costs, refer *to Sales & Marketing Management* magazine's annual "Survey of Selling Costs" and the "Official Airlines Guide." Consider the effects of special promotional airfares if your meeting date is relatively near and *if the airline will guarantee* the rates quoted now. For video conferencing and production assistance, see Chapter 20.

* For quick local estimates, use S&MM's Survey "100%" (average) dollar figures for hotel costs, taxis, etc., multiplied by number of participants/cities contemplated. Airfares cannot be averaged; calculate carefully, or call for quotes.

That is, average hotel costs vary so greatly among our metropolitan areas, as established by *Sales & Marketing Management* magazine's annual "Survey of Selling Costs," that you cannot ignore the differences when choosing sites.

Soon after the first "Survey of Selling Costs" was published (in 1973), we participated in presenting a special program created by the magazine to give its prime advertisers a better understanding of the meetings market. In our segment of the program, we created an exercise which (when used in conjunction with the survey and published airfares) permitted the participating guests to demonstrate in workshop the substantial differences in costs between 1 central or 4 regional or (arbitrarily) 35 local meetings. The lowest cash-expended cost was for the 4 regional meetings; next, the 35 district meetings, if the cost of *purchase* (and future use) of hypothetically needed video recorders was separated from travel costs. If extensive equipment rentals are needed, local meetings can be more expensive than regional; if special equipment is not needed, local meetings are less expensive than regional. Fewer hotel nights and air tickets also help save in both instances as against central meeting costs, which are always the highest.

Dollars-expended savings projected out at 25 percent in favor of regional versus one central meeting, even after providing for the time and travel costs of the presentation team and multiple equipment rentals. That's for an identical program which gives up only simultaneity of delivery to achieve great savings!

So far, we have considered only direct, paid-out costs. But the indirect costs of salary for participants, coordinator, and supporting staff can be enormous. Regional and local meetings can save significantly in indirect costs too, because of the paired concepts of less time in meetings/less time off jobs.

Meeting time costs money, too. Consider that an employee works no more than 50 weeks per year; if all were 40-hour weeks, only 2,000 hours maximum are available per year. So the direct salary cost per person per hour is one half the *thousands* of base pay; that is $15 hourly for a $30,000 salary level. Now double or triple that $15 hourly cost depending on the company's overhead multiplier; 300 percent of salary is considered normal these days to pay for fringes and secretarial support and so on.

Now, how many hours of each person's time do you need? And how many people must you engage during that time? Adds up, doesn't it? Now consider executive time, supporting staff time, and "invisible" expenses, such as inspection trips. That takes care of the salary costs.

But what about the off-the-job costs? Before the people can surpass present levels they must make up for the time "lost" in the meeting room. That break in sales could manifest itself later in a dip-and-peak sales pattern that could complicate delivery and even cash flow.

And last, a concept we brought to costing years ago: at the company's current rate of return on the sales dollar, how many dollars in sales volume must be generated just to pay for the meeting? Now that's a sudden death question that should make the case for cost-effective planning.

It's no easy job, costing a meeting. Nor evaluating benefits. But that task is both doable and essential. It takes only time and attention to detail. Scrupulous attention to detail.

Let the Locations Comparison Sheet and the two-part Cost Justification Work Sheet (both in this chapter) guide your thinking. When you've completed these guides, you'll know both the cost and the value of the meeting you're planning.

Sales Meetings That Work

Cost Justification Work Sheet

(Assets)

Re: Message (Meeting Title): ____________________________

Benefits of the Meeting:

1. Direct dollar benefits:
   - Skills learned/improved here will add ______% to overall sales within ________ months — $________________
   - Market share for product will rise ______% over previous month/quarter/year — ________________
   - Long term revenue for this new product is projected at — ________________
   - Attitude change/reinforcement will — ________________
   - Eliminate negative impact of (type ______)
2. Other considerations; arbitrary value:
   - ____________________________ — ________________
   - ____________________________ — ________________
   - ____________________________ — ________________
3. Costs reassignable to related functions:
   - Allocable to training budget — ________________
   - Allocable to industrial or human relations — ________________
   - Allocable to public relations or advertising — ________________
   - Balance charged to sales budget* — (________________)*
4. Opportunities for future reuse:
   - New-hire training — ________________
   - Dealer training — ________________
   - Customer/public information/service — ________________
   - Benefits grand total: $
   - Reenter: Costs grand total: $
   - Subtract: Net worth (loss) of meeting $

Conclusion: Can this meeting pay its own way? (Yes) (No). Why?
If justified, restate reasons as Return on Investment.
If not justified, rethink objectives or find a better way to achieve them.

*This figure ($__________) multiplied by company's current profit ratio requires $____________ in sales volume just to pay for our portion of the program.

Sales Meetings That Work

Cost Justification Work Sheet

(Liabilities)

Re: Message (Meeting Title): ______________________________

Cost of the Meeting:

1. Meeting room expense: $__________
   Rental charge, if any __________
   Sales aids, catalogs, etc. __________
   Other support materials __________
   A/V presentations __________
   Stage: sets, lights, sound, unions __________
   Production assistance, if any __________
   Crating/shipping __________
2. Program development:
   Sales/training staff input time __________
   Technical/consulting expertise; time/fee __________
   Writing; in-house/contract __________
   Visualizing; contract __________
   Other assistance __________
   Printing, exhibits, etc. __________
   Pilot program/test run __________
3. Facilities; ______________ persons
   Rooms/beds; _____ x ______ days x $______ __________
   Meals; average per diem of $______ x ______ __________
   or:
   ______breakfasts @ $______
   ______lunches @ $______
   ______dinners @ $______ __________
   Gratuities and tips __________
   Other charges __________
4. Transportation:
   Airfares, estimated __________
   Taxis and airport transfers __________
   Local daily shuttle bus __________
   Rental cars: ______ x $______ per day/mile __________
5. Optional:
   Spouses; plus 100% of accommodations/transp __________
   Side trips, excursions, sports, etc. __________

6. Staff time; ______________ hours program time (Formula: $"N"000s salary @ 100% overhead = $"N" cost per hour's time)	
Executives; _____ x $_____ per hour x ______ hours	__________________
Managers & supervisors: ____ x $______ per hour X _____ hours	__________________
Salesmen; ____ x $_____ per hour x _____ hours	__________________
Presentation team; ____ x $_____ per hour x _____ hours	__________________
Costs grand total	$__________________

12

Building agendas and control

To this point everything discussed has been in the realm of ideas and generalities. But as soon as one begins to deal with the agenda, one deals with practical methods and specifics.

Key among them are *(a)* the size and duration of the meeting event(s), as determined at least in part by the dollar considerations reflected in the Cost Justification Work Sheet, and *(b)* the specific purpose(s) of the meeting as determined by the message and corresponding strategies adopted. Purposes tend to dictate agenda formats. These interrelated concepts need to be examined in detail.

When deciding on the size of the meeting group(s), the main question becomes, "Is the big crowd really productive?" Some meetings of large size are unavoidable; for instance, the annual stockholders meeting or the association's annual business meeting with convention attached. Both are legally required, and all qualified individuals must be permitted to attend. Dictated size dictates formats.

But for most corporate meetings, especially in the sales department, size is discretionary. Size can become a handicap and itself an unnecessary expense, as the Locations Comparison Sheet indicates. In a sense, the large assembly meeting is a cannibalistic creation which feeds on its own size. When the crowd grows so large that the product itself cannot be used as a tool, then the cost of making maquettes or slides is an extra cost of size. And although the initial cost per person of a slide presentation is high for the first 50 or so people, any substantial increase in audience size (which should, theoretically, substantially reduce cost per person) simultaneously requires larger screens, which in turn ultimately require larger rooms, more expensive equipment, and more elaborate presentations to fill up the huge stage and screen in that mammoth room.

The hidden, unproductive costs of the big central assembly meeting—or show—are staggering. The staging and lighting costs and the difference in airfares between regional offices and the single host city are a "central" cost. The use of larger, more expensive hotels is often a direct consequence of size: motels lack ballrooms. And since the ultimate consequence of the huge auditorium-type program can be a total loss of the training opportunity (if breakout workshops can't be accommodated), the central program can become preponderantly wasteful of everything put into it!

The complicating factor is, of course, that "large" and "small" are subjective judgments based on the norm for the given company; but a "small group" as defined by psychologists is usually a group of 5-9 persons. They often function without an appointed leader, depending on who has the needed information and expertise for the given problem. Hierarchical titles don't matter—so it's a true merit system.

Your problem in preparing, therefore, is to define the size category of your group for each given meeting. This need is further strengthened by the need, for the large group, to be explicit about rational ideas; and for the small group, in addition to have an absolute authority deliver the material. One-way speeches will pass any group if they're well prepared. Don't ghost writers prepare drafts of Presidential speeches? Sure, the President will personalize them; but even you'll change even your own script at the last moment on occasion, if not always. But the smaller group (which we'll define as smaller than classroom-30) will unmask a posturing lecturer and will brand him a phony. Small groups can be politely vicious, and there's no full recovery for your speakers or your credibility if you permit such goofs.

Apart from the degree of preparation needed, there's no other significant difference between large and small groups, despite industry claims. When the first edition of this book was published, it seemed totally comprehensive and unchallenged to most of the cognoscenti of the field...leaving only the topic of small groups as the unspoken category. Mea Culpa. Large and small meetings are prepared in exactly the same ways—only more so for the latter. That doesn't require a whole new technology. It does require common sense. Wannabies and other persons with marginal assistance for sale simply created an unneeded new niche. Take that for what it's worth—an ersatz difference that's intended to help them to part you from your money. That's just another indication of the extent of the industry's pretense to expertise. We don't think much of such pretense...nor should you.

It's probably very comforting to the disloyal opposition to claim that only this writer has those crazy ideas. But other direct statements can be attributed to major business personalities: Lee Iacocca and Don Peppers.

In his autobiography, *Lee Iacocca: An Autobiography,* Iacocca wrote the following:

> "Of course the more common way to communicate with your people is to talk to them as a group. Public speaking, which is the best way to motivate a large group, is entirely different from private conversation. For one thing, it takes a lot of preparation. There's just no way around it—you have to do your homework. A speaker may be very well informed, but if he hasn't thought out exactly what he want to say today, to this audience, He has no business taking up other people's valuable time."

Several observations: First, it sounds a lot as if the man is saying, *Have a concise message*. Second, he's making a distinction between private small talk and group communication. Third, he's telling you not to wing it—that suggests your making an agenda. Fourth, he believes that your practice of the message prior to the event will help to get you to your goal of valid communication. And all of that in one paragraph from a man who has proved that he knows how to get things done.

As stated elsewhere in this chapter, a meeting without an agenda is a bull session; and Iacocca says "prepare" because a large group is "entirely different." General knowledge—not our discovery. How does the meetings industry justify trying to convert it into something arcane?

To clarify: any agenda meeting is different from a bull session (his "private conversation") because of the direction given on and by paper, often called "road mapping" by trainers. Much different—but only in the need to prepare: people have learned in much the same way regardless of topic or purpose for over 5,000 years of recorded history! The brain probably hasn't changed recently.

Numerous comments regarding preparation, notes, and presentation styles are contained in *Life's a Pitch*, by Don Pepper, whose business life consists of persuasion techniques.

So prepare. Distribute an intelligent printed agenda for each member of each group addressed, even if they are absolutely identical in composition to the last group. For practical purposes, every company field office can be considered to be identical (by normal averaging) to every other unless and until you have firm facts to the contrary. If you must demonstrate, then rehearse the full demonstration, preferably several times.

So if you won't take it from us, take it from Lee Iacocca: Prepare! With a little practice you could make your meetings look even more professional! For free...no matter the size!

In this context, you can better appreciate the advantages of the video conferencing techniques. Because people accept the electronic intermediary as not compromising a straight-from-the-horse's-mouth presentation, video conferencing is an ersatz central assembly meeting without the travel, and with breakouts held in the field instead of in adjoining hotel rooms in the central city.

Other communications media, such as video tape and movies, sacrifice simultaneity and feedback/participation opportunity and so are not substitutes for video conferencing. On the other hand, video conferencing was originally expensive (although no longer), and that put two questions to you. First, is simultaneity essential? Second, is direct audience feedback with the top executive essential? If those answers are no, your decision is made.

If you take the districts route, your decentralized program can be packaged with lectern scripts, A/V segments, workshop exercises and workbooks, and explicit instructions for the local manager. If you go the regional route, exhibits and displays might be part of the "convention"; you can construct several sets or ship the original around. The last is the road-show concept, of course, and few managers welcome road duty. But if presentations crews are rotated (or the program dates scattered) even that one human disadvantage is eliminated. The road show assumes, of course, that materials and authorities are cheaper to ship than to duplicate or record. If not, go the simultaneous meetings route, and get all your feedback within a few days.

Once location(s) and size are more or less determined, there's still the consideration of program duration and calendar scheduling. While there's a tendency among financial people to "amortize" the transportation costs by packing the agenda, that diluting of concentration adversely affects your purpose.

According to legend, when Lincoln was once asked, "How long should a man's legs be?" Abe answered, "Long enough to reach the ground." If you know what the meeting's objectives are, you also know when those objectives have been achieved. Then stop!

Don't belabor the issues; don't do all the accumulated laundry in one load. Conversely, never cut back on the needed time (proved by test run, if necessary), especially because group efforts always consume more time than individual test situations. Slippage is normal with groups, and size aggravates the problem.

Yet programs don't always cooperate by dividing themselves into neat, day-long blocks; so sometimes you need to choose whether to go long or short. It's not all guesswork. One of the curiosities of companies is that their employees develop a group personality. After one or two sessions, an alert Meeting Manager can sense the type of program and the duration of time over which the audience will respond best. Honor it. You'll find that the attention span is longest for programs that appeal directly to audience needs. And there's not much excuse for any other kind.

Keep human nature in mind, too. Since employees would rather meet on company time, and since non-payroll associates such as distributors and dealers would rather not waste their business hours in your meeting room, schedule accordingly.

For payroll people, estimate that one long day (with an overnight stay preceding, if necessary) is better than two partial days. Mondays are best for starting, but never begin on Friday for a one-day event. Consider full or partial weekend stays when the meeting is held in a geographically desirable area so spouses can join at their expense; when more than two weekends away are involved, send the people home for the third or fourth, or pay the spouses' weekend expenses.

For non-payroll associates, schedule tightly for one evening, at least one hour but not more than two, preferably before they go home to dinner. Never request trips or overnight stays without clarifying expenses in advance. Plan a series of meetings with non-payrollers only with their advance approval of the idea and preferably the dates.

For all the emphasis on brevity, don't overlook the need to provide a program that has enough substance to justify the expenditure of time and effort on the part of all participants. There's no way to pay for boredom or to buy off the resentment that comes of over promising and under performing.

Apart from size and duration as determinants of format, as mentioned, is purpose. That purpose is best summarized in a statement of objectives. A complete statement contains *(a)* a behavior (what participants must be able to do or do differently); *(b)* a minimum performance level for the new skill; and *(c)* valid ways to measure achievement, immediately and long term (details in Chapter 13).

So that potential meeting formats do not color your vision of objectives, complete the accompanying Objectives Profile now before going on to special agenda formats.

Special formats and agendas. Although there are many variations on the basics, there are only two basic types of meeting structures: *(a)* the solution-delivering format (following a lectern address, workshops provide specific training) and *(b)* the solution-seeking formats (used either to gain general information, exchange and act on opinions, or to identify and/or solve problems).

The preliminary agenda must reflect the specific behavior and performance level to be accomplished. Whereas a brief local meeting might have only one objective in a short agenda, the central assembly meeting, by its nature and cost, is usually composed of several substructures, each with its own objective.

Notice that the term *solution delivering* demands more than the mere transmission of information in a one-way flow. There is no solution provided until each participant understands how to turn your message theory into his own practice.

As we have seen, that's why the maximedia spectacular fails the education task expected of it. While the spectacular might transmit some information, it's too expensive a way to do an inadequate job!

Sales Meetings That Work

Objectives Profile

(Make one for each objective or major program element)

Message:

1. Meeting Objective (Participants to be able to do):
   Minimum acceptable skill level:
2. Problem(s) involved, if any:
3. Alternative solutions to problems:
   a.
   b.
   c.
4. Apparent action required by solutions:
   3-a.
   3-b.
   3-c.
5. Interim decisions required:
6. Problems generated by:
   3-a.
   3-b.
   3-c.
7. Resolution of problems:
8. Final decision among alternatives:
9. Objective revised or confirmed, accordingly:
10. Valid measures of achievement (quantitative and/or qualitative):
    a. Pre-program analysis/testing
    b. Interim testing
    c. "Graduation" testing
    d. Post-program, near-term results
    e. Post-program, long-term results
    f. Feedback provisions:

It's important to recognize that regardless of whether you are holding central, regional, or district meetings, you must ultimately reach the same number of participants and enable them to perform to the same standards of measure. Such how-to elements are a matter of scope (covered in Chapter 13), not agenda or objective.

There are practical limitations. Only small groups can hope to concentrate on problem-solving exercises; large groups must hold to solution-delivering material in assembly, although break out groups have more latitude.

In the balance of this chapter, we will work with guidelines for the solution-delivering format and for the two main aspects of solution-seeking formats common to corporate meeting rooms, the problem-identifying agenda and the problem-solving agenda.

Delivering solutions. One-way flows of information are legitimate means of communication but they do not require a meeting and might better be served by letter or telephone.

The well structured solution-delivering agenda, therefore, includes such exercises and workshops (and any other needed type of practice session) required to convert the theory of the message into cognitive or dexterity skills. Workshops are the general device used to link an authority and the audience via specific teaching/learning sequences.

Sales Meetings That Work

Preliminary Agenda

(Solution-Delivering Meeting)

Message:

1. Purpose of the meeting:
2. Who should attend (by name, job title, or department):
3. Who should be informed even if not attending:
   Prior: Of results:
4. Details:
   Time: ______________ Place: _________________
   Duration: ___________________
5. Topics to be discussed: Authority (speaker): Time allotted:
   a.
   b.
   c.
   d.
6. Training sessions to complete (or programs to begin) as a result:
   Topic: Skills/tools: New/modified:
   a.
   b.
   c.
   d.
7. Prior preparation required of participants:
8. Action to be taken if meeting objectives (are) (are not) realized:
   short-term:
   long-term:
9. Future meetings (programs) to result:

Unfortunately, some workshop planners—to avoid the implication that executive or professional participants are being taught or trained—use the terms *clinic* and *seminar,* ignoring the obligation of the former to provide corrective action and the latter to guide independent (seeking) study. Such misuse has made the distinction of program formats by these terms almost meaningless, even when properly applied.

When you have answers to offer, this is your category!

Seeking solutions. Most management meetings tend to be of the "What are we going to do about..." variety; that is, they are *solution-seeking* (also termed “Problem Identifying”). Such meetings can be loosely structured, with advance preparation and a tentative agenda; they can be unstructured, as bull sessions; or they can be highly structured by any of a number of established techniques.

Highly structured solution-seeking groups in relatively large numbers meeting for a finite period for a specific purpose are commonly known as conferences.

Conference techniques include:

Discussion: Task-oriented, systematic talk about a specific topic. We’ll return to this idea.

Buzz groups: Any number of teams of about six persons who discuss, for about five minutes, their assigned topics and then report decisions or conclusions to the total audience.

Committees: Teams with specific assignments or functions acting as an entity to discuss and research as necessary to obtain the facts and/or solutions reported to the larger group.

Role playing: Participants act out interpersonal problems so as to gain insights into others and themselves.

Case histories: Analysis of real or hypothetically realistic situations that exemplify principles under discussion.

Loosely structured solution-seeking gatherings of few (ideally, five to seven) members for a task-duration are known as *small groups* and differ from casual groups and committees in their cohesiveness and *group-think* characteristics. Brainstorming, for instance, is a small-group function. Also in this category is the little-understood and under-appreciated *leaderless small group discussion* (LGD). Since five to seven participants is its ideal size, its real significance to companies lies in the average field sales office ratio of one first-level manager to eight or fewer salespersons. LGD techniques are complex. The best overall introduction is given in *Discussion and Group Methods,* by Ernest G. Bormann (New York; Harper & Row; 1969). His style is direct and his bibliographies are spectacular.

The discussion technique is unique among all because of its flexibility. It can be highly structured or loosely structured; it can be used by small, medium, or even large groups. It can be subjected to imposed time and topic limitations or allowed to flow as it will, according to the evolving information.

Discussion is simply *purposeful talk.* Small groups permit the luxury of free-wheeling commentary; but in large groups—to prevent chaos—control mechanisms are necessary.

The *discussion group,* therefore, can function according to any of the following techniques:

Debate: Presentation, defense, and advocacy of one of two conflicting positions; it needs audience participation to complete a conference function.

Forum: The audience participates, usually by questioning forum guests, with or without prior formal presentation, to elicit information and get clarification of points made here or elsewhere. A common format for covering public issues and political positions.

Panel: Free flow of information and opinion on a topic By panelists, with or without brief preceding statement of position.

Symposium: Set speeches on a topic or aspect of a topic by designated participants, who might or might not question each other afterward.

Interrogation: Systematic questioning of an authority with intention to challenge his theories or heighten discrepancies, inconsistencies, and so on.

Descriptions of all the conference/discussion relate to the pure format; but in both theory and practice, formats can be blended and modified in any way that suits the needs of the meeting planner.

Notice that the nature of the problem you must solve will tend to make one of those techniques better *in this instance.* For another problem, another technique might serve better. *Never* impose one of these techniques on your problem: that's a facet of medium over message!

Notice also that the conference/discussion techniques all require the *exchange* of information as an integral feature. That alone distinguishes them from the solution-delivering formats and from the one-way flows, such as speeches. Without that exchange, there is no true conference. It is the presumption that something will be done with the product of the discussion that differentiates it from the bull session: what do you *do* after discussing the scores of yesterday's ball-games?

Finally, all of these techniques can be slotted into an agenda, which qualifies them as meetings; with the addition of exhibits, displays, and banquets (or any other nonagenda communications formats) they can help carry a convention, which is created by the mix of communications formats. Size and duration are irrelevant: meetings can last several days and conventions can last a few hours. Don't let the industry's own confusion stampede you into poor choices.

Solving the problem of problems. If the majority of management meetings are solution seeking in nature, the majority of those are problem oriented. Many serious problem-solving meetings end badly because "solutions" are often prematurely advanced against inadequately defined problems. The result is "solutions" that can't work.

That happens in part because of human nature and in part because of carelessness. Human nature affects problem solving because most people find life more comfortable if they ignore incipient problems and let them exist as nebulous gray areas. Having learned to avoid the defined discordances that demand action, they become almost neurotically unable to confront and define problems from any source. The old conservative cop-out, "Let's wait and see," is in reality an attempt to avoid confronting the problem by waiting for it to eliminate itself. That's also poor management, however common.

Occasionally there's another category—the unrecognized problem. Such problems begin to make themselves felt as areas of complaints. If no one articulates complaints, the problem can become quite serious before persons involved compare notes. In this context, complaints are a healthy and beneficial phenomenon. Here's how to make good use of them.

A procedure for problem identification:

1. In advance, list every significant related problem of which you are aware; define each succinctly; look for "holes" in apparently related problem areas.
2. List tentative solutions, if any exist; keep in mind that a problem previously considered "solved" might have been too narrowly defined and now is showing variations.
3. Earmark the known unsolved problems for group response; on the basis of past conversations (and maybe additional phone calls), try to establish parameters on the suspect areas.
4. At least a week prior to the meeting date, announce an open discussion on problems and complaints; direct each participant to bring notes and documentation on any situation(s) that troubles each or his or her subordinates. Do not require them to identify and define specific problems and solutions or they'll tend to turn off.
5. At the meeting, create the feeling of an open session by asking the nature of each participant's main problem or complaint; jot each problem on a blackboard (or other easy-to-change pads). As each new main problem is mentioned, ask how many share it, and record that number. The group should ultimately act first on those areas common to the greatest number of participants.

6. If the group misses any points you saw (item 1 above), offer them now. In their opinion, are these prime or secondary? Guide the group without prodding—this is a discovery session.
7. Regroup all individually stated problems from all sources into broad categories of logically related topics. Direct each participant to strike from her or his personal list of remaining second-level problems all items that are apparently covered in the newly regrouped structure.
8. Call for all remaining problems; slot each into its logical category, if possible; make a new category whenever the participants agree one is needed. Continue to keep count on the commonality of each item offered.
9. Attack what the group considers to be the most serious or most common problem, using the techniques outlined under the problem-solving section following. When the key problem is either solved or found to be unsolvable today, take up the next.
10. Treat all unresolved problems as candidates for a subsequent problem-solving meeting. If appropriate, assign committees to work on the definition and information-gathering functions regarding each complaint area not satisfactorily dealt with.
11. Comment on the ease with which they can adapt today's format to their own needs. Thank the group. Set a new date, and adjourn.

Whether or not each problem is solved in a problem-solving meeting, do not abandon it. Acknowledge the unsolved problems in an all-group memo, and keep working until all problems are either resolved or eliminated.

Unrecognized problems can be costly. Customer complaints cost a salesperson valuable field time and cost the company good will-both far more costly than analyzing complaints and solving problems.

A procedure for problem solving:

Discussion—purposeful talk—is one of two key elements in problem solving. The other is judgment, based on rigorous scrutiny and analysis of facts.

Don't confuse brainstorming with problem solving. Brainstorming is an attempt to produce a quantity of ideas under rules of *suspended* judgment. The idea is to say anything appropriate, no matter how unlikely, in an atmosphere of absolute freedom from criticism in the hope that the list of ideas will include something worthwhile. Sometimes it does, based on later evaluation.

But evaluation is integral to the procedure in problem solving; carelessness or emotional decision making can lead to useless or even damaging "solutions."

Over the years, various think-tanks have studied the concept of problem solving, and the following might be considered a good generic outline of workable technique.

Sales Meetings That Work

Preliminary Agenda

(Problem-Identifying Meeting)

Problem/complaint area:

1. Purpose of the meeting:
2. Who should attend (by name, job title, or department):
3. Who should be informed if not attending:

4. Details:

   Time: ______ Place: ______ Duration: ______

5. Topics to be discussed: Time allotted:
   a.
   b.
   c.
   d.
6. Apparent "holes" or curious relationships worth exploring.
7. Prior preparation required of participants:
8. Objectives of discussion:
9. Action(s) to be taken if meeting objectives (are) (are not) realized in the first meeting:
10. Future meeting/programs to result:
    Near term:
    Long term:

Problem-solving outline:

I. Define the problem (using preceding problem-identifying agenda)
   A. If problem is fully understood now, state explicitly And/or quantitatively
   B. If not fully understood now:
      1. list all untoward or suspicious events/circumstances, are known to impinge on the problem area(s).
      2. if the main problem seems to be made up of several interrelated problems, break out each on a separate path before continuing.

3. list other events / circumstances / curious relationships not yet fully explained which might be part of the problem.
4. condense and/or combine those lists:
   a. grouping like items;
   b. seeking new relationships not previously understood.

II. Define the solution
   A. Stipulate the "solution criteria"; those conditions to be fulfilled before problem is *solved.*
   B. Partial solutions: Acceptable? Under what conditions?
   C. Be certain solution will not create new problems.

III. Begin creative analysis process
   A. Examine each group/related/condensed item
      1. break out each area into logical components.
      2. break out each component into smaller elements
      3. continue break-outs until each smallest-practical problem element is identified
   B. Examine the break-outs and determine
      1. is any of these a clear cause of problem?
      2. are any groups likely to be the cause?
      3. would any element's resolution result in a partial, use-ful solutions?
      4. if none, seek further relationships.
   C. If several possible solutions present themselves simultaneously, list all. (Some choose to brainstorm at this point and within context.)
      1. be inventive; reach; what if?
      2. accept and do not ridicule *far-fetched* suggestions, but subject them immediately to criteria established.

IV. Recognize solutions (at any point in the process)
   A. When any possible solutions pass preliminary critiques, Examine fully regarding criteria II A, B, C.
      If two or more possibilities pass criteria, select the least complex/most practical/most advantageous, according to need. Adopt the best and run with it

1. announce new policy/procedures
2. commit: which attitudes/habits/skills are affected? How to re-educate or retrain?
3. create any needed support/tools

V. Plan for re-examination and feedback
   A. Is the problem really solved? If not, recycle.
   B. Have any new problems been created? If so, recycle.
   C. Can further improvements be made after trial period?

That path to problem solving can be used by you alone or by a small group or even by a dozen or more people IF the problem-solving meeting is held to its purpose and agenda (a problem-solving agenda follows). To prevent the meeting from turning into a respectable-looking bull session, prepare meticulously for each of these indispensable steps:

A problem-identifing/-solving meeting plan:

1. Prepare a problem-identification agenda for discussion. If you are responsible, at least in part, for solution of the given problem, complete the identification process; call the meeting only if you fail.
2. Prepare a problem-solving agenda for discussion. Again, if you are responsible for its solution, complete the problem-solving process according to the path already provided; call the meeting only if you fail.
3. If meetings seem necessary, discuss the problem definition, solution criteria, and preliminary agendas with associates qualified to comment on the problem. Adjust the material to reflect valid suggestions and criticisms.
4. Revise the original preliminary problem-identifying and problem-solving agendas into the working agendas.
5. Announce the meeting; distribute the working list of complaints (if at the identifying stage) or working

definition (if somewhat advanced) as an integral part of the announcement. Outline the criteria for solution, if any, to set participants thinking in advance of the meeting.

6. Require participants to come prepared with documentation, statistics, and facts which have a direct bearing on the complaint/ problem area(s). State that they are not expected to arrive with ready-made solutions.
7. In conference, give the participants free rein on discussion as long as they observe the agenda(s). Interchange of opinion is crucial; criticism of suggestions is essential to avoid superficial, faulty "solutions." If the brainstorming variant is used, be sure to evaluate all suggestions immediately following the free-wheeling input session.
8. If the group believes the definition or agenda is faulty, amend it and proceed accordingly, or fight it out. Make every decision on criteria/agenda before proceeding with related analysis.
9. Honor the (original or amended) agenda(s). Do not get bogged down on small points, and do not continue if discussion founders on a point beyond which, lacking facts or agreement, no further decisions can be made. Adjourn and reconvene when necessary material is in hand. When rethought, the material already in hand might provide the insights needed for solving the problem without reconvening.
10. Record or otherwise transcribe all proceedings for a permanent file. At the end of discussion on each element, summarize—for group approval—a running recap on direction and achievement.
11. If a valid solution is produced at any point, whether or not the entire agenda has been covered, examine it thoroughly, hail it if it meets all criteria for solution, and adjourn the conference. Adjourning ahead of

schedule wins honors. Otherwise, adjourn when you have all the information you need or can get now; re-analyze personally before calling the next meeting.

12. Send a thank-you letter to each participant, noting that his or her contribution to the effort helped the conference to succeed. If you skip the letter, hurt feelings, counterclaims for credit, and sour memories could mar any future attempts.

If you observe these points, success is highly likely. But if several adjournments do not provide the basis for a valid solution, consider whether *(a)* the complaints/problems are not properly identified; *(b)* the problem is not properly defined; *(c)* the solution criteria are not valid; *(d)* a possible solution was suggested but not recognized; *(e)* the problem has no solution and so the conditions producing the problem must be modified—that is, eliminate the unsolved problem at whatever cost. Or endure it—your choice.

Sales Meetings That Work

Preliminary Agenda

(Problem-Solving Meeting)

Problem area:

1. Definition of the problem:
2. Can the problem be eliminated? (Yes) (No). If:
3. Criteria which must be met by an acceptable solution:
4. Order of discussion of topics within definition and criteria (beginning with the least-dependent item):
5. Who should attend (by name, job title, or department):
6. Who should be informed, even if not attending:
   Prior: Of results:
7. Details:
   Time: ____________ Place: ____________ Duration: ____________
8. Prior preparation required of participants:
9. Action to be taken if meeting objectives (are) (are not) realized:
10. Future meetings (programs) to result:

Creative meetings bring out the best in people, and that's what good management is all about. Test yours on the accompanying problem-solving agenda.

Implementing solutions. Once a problem has been *solved on paper,* the solution must be implemented before the problem is *solved in practice.* Such implementation usually requires that some attitudes and skills now current be augmented, reinforced, or even changed. To accomplish those ends requires not only a general description of the problem and its solution(s) via a lectern script, but also the presentation/recommendation of tested methods and procedures that will make the solution practicable. In short, you need workshops and/or training kits. (See next chapter.)

And if you begin to get the idea that most meetings are problem-solving sessions, you're beginning to get *the idea.*

Another Viewpoint. Relatively new on the meetings horizon for the new millennium is the concept of appreciative inquiry. We have not added it to the established methods above because it has not (yet?) been accepted as a "standard" format by any consortium of social scientists.

Briefly, as this writer understands it, appreciative inquiry seeks to determine what might work better (or has already worked—historical fact or imputed claim?) And then targets innovative ideas and potential methods to create whatever the group thinks might work in the future.

Wonderful—if it really works. Simple. You don't even have to think—just take surveys. However, that seems to me to be Feel-Good-Plus-More-of-Same. That might or might not be the attitude of the concept's creator, David Cooperrider of Case Western Reserve University. He is the foremost proponent as well as its originator. Few others seem to be totally committed. Yet.

On reflection it seems that appreciative inquiry might proceed from a misreading of the problem solving technique.

Yes, problem solving has been around for a while, but that doesn't negate it as a worthwhile model. Yes, many users take the easy route and depend on past solutions to provide future answers; and that doesn't always work; probably it never really does. But that's the fault of the users, not the problem solving model.

The underlying mismatch might be the assumption that appreciative inquiry itself assumes that the problem solving technique necessarily involves backward-looking solutions or precludes forward-looking solutions. Neither of those assumptions is true. Moreover, if looking back is a problem for problem solving, then isn't it also a problem for appreciative inquiry, too?

However, we might take a caveat from those key discrepancies: Be sure that your definition of the solution being sought actually includes new ideas and concepts that might not have been tried before. That is not to say that the new and untried are *ipso facto* superior to the tried and true—only that you should not define your proposed solution identifiers too narrowly.

Meanwhile, you might give the appreciative inquiry model much more thought before you jump on the bandwagon. It's brand new and might be nothing more than one more of the fads that perennially sweep the meetings and training fields. Those fields are only cousin variations within the group communications field, but trade magazine separated them in order to create distinct advertising bases for their own marketing. People learn in essentially the same ways no matter what the purpose or what magazine appellations might be used to separate the purposes.

Worse, there are no proofs of efficacy yet offered. We can never be sure that such newly proposed concepts are in fact work-able in the last analysis or whether proponents have learned from the McLuhan incident that far-fetch ideas get more attention from the press and so might be rewarded with fame and fortune for the originator, whatever its perceived or actual benefits or losses to the user. It's especially sad when trainers believe and distort.

This might be an unfair analogy, but if you were drowning, it would hardly matter how good it would feel to be out of the water, nor would there be opportunity and time to interview past survivors to see how they did it and how best you might escape. So determining what's wrong now (problem analysis) and how to escape (solution) might work better. That's the key difference between the two approaches, as we see it.

It is not our place to tell you how to value these somewhat incompatible ideas. But however you decide to approach them it's never too late to think!

The complicating factor in designing any meeting or any approach to the solution of problems is, of course, that each meeting is different from any other in at least some small degree—either of message or of presentation or of participants—as well as in the likely surrounds at a distance.

Differences are likely to be more substantial than meeting group size, although size might have some bearing. The silly designations of "large" or "small" are subjective judgments based on the norm for the given organization, wherein 1,000 could be small. If the group is smaller than classroom-30, then we suggest that it is then indeed small. All others are large! Someone must set a standard gauge eventually, and we've already helped to set many of the others. So humor us.

Yet, a "small group" as defined by psychologists is usually a group of 5 to 9 persons. Leaderless small groups often function without an appointed leader, depending on who has the needed information or expertise (if any) to apply to the given problems. Therefore such a group is an ideal task force for attacking really serious problems immediately. The group know who knows best, if anyone does. That's an aspect of teamwork where teamwork is rarely recognized or appreciated. That's also a true merit system, and it's contrary to the non-merit but common "networking" system in fashion today, wherein contacts, not necessarily merit, control most results. "It's who you know," is their rallying cry;

but "what you know" will serve you in a pinch. Go with quality, always.

Your early problem in preparing any meeting, therefore, is to define the appropriate size category of your group for each separate meeting. This need is further strengthened by the need, for the large group, to be explicit about rational ideas; and, for the small group, in addition, to have an absolute authority deliver the material. One-way speeches will pass most large groups if the speeches are well prepared. Don't ghost writers prepare drafts of Presidential speeches? Sure, the President will personalize up to the last moment, but even you will change your own scripts up to the last moment to serve the occasion better, even if you wrote the script(s) yourself.

However, any small-sized group (probably under the classroom-30 count) will unmask a posturing lecturer and will brand him a phony. Small groups can be politely vicious, and there's no full recovery for your speakers or your personal credibility if you permit such goofs. Credibility is the key discrepancy between sizes!

Apart from the degree of preparation needed, there is no other significant difference between large and small groups, despite industry claims to the contrary. That's our opinion based on our having created meetings and other group communications events for groups from 6 persons to crowds of 6,000—in the same room! Does your group fall into that range? However, when this book was first published, size seemed totally comprehensible to most user-readers except that I hadn't stipulated it as described above. Therefore, the opportunists in the industry hit upon "small" as a new category. Of course it's not, if you know what you're doing. *Mea culpa.* But now it's explicit—sorry we didn't state it clearly in 1983. As if you couldn't have figured it out.

Small meetings do not require a whole new technology or methodology. They might require a new understanding of methodologies and procedures on your part—*function*, not size. And they do require common sense, which is often in short supply. The meeting industry's Wannabies and other persons with marginal assistance for sale simply created a new selling niche, regardless of what the niche was actually worth to you. Take that for what it's worth: an ersatz difference intended to help them to part you from you money more readily. It's in the same category with tales of left-corner screen matter—that disappear off-screen whenever you shift focus to that left-corner screen area. Or don't your people do that?

Or what about those marvelous-looking graphs that state print size for certain screen sizes and distances. Common sense? The eye is a lens, folks. When you can see with your naked 20/20 vision at any distance is what you can see at ten or twenty times that screen size and distance if the item image, screen size, and viewer placements are also varied by the same percentage multiples. Yes, you can read a postage stamp if it's enlarged fifty times and seen from a distance that's fifty times your arm length. Or 500! Just calculate your ratios for each room. Proportion, not bluster! But it's just one more clear indication of the meeting industry's pretense about offering usable expertise. It fills pages with "text" that sells (and accompanies) ads of products and services. Does that really help you?

Want a second opinion?

> *to this audience* (Iacocca's emphasis) he has no business taking up other people's valuable time.

Remember that communication is understanding signaled by an appropriate response. No response? Then no proof of communications achieved. Applause is appropriate only for entertainment and other present-moment satisfactions, like huge birthday cakes and deserved awards.

Notice that Iacocca says specifically to "prepare." We say, 3x estimated running time because a large group (unspecified size; we'll say over classroom-30) is "entirely different." In its demands, yes. Much different—but not prepared so differently in learning techniques. People still learn in much the same ways...after thousands of years of recorded history. Human brains probably haven't changed recently, even if fashions and electronic delivery have.

To clarify: Any agenda meeting is different from a bull session because of the direction given by and on paper. So prepare and distribute and intelligent agenda for each group you address even if they're essentially identical in composition to the last. Because of averaging, most district offices can be treated as "identical" to all others when planning, unless a trusted someone has experience to the contrary. Be aware that most managers will disagree, saying, "We're different." Probably they're not. So just ask for several reasons why they think so. And try not to laugh. If you must demonstrate a product or other tool, then rehearse the full demonstration, preferably several times.

Now, a story on Lee Iacocca: Iacocca appeared on a program that our company and we were coordinating for a Mobil Oil Company Dealer Convention in the early 1960s. He arrived on the night before to prepare, as did his assistants, who dropped some cases and disappeared for the night. On the following morning, they couldn't locate the lenses for the rental visual projection equipment that they had insisted on providing for themselves. They stated,"We don't understand—the stuff was right here last night, when we checked." They hadn't really checked on the previous night; they needed an excuse, and our coordinating company was a handy target by implication.

Our client was not misled. He knew that if all went perfectly, he would get the credit; and if anything went wrong, we (as his convention coordinators) would get the blame. So it was not in our best interests to sabotage anyone. We simply ran Iacocca's slides on our machines; of course it worked. Later it turned out that the rental equipment lenses were tucked under a fabric shield over the opening of a deep cover—and would have been discovered in any actual check beforehand. Be careful when you choose assistance, because if you don't know the worth of your assignee, the work might never be done!

Another example: On another occasion, at an association's training session that we were writing and coordinating, one of their small member company's presidents decided that he could use that same account's dollars. So he hazed our staff until he became predictable. During his portion of the training presentation, expecting his games, we held the script prominently in hand at the projector in the rear; he winged it beyond recognition and then asked for additional slides, as if the fault were ours. The client understood instantly. That account did come back to our company in the next year, but without that member. Enuf sed. Caution always.

Can that stuff happen in smaller surroundings? Why not? One person in an AV service studio often found errors to correct and usually spotted them before anyone else did. Terrific proofreading! Eventually it became apparent that he was *causing* the problems that he took credit for correcting. Large egos with small ego strengths can work some incredible horrors.

Also, a small visual producer company favored by our key person billed our company for a greater number of slides than were PO'd by count, even though the PO stated that additional items (if any) would be separately PO'd. But the supplier refused to consider the facts and insisted on payment in full. Later, our secretary confided that someone (specified) at our own firm was suspected of taking kickbacks—charged to our company. It was simply not that obvious ever before, until given the very explicit PO we issued. But the fact-of kickbacks is becoming increasing known to company auditors. You might be invited to take—and also to account. Smart guys decline the former.

Take the lesson: Politics is politics, and greed is greed. You'll probably never know when someone unknown or unsuspected is gunning for you...or even whether you might get into the cross hairs from time to time by accident. So when you create or coordinate a program, examine everything. If there's time, examine the first examination: double check everything! If you do that, you're far less likely to go wrong—and surely likely to go right.

Meetings management is about control, not budget, even though budget is your prime attraction to the suppliers of that field! Outside help can be great—but it's not essential to your meeting's success. Intelligence and common sense are!

13

Structuring training and workshops

Many attempts have been made to distinguish between education and training in the industrial context. Criteria have included such considerations as who pays, on whose time conducted, and immediacy of usage—all of which we consider irrelevant.

The only line of demarcation that seems to work consistently is that of focus: are we equipping the learner with the concepts and generalities that will help him solve specific problems in the future (education); or are we preselecting from all available information in the field only that which will help solve the specific problem at hand (training)? That's macro function versus micro function...and, to a large extent, theory versus practice.

In this context it's clear that companies usually *train* employees. Of course education is valuable to the organization; top executives are being educated when they attend programs on corporate responsibility (business) or social responsibility (professions). Here they learn ethical principles for application in the decision-making process. Lower-level employees are rarely given educational programs, although the company might pay tuition for courses of benefit on the job. Some companies pay for advanced college degrees with the expectation that the individual educated will perform better on the job. By all definitions except ours, these purpose-oriented situations would distort the education/training designation and maybe lead to faulty emphasis and wasted effort.

What the macro/micro focus makes evident is that most of the programs conducted at lower levels are training programs whether or not a classroom is involved. The fact that most corporate training departments are so little involved in the firm's daily programming indicates how little the training function is appreciated.

Although the need to train is ubiquitous, there is absolutely no standard training format. If any method converts theory to a single individual's personal practice, that method is training. And it's valid. That does not necessarily imply that the method is the best possible format, or that it is complete, or that it cannot be improved. Yet it is valid.

Over the years, numerous fads have come and gone in the training field. Old timers have seen wild swings from it's-gotta-be-programmed-learning to it's-gotta-be-simulation-games to it's-gotta-be-computer-assisted. Those formats—and many more—are useful in specific situations. Yet none of them can be said to be best or usually workable. These formats are containers—if there's no message inside, they can't accomplish anything. And in this sense, the container is simply another medium, which might or might not serve the message properly.

Then how do you select or create the proper format?

According to the numbers. The number of people who must ultimately be reached with the new information or techniques will, in large part, dictate the types of formats that are needed for the tasks. The best format could be different for every different segment of the overall training program. What matters is that each be best according to what must be accomplished in that segment.

By definition, expertise is uncommon; therefore the number of authorities on any given subject will be few. On the other hand, there seems to be no lack of trainees. Major programs are often constructed for groups which might be not only large, but also indeterminate. A major corporation or association could be preparing a program to be used, for instance, with all new-hires for a number of years ahead, numbers unknown or virtually infinite. On the other hand, if only a few individuals will ever be trained in an esoteric discipline, one-on-one training on the job would be the logical method.

We're talking about scope in the movement of information and practical ability between the authorities and the meeting participants. The scope of the program—the sheer numbers of people who must ultimately be trained—will dictate many format responses.

To see the effect of group size on format, take as an example of scope the simplest of problems—how to dial a telephone. That skill can be programmed in several formats:

1. The authority can train each person in the company individually or in small groups by explanation, demonstration, and individual practice; or
2. The authority can script the presentation and conduct the initial training session; then offer the script so that each newly-trained employee becomes a trainer for others; or
3. The authority can both script the verbalized information and demonstrate by proxy (sketches, photos, videotape); with instructions to the unknown recipient trainer included, the total package can be sent out and adequately controlled by anyone—even someone who has no prior knowledge of how to dial a phone.

Every training meeting you ever structure will be a variation or combination of those three basic formats. It is the *control structure* of those formats—the physical and capability demands made on the authority/trainer—which determines how the given group can and should ultimately be reached.

Notice that the theories of electronics and switching mechanisms have no part in the nucleus program—how to dial. The former would be contained in an education program, which is not essential to the narrow task of dialing; in fact, the basic electronics theories go far beyond dialing—too far to be of value.

Stripping any potential program to its essentials lessens the bulk of the apparent task and heightens the meaningful relationships of the information selected for presentation For those whose job requirements go beyond simple dialing, you might add complementary sequences on the related theories of answering the phone, and so on. Each new sequence can be packaged in parallel to the original; and so a cohesive, easily coordinated master training program will have been created. Painlessly.

Yet for all its wide applicability, the breadth of any one unit of information/training will never exceed the need or the capability of the individual learner targeted for "how to dial" training only.

Notice how the authority/learner ratio and capability change dramatically with each of the three main format variations. *Practicality* is as important a consideration as *possibility.* It is certainly possible for one individual to teach thousands, but the elongated time span and waste of expertise are inefficient. Practicality says that few tasks are so complex that only one authority exists; therefore it's possible to reproduce expertise to the small degree needed without loss of effect.

When you begin to view each new message in terms of the scope of the overall assignment you will more easily be able to select the workshop/rehearsal/practice elements that will build the particular skills desired.

When you let the scope of the impending program guide you into the most workable formats, you'll find that the opportunity to go beyond the meeting participants' needs with information is as unlimited as your imagination.

Here are some of the ways in which some of our clients were able to package programs so as to assure their effectiveness in the field *after* the meeting:

- A three-hour special-market study with new presentation tools, calculated to make sales people feel and talk like authorities in a prime market; market information they gathered and reported back formed a check on usage and kept program data current.

- A short course on human physiology in relation to the determination of personal comfort (ergonometrics) in the workplace; built sales people's confidence in new office chair; enabled them to teach dealer staffs to "fit" adjustable chairs to company buyers.
- A structured-but-branching sales demonstration of car telephones enabled salespersons to guide the discussion along patterns of usefulness to the prospect, rather than confusing technology.
- A full morning's money-oriented training meeting designed to teach office open-plan equipment salespersons how to talk finance and tax write-off advantages with comptrollers of prospect corporations.
- A 10-hour recruiting and hiring seminar in which the personnel and training managers, as a team, taught field sales managers how to select and motivate higher caliber new hires.
- An eight-hour industrial product knowledge program (variable in two to four sessions) enabling the manufacturer's sales managers to teach the industrial distributor's sales personnel, aided by his own account rep. Further developed into an eight-lesson self-help guide for new distributor hires.
- A two-hour product training program enabling distributor account executives to teach retail sales clerks how to sell the features, advantages, and benefits of a major household appliance.
- A "refresher kit" used by regional sales managers with their distributors; sales people used the kit to recap and highlight national trends, statistics, and quotas first announced in a major central meeting; a lever for larger orders.
- A three-part program created by an international industrial chemicals firm enabling field salespersons to

upgrade the attitudes and job skills of kitchen employees of industrial feeding customers. Repackaged and translated into multiple languages so airlines could upgrade flight-kitchen standards around the world.
- The creation of a coordinating syllabus so district sales managers could integrate existing training packages with scheduled new programs to the best advantage of each salesperson; noted "holes" in the ready-training fabric to be covered ad lib by managers until packaged later.
- A slick, illustrated booklet used as a training/conviction manual by an international airline for its sales staff; then used to sell the airline to independent travel agents and group tour promoters; passed through agents to travelers as a trip guide.

The last two programs indicate how much the complexity can vary. Although the syllabus-related training session for managers was in a single ringbinder, it encompassed descriptions and decisions on literally hundreds of items of training for which the manager was responsible—everything from pre-hire to first promotion of the new salesperson. Its flexibility permitted customizing of the training regimen of the people longer on staff. And it identified elements of the total training program that could not be delivered, in some instances, within two or three years. Manager training and discussions occupied two full days to cover collateral theory, establish priority of need, and obtain their input.

By contrast, the airline brochure was nobody's idea of how a *training* tool should look: it was consumer-public oriented and bore absolutely no technical or industry information. Yet it sold hard the only thing an airline really can *sell* beyond service: the glamour of the destination, creating credibility in the process. The "training" was accomplished in perhaps a half-hour's discussion plus a role-played sales call. After the initial actual sales call, agents called in for additional copies, providing a record of key producers.

Similarly, some of the programs were relatively elaborate, with printed lectern scripts, visuals, and workbooks. Others were essentially Roman numeral outlines (to I-A-1 detail) which guided field managers in organization of material but required them to fill in details according to local conditions.

Notice how often the package concept surfaces. When you are alert to possible reuse of materials, you will find that with very little more effort (or relatively minor changes) a good deal more mileage can be had from the materials prepared for the meeting room. It's mostly a matter of structure, of your recognizing the scope of the ideas and their potential application.

These examples also illustrate the interrelationship of the internal sales meeting and the related needs of the dealer or distributor. It is essential, therefore, that material presented to the sales force be expressed in the customer's own terminology. If you use company jargon, you force each sales person to reinterpret before making the customer understand; and in the process each one of the interpretations will probably stray from your intent.

Obviously, before you can construct such programs, you must know what you intend; that is, you must be able to specify the *terminal behavior* of the trainee. In the training field, a complete statement of objectives describes: *(a)* precisely what the learner will be doing when he demonstrates that he has reached the desired objective, whether cognitive or skill learning; *(b)* the conditions (problem difficulty, time or coaching restrictions, and so on) under which the learner must demonstrate competence; and *(c)* how and by whom the learner will be evaluated, and the passing grade if perfection is not required; consistency of scoring is essential.

Your program must include the information and workshop exercises that fulfill the needs expressed in your statement of objectives. Nothing less is sufficient; nothing more is pertinent.

Sales Meetings That Work

Training Profile

Message/Problem:

1. Complete statement of objectives:
   a. Educational intent:
   b. Terminal behavior/performance:
   c. Conditions:
   d. Evaluations:
2. Skills and attitudes to be (changed) (reinforced) to achieve those objectives:

Item: Changes required:

__________________________ __________________________

__________________________ __________________________

__________________________ __________________________

3. Alternatives to a (training) meeting, if any, and reasons:
4. How can those changes be measured:
   a. During the meeting's workshop sessions (consider tests, role-playing, demonstrations, etc.):
   b. Short term (after initial interval of 2-4 weeks); including:
      (1) Manager's standard-form appraisal of man's actual sales presentation;
      (2) Man's dollar performance measured against quota assigned:
      (3) Man's dollar performance measured against his coworkers (contest?);
      (4) Other measures:
   c. Long term (after 2-6 months); including:
      (1) General company improvement target of ____% in (period).
      (2) Man's own achievement of ____% improvement (absolute) or (compared to what/whom):
      (3) Freedom from defective performance as measured by:
      (4) Other measures:
5. Does the corporate training manager agree that the needed skills and attitudes:
   a. Can be achieved/reinforced/changed by the tools selected on the message Profile? (Yes) (No). Discrepancies:
   b. Can be measured by methods outlined in Item 4 above? (Yes) (No). Discrepancies:
   c. Will be achieved by this audience (as outlined on the "Audience Profile"? (Yes) (No). Discrepancies:
   d. Resolution of discrepancies:
6. Do the measures provide for controls to separate general market conditions from the individual's own achievement? (Yes) (No). Describe:

7. Are the results of the training methods fully predictable based on past experience? (Yes) (No). Is a control test run of program required? (Yes) (No). Why?
8. Can additional objectives be achieved with a different audience (distributors or dealers, etc.) by slight variations in concepts expressed in Items 2, 4, and 5 above? (Yes) (No). Describe:
9. Should incentives be used (Audience Profile)? Why?
10. Any adjustments needed in complete statement of objectives (Item 1)?
11. Complete statement of objectives, confirmed or revised:
12. Final statement of measures to be applied:
    a. At meeting:
    b. Short term:
    c. Long term:
13. Acceptable performance criteria based on Items 11 and 12 above; describe; meaningful and useful?
    Quantitative:
    Qualitative:
14. Is the total anticipated cost justifiable on the Work Sheet? (Yes) (No). Discrepancies.
15. Resolution of discrepancies, if any:
16. Final decision on the training value of this meeting:

Elements of the program will be determined by your needs. Your format might be *(a)* wholly live, *(b)* partly live and partly packaged, or *(c)* totally packaged. Do not be too quick to adopt the generic "name" formats, such a programmed learning, computer-assisted instruction, or simulation games; those names alone cannot assure you success in your meeting room. Each of these generics has some advantages and weaknesses—give full consideration to both sides of the scale before adopting one.

Here are the key concepts involved in each:

Programmed learning. Complex, requiring the cooperative efforts of authorities, trainers, psychologists, and maybe sociologists; requires abundant control testing. The true PL format is rare. But untested, uncontrolled quack versions still proliferate by invoking one of the highly visible features of PL: small bits of information sequentially presented in "frames." Frame formats often accomplish more than the unstructured materials they replace, usually because the original text was poorly organized. No one has ever *proved* that a PL format outperforms other formats properly prepared in their own disciplines; but HumRRO has found that PL benefits are limited to linear operations and sequential information. Framing has a tendency to destroy concepts, which are synergistic, not cumulative. You might say that a hamburger is a programmed steak: chemically identical, but changed for all time.

Computer-assisted instruction. Two distinct uses of computer capability. First, when programmed with facts and go/no go instructions, the computer can respond as a teacher to the particular choices and errors the student makes on the formulated lesson; unprogrammed questions cannot be asked/answered. It's expensive. Second, as a huge adding machine the computer can project in seconds the consequences of any economic decision a manager might make in simulation game decision situations—raising or lowering prices, competitive response, favorable or unfavorable market conditions. Several years' consequences can be seen in minutes or hours in the training room instead of in the annual report. Expensive to program, but cheaper than an Edsel.

Simulation games. Reproduction of reality is the essence of these games. All applicable theories and methods of the subject being studied are embodied in the rules and action of the game. The game, therefore, is as useful as it is believable as real life. Research has demonstrated that games are a good way for some people to learn concepts, especially those who are not skilled in the traditional classroom study and testing techniques. However, games are *another* way of learning; no one learns more via games than via well-structured formats of other types. Used as a companion piece for traditional formats, games might by novelty or actual applicability help to lift understanding toward the 100 percent mark among large numbers of trainees. It's extremely difficult to construct a game which is credible, useful, and valid over a long period of time, as one must be to justify the cost of its creation. Seek professional assistance if this seems your best format.

Whenever you plan workshop sequences for information you have mastered, ask yourself "How did I learn it?" and "Is there a better way?" Those questions will put you on the right track.

When push comes to shove, it might be deeper than that. Max Planck, who won the Nobel Prize for physics and was Einstein's mentor, noted:

> "Great scientific theories do not usually conquer the world through being accepted by opponents who gradually convinced of their truth have finally adopted them. It is always rare to find a Saul becoming a Paul. What happens is that the opponents of the new idea finally die off, and the following generation grows up under its influence."

Distance Learning: Although it seems that DL has arrived in training and other forms of communications crash-bang with the computer, it has in actuality been around for a long time. If you doubt that, read the very fascinating book by Edward T. Hall, entitled *The Silent Language*, first published in 1959. Regarding what he defines as technical awareness: "Its very explicitness and the fact that it can be written down and recorded and even taught at a distance differentiates from the other two types of integration"(formal and informal awareness). To Hall, an anthropologist, all the behaviors of any cultural group can be seen as attempts to communicate.

Then let's get our bearings:

a) A lecture is a lecture is a lecture. Thanks, Gertrude.
b) A lab/workshop is a workshop is a workshop.
c) "Distance learning" is a relatively newly-used term, but it's long been a *fait accompli*, especially in Mexico.

d) There's not a significant actual difference in preparation between a lecture developed for a college classroom/ lecture hall for more than 100 students or a broadcast of that same lecture and same teacher to one student at 100 locations...if all speakers can see each other, assuming permitted questions. And that argues for two-way video conferencing.

Most lectures are a one-way flow of information in any case, and few allow for questions or even limited participation. Conferences demand interaction, and labs/workshops need that plus instructors or proctors. If those are the key differences in structure, and if you're prepared to acknowledge that and work around the demands, then you can easily *go* via video conferencing.

If an when a laboratory or workshop experience is needed, then it matters little whether the workplace is provided in one location or another or in multiples, so long as the seeing and facilities are appropriate. So it's possible to deliver a workshop in multiple locations nearer the location of the participants/students. The video program's chosen authority is still the authority. And if the sites chosen are appropriate, then the video authority or a local expert can supervise. Which would be more workable? More desirable? Choose. Life is full of trade-offs.

Then create the instructions for your workshop portion and send them ahead to the remote sites in sealed, numbered envelopes. At the logical points in the original script for sending students to the labs/workshops, then the distant learners will be sent to their local sites with their expert (or a proctor, if no expert is suitable or available). Most business meetings are not rocket science. Two-way video will allow the lecturing authority to oversee everything to about the same degree as if he were in the (huge) lecture hall personally. The difference is that the university's "personal touch" for only a few hundred students can now be expanded to include corporate thousands. Don't overwhelm the authority with sites. Better to have multiple teaching days for the same material—or capture it on tape and repeat it.

Now slot your needs. Use common sense, because the message dictates its own needs. Video conferencing is being done regularly—simply not by you? But it's never been such a great substitute for travel before because of the old, now eliminated, jerky-frame structure. Give it a try before your boss asks you "Why not?"

Now consider again the fact that the training industry seems to be recognizing that nothing new has been introduced in the past fifteen years or so (longer than some of its practitioners have been in the business), and you see an industry as ripe for rip-off as the meetings industry has been. Under-qualified and probably incompetent trainers-by-title have flocked together under the banner of "let's do the newest thing"—even though the newest things were computers (a delivery mechanism only) and could contribute absolutely nothing to the message or participant understanding of the message. The computer has built-in patience for repetition.

In a phrase we developed decades ago to serve a telephone company during the deregulation period: *we have now learned to travel the message instead of the messenger*. To that thought add "or the participants," because they don't *need* to travel anymore. Culture aside, there is now no difference between teaching someone in a far country or in teaching someone in another room on the premises. Simply prepare the identical materials for presentation in a manner different from supervision by the speaker directly, but nevertheless properly and competently, so as to foster under-standing no matter who is proctoring the far ends. Barriers? Just train-the-distant-trainer, who can translate into local methods. The radically-new cannot be appraised by the old standards: it's time to re-think your approach to instructional sessions—meetings or classrooms.

Distance learning works. Our major corporations have been cooperating with our colleges for decades with the one-way connection featuring the professor's face. In a land of difficult terrain and tiny villages, The Board of Education of Mexico broadcasts all its instruction so as to be received by everyone simultaneously and equally via the receivers provided. The U.S. Army has been video conferencing for decades. Site-dependent people haven't really recognized that they have an alternative—how long will you remain in that benighted group?

All training is based on common-sense principles—they've been around for thousands of years. But trainers of the past were not confronted with the numbers generated by today's national and international markets and so a special discipline has grown up. While the training field does not have all of the answers either, it should be able to help steer you around the shoals of workshops, exercises, and testing. And don't let anyone say tickets are needed first.

If you have no background in training but are required to manage a major meeting, ask your company's training manager for assistance in formulating your workshop program. You might begin your conversation around the elements of the Training Profile in Chapter 13.

Face it: The easy excuses are gone. If you are personally recalcitrant, then work on it. Meanwhile, there's been a paradigm shift in communications methods. Too many of the people who grew up with electronic marvels might be rushing you. How nice it can be when you can say honestly that you were in the vanguard of users! If your company does not have a training manager, and if you can expect to be charged with future meetings as well, you will find help in the publications of the American Society for Training and Development, Washington, D.C.

One way or another, complete the Training Profile before continuing with your planning of other elements.

14

Shaping the program

So far we have dealt with ideas for message, media, and related protective measures, but only as abstract ideas on paper. The next step is to express those ideas as agenda components, as a program. In doing that, you begin to convert the ideas into the reality of the meeting event.

It takes people to convert those ideas. People to teach. People to offer expertise before and during the event. People to oversee production of components. And people to work behind the scenes to make the event happen.

This chapter and the two following will together cover all the speaker and support committee functions. Because speakers are part of the shaping process, while committees are not, the former will be treated here as a component or tool.

The word speaker is not a catch-all, meaning merely "one who talks." It does not in the least imply that one of the innumerable public speakers can be substituted for an authority on the specific problems/topics on your agenda.

No one should ever be permitted to take the lectern before a large group unless *(a)* he is an authority on the matter being discussed or *(b)* a recognized authority has prepared the material to be delivered and the speaker acknowledges that source.

If an audience discovers on its own that any speaker is not indeed an authority, they will reject the message, however valid it might be. Furthermore, being the center of attention requires the speaker to be prepared, quick, decisive, and right: errors or careless slips made on the platform seem to be magnified, and if the crowd doesn't riot, it might just tune out. Because it constitutes feedback, the riot is preferable.

The need for credibility and expertise cannot be overstated. Behavioral studies have proved that people accept suggestion and are swayed in direct proportion to the speaker's *perceived authority.* Advertising capitalizes on that mental set when it dresses actors in medical smocks to sell home remedies. Once convinced, the same audience tends to forget who said it (only an actor) and retains, if anything, the impression the actor conveyed: sound "medical" advice.

Therefore, you must exercise discretion in selecting the individuals to whom you entrust your spoken message. Program *the* authority on a complex topic, even if he's not the head of his department; let his chief comment and introduce him if politics matters. Schedule highly respected individuals to increase the chances of acceptance of a debatable position. Never let a high-profile type appear simply to satisfy his ego. Conversely, if a knowledgeable *unknown* is at the lectern, he will make his expertise apparent despite (and even because of) challenges from the audience.

Finally, the speaker who betrays his authority—goofs—probably will lose the argument, whether right in a basic position or not. The human mind has an impressive ability to retain negative impressions of speakers. Beware of phonies!

Yet, as the Hawthorne Effect indicates, people want to cooperate and will bear disadvantages leading to a valued goal. That means you can schedule an authority as a leader of your workshop session even if he has never conducted a session before. Just present his credentials, admit that it's his first time, and ask for the audience's comments and criticisms following. That's a good learning experience for both par-ties. Of course a skilled meeting leader sits in as *facilitator* to keep the program aspects flowing.

The meeting facilitator, should you use one, is a person whose expertise lies in the meeting *process* itself, not in the subject matter of the meeting. The facilitator usually does not speak, does not take issue with the speaker's position, does not get involved in discussions. He does make sure the agenda is honored, and settles matters of procedure if conflicts develop. If he does his job well, he tends to blend into the wallpaper.

The *moderator* of a panel or workshop is, by contrast, a featured speaker, even if used merely to link events. This person's commentaries must sound like he knows the purpose and direction of the program and why each of the other speakers was chosen. This is the one who gives cohesiveness to the program by the rationale he expresses. It's the same rationale you used to construct the meeting and will use to justify its components to top management, but it's restated from the audience's viewpoint. Simple but critical. For safety, you should write the person's remarks yourself. Even if you yourself serve as moderator, you should put the rationale in writing: don't take a chance on forgetting important elements. An outline will suffice for you and anyone else deeply involved in the planning; for all others, provide verbatim comments. Just call it an *overview* and present it in the opening portion of the program. It's the Big Picture.

As you begin to consider authorities as potential speakers, you'll notice that they immediately fall into the category of company staff or outsiders. If the latter, they can be recognized authorities on the prime topic or accepted authorities on some aspect logically related to the message of the meeting (a psychologist speaking on values in personal and company life would be an example). The drawing-card personality with the homogenized message is an entertainer in every respect and should not be confused with experts, as your agendas identify them.

Here's how the different groups affect the planning:

Staff authorities. When a crucial topic is beyond the speaking or leadership skills of the staff person who knows most about it (not uncommon among scientists and engineers, whose discipline is nonverbal), consider augmenting that person with a better speaker from his or her own department or from the company's marketing team. Let them work in tandem at the lectern, with the pinch hitter swinging at the complex ideas and the key authority fielding the technical questions.

For a long-term solution to the problem, make arrangements for the marginal speaker to see a local high school speech course instructor, preferably the argumentation or debate team coach, who makes a living turning undeveloped skills into convincing competitive prowess. Coworkers wisely coach associates only in an emergency or on relatively small points of delivery.

In a large assembly meeting, all speakers must be able to project-to make the message heard and felt. But in small groups a true authority, although a mediocre speaker, will sometimes make a great instructor simply because a high conviction level transcends his lack of ease. Find a pretext to test or rehearse the person in advance of the meeting; a dry run with a couple of trainees to "test the exam structure" is a perfect cover. Never let an unknown quantity jeopardize the results of all planning.

With the Preliminary Agenda in hand, approach the selected authorities with a request that they speak on the specific topic, covering specific material to accomplish specific goals. Next, suggest the presentation techniques and tools that seem best to serve the training objectives. Then ask for the authority's own comments and preferences for techniques and tools. Nearly all, if given first a direction and then a choice, will gladly follow your lead. Even when disagreeing, since you approached them rationally, they will explain why changes might be necessary.

In general, the staff people you approach will share your *field,* or frame of reference. They will be able to appreciate and respond to your entries on the various profiles and guides. That's not true of the outsiders; and in practice you might not want to show confidential material. Here's how you can work it out.

Guest authorities. Guest speakers from affiliated companies or government agencies should get special handling in the public relations sense, but they should be expected to meet the same message and competency criteria as everyone else. That means getting high recommendations from business associates and associations—but also hearing the individual speaker if at all possible. Paid professionals with allied expertise usually appear with some regularity; those who are most secure about the value of their service will encourage you to sit through a presentation to another group before contracting. A professional expects to tailor a presentation to your needs (time allotted, points to be emphasized, and so on), and (as a professional) is able to work under whatever conditions your own staff can accept.

There are some differences in response:

Guest speakers generally have a personal or business interest in your topic and/or company; if not, they wouldn't be willing to appear. Whereas business associates usually understand the common cause and expect to adjust to it, government agents tend to have a prepared script from which they don't depart. They might drop portions not related to your needs, but if they agree to appear they usually tell you what they would like to do. They also have a notorious no-show record (substitutes are provided, and it might be a different body mouthing the same words). In general, the government agent you can learn to do without.

In any case, if either of these types agrees to speak on your program, the costs they incur, if any, to create visuals or take-away materials must be paid by you. In practice, most persons who speak frequently already have their own visuals and no cost is involved. View the visuals when you audition the person—many existing support materials are shamefully inadequate. Don't be embarrassed to talk specific dollar ranges for materials before contracting; as a matter of courtesy those materials will belong to the speaker even when you pay.

You are obligated to offer to pay expenses; they might accept; but rarely or never are you asked for a fee. That means you are always in the position of *suggesting* direction and *requesting* changes. If they don't bend, your only remedy is to say, "No, thanks." Your control is compromised when you deal on this basis; be sure your gains are substantial before you commit.

Paid professionals are easier to work with. They have a business message that you value or you wouldn't approach them. Because you will pay a fee you have some employer rights. You can ask questions and state preferences and expect certain minor changes. You do not have a right to demand total rewrites—in that case, you're talking with the wrong person. All changes should be agreed upon on the basis of mutual understanding of reasons and needs because rabid horse-trading can damage. You will probably pay travel expenses above fee; but set specific limitations (airfare, hotel, and meals; no liquor, and so on) or the tab might astound you.

Paid personalities are perennial problems. Most are "famous" for something and behave like Hollywood starlets: their material is sacred and inviolable; their message is so profound that it dazzles all, from ladies' teas to presidential cabinet meetings. Because they deal in a one-way flow of information and present-moment satisfaction, they are strictly entertainers—even when they touch on wars, starvation, or busing. They survive because they sell tickets to banquets nobody would otherwise attend. Unless that's your predicament, stay away!

Under duress? Consult the web under both "speakers" and "trainers" to find alternative talents for either need among the less publicized purveyors. Gale's *Speakers and Lecturers* is no longer available. The Federal government's site www.alx.org might help, although minimally, as might quasi-commercial sites such as www.referenceUSA.com. Those three main categories should describe every type of speaker who could ever appear at your lectern; don't make unnecessary concessions. Do stipulate due dates for your receipt of the preliminary outlines of their presentations; biographical material, if needed; final outlines or scripts; lists of A/V needs, and so forth. Once you schedule, manage! And control via PERT (next chapter).

Besides the speakers, their support materials and other required learning aids and tools are the other great shapers of program. As mentioned before, the type of tools to be used is a decision that virtually makes itself based on prior decisions: the objectives of the meeting; the means by which achievement will be measured; the complexity of the individual topic; the take-home requirements for training material; and the time available for practice and rehearsal during the meeting.

Naturally the skill of the speaker as a speaker and as an authority has a direct bearing on packaging or media, although this should not sway decisions on content. You decide whether and to what extent to indulge his preference for presentation methods or minor tools-as long as his chosen method is adequate for the group.

In small groups, for instance, it makes little difference whether the speaker uses standard 2x2 slides or an overhead projector or prepared charts. For a medium-sized group (the classroom-30), the charts might be inadequate, and the overhead projector might be borderline. In a large assembly meeting only the traditional slide will survive enlargement with requisite brightness.

In small groups the speaker's choice of design sketches, photographs, or product (maquettes) can be used; in large meetings, control of attention is a prime consideration and prevents hand-outs and pass-arounds: only projected visuals will suffice.

All of the tools mentioned in Chapter 6 are self-explanatory with the possible exception of psychodrama and sociodrama. The key distinction between the two is in who "believes" or benefits—the actors or their audience.

In psychodrama, the therapeutic progression from role playing, the problem attack situation is usually unrehearsed. Participants really project themselves into new roles, actually believing and suffering the interpersonal conflicts; meanwhile, the audience observes, learning vicariously. In the sociodrama, the actors (probably rehearsed) are not believers in their script, but they attempt to involve their audience emotionally. Catharsis and new understanding of others is the goal of both.

As with anything that enjoys ready acceptance, the quacks have moved in on these forms. *Never* stage a psychodrama without a trained psychologist in the room; and it's wise to have an industrial psychologist check the premise of your sociodramas in advance of the first performance if sensitive issues are involved. When dealing with the human psyche, business has no right to experiment or err.

As previously mentioned, the major distinctions between the assembly meeting and its breakouts, on one hand, and the small meeting, on the other, are two: *accessibility* of authority and the *placement* of the workshops.

In the assembly, the prime authority is virtually inaccessible because question-and-answer periods are inadequate to full understanding even though they create the illusion of audience involvement. Breakouts put the second-string authorities in touch for the real work of learning theory and practicing skills. Still, it is not practical to schedule a breakout session following every important presentation in the assembly room—and that distorts the placement of the workshops.

In the small meeting of not more than the classroom-30, all persons are in the same room at all times, having constant access to the authorities and having constant reinforcement by drill, quiz, and practice session exactly where those elements are required.

As we said, the large assembly that cannot provide breakout space or sequences must send the practice sessions back to the local region or district—it cannot simply ignore that need. At that time, such continuations of the central meeting themselves become small meetings on a separate agenda. The total structure, however, is the master program for that message/problem; either half alone is incomplete. That fact must be reflected in the master planning.

Workshop sessions are an indispensable part of any training/solution-delivering meeting; only their placement—not their existence—is guided by subjective judgment.

How and where the workshops will be conducted will at least in part determine the degree of advance preparation required and, therefore, the cost. Whereas the meeting leader can hand out a dozen photocopied sheets during the course of a morning to a small group, photocopies are often more expensive than offset printing when hundreds of copies are involved. Moreover, when you have hundreds of copies of a dozen handouts, separate envelopes (hand stuffing?) are usually required and binding as a booklet might be better. Costs rise quickly.

So there are choices to be made in *discretionary spending,* and that, in turn, affects the flow of the program-its shaping via the theatrical principles of *timing* and *pacing.* With practice, you will master all three.

Discretionary spending. No matter how objective you hope to be about assigning money to various individuals and projects, your very concern for the cohesion of the program as an entity will make a number of subjective decisions both necessary and justified. Deliver to each speaker (within the confines of your budget) the sum of money he will require to do the basic job as you understand it.

Your original budget projection should reserve funds (or a specific percentage of all available funds) for your own discretionary use or you'll be at the mercy of all the speakers, fulfilling their own preferences and tastes and overrunning budget in the process.

If you earmark discretionary funds you have the means and the opportunity to package in such a way as serves your purposes. For instance, once the basic requirements of any given speaker are provided for, you can decide whether the talk is so important or interesting as to deserve further development as a package for subsequent use. The extra funds will probably show during the meeting.

You will also be able to decide whether a relatively unskilled speaker needs additional help via another authority or the reproduction for handout of some of the basic projected visuals.

Depend on your own feeling for relative needs, because few speakers ever believe that they have been given adequate funds. Even *adequate* is a relative concept, dictated for each speaker by the statement of objectives for his segment of the program.

Most money will go for visuals—which as HumRRO has determined can be printed or projected with equal success. Visuals can be easily separated into one of three categories: *(a)* the type of study plate for which, because of detail, there is no auditory substitute (such as statistics, formulas, and schematic drawings); *(b)* the type of conceptual renderings which express relationships between facts, statistics, allusions, and so on; and *(c)* the cosmetic group of simple illustration of minor points or filler-type material added to avoid visual lapses on the screen. The last group is highly dispensable in the workshop because it is extraneous or attention-dividing as well as costly; it might be needed in a packaged presentation for smoothness and continuity—a production value.

Be alert to filler materials. They tend to indicate holes in the logic and continuity of the script; and if the script defect is remedied, the filler visuals will not be needed.

By pleading poverty you can avoid giving extras to the speaker who seeks them for ego reasons; by augmenting you can underpin the crucial elements. By both methods you can wield a subtle and powerful effect on the total program's pace and strength.

Pacing the program by sequence. Your fully developed Preliminary Agenda for the contemplated meeting will include various topic areas that must be fully treated in the program, but it does not automatically reflect the best relationship of those components to each other.

For all practical purposes, one begins with understanding the complex program and proceeds to the simple classes; That's accomplished by first stating the complex terminal behavior and then going step-by-step *backward* over the progressively less complex foundation material. It's fairly easy to work such relationships out by simple logic. Workshop from simple, upwards to complex...which is likely to seem less complex thereafter.

Yet there are choices that require value judgments. For instance, a new, structured sales presentation could be unveiled either before or after the nuts-and-bolts portions have been mastered. Although the big picture is helpful up front, you would telegraph and so lose the power of surprise were all workshop pieces gathered for presentation near the end of the session. Solution: Describe it briefly early in the program (overview), but save the punchy, verbatim sales presentation till the end, where it is best practiced.

Good sequencing requires that you separate the bone-crushing sequences with easier material, practice sessions, and even rest periods so as to create psychological relief and slow the fatigue point of the audience.

Pacing the program by elapsed time. Elapsed time has much to do with the feeling of cohesion not only of the individual topics, but also of the overall program. The amount of time over which a given amount of information is spread directly affects the audience's appraisal of it as a thin or heavy program. That, in turn, colors their appraisal of its significance because emotional reactions can dominate judgment.

If your Preliminary Agenda lists seven topics to be covered in four hours, each will average about one-half hour; but each must immediately be weighted against the others—assigned more or less time in direct proportion to its value in relation to both the other six topics and/or the final statement of objectives.

If you believe you can adequately discuss, practice, and test each topical component in its adjusted time allotment, do so. If you cannot, either drop several topics, if that's feasible, or extend the program to a full day or longer. Don't let arbitrary cutting damage your program.

Once you have made a time assignment that you can justify, fight for it. If you've truly miscalculated, compromise; but it's human nature for each speaker to feel the "need" for more time, just like the "need" for more money. And if you haven't the authority to make your time limits stick, why are you managing the meeting?

Sometimes the topics on an agenda are not related to each other in reverse order of complexity. In that case, your feeling for pairs of topics or speakers which are complementary will help make the lineup more logical than arbitrary. The feeling of logic in the program helps sell its message.

The overall flow, or continuity, created by a proper tempo (the feeling that the succession of events is neither rushed nor tedious) is referred to as the *pacing* of the program, a theatrical concept. Similarly, *timing* is the sense of the exact moment to proceed (exactly when the learner has heard enough and feels psychologically ready for a new direction). Timing and pacing are reflected in the business program in the fine tuning of such small elements as coffee breaks and quizzes as well as in the bold strokes of the agenda.

When a program has been properly paced, it takes on a rhythm of its own; and even on paper it has a feeling of liveliness akin to that which is felt during the actual event. Such a sensitivity to the paper product can be developed, and the Meeting Manager who has it knows instinctively when he has constructed a superior program. That's why he has so many.

The working agenda. In distinct steps up to this point, you have evaluated the message, created the Preliminary Agenda with a statement of the training objectives, evaluated and selected prospective speakers, identified the tools needed, and paced the whole. Now you are ready to transcribe the Working Agenda.

If you have properly combined the topics for their synergistic effect on each other, then creating the Working Agenda is mostly a matter of translating allotted time blocks into clock times.

Six hours of hard work is considered a full day. Stretched out by lunch and coffee breaks, it fills the traditional eight-hour workday and leaves participants tired but not exhausted.

In assigning clock times, when topics don't cooperate to deliver neat three-hour mornings or afternoons, put the longer section in the morning, but don't go beyond four hours in any case. Some trainers with heavy schedules also require evening study or talk-over groups; these should be relatively unstructured so the individuals can feel somewhat free to program their evening hours. It gives psychological relief from rigid scheduling while acknowledging that the people are mature enough to do the assigned work.

If you have been honest with yourself in drawing up the profiles and guides, then your working agenda will be solid. If the duration is no longer than needed, it's well paced.

Your feeling for the intrinsic rhythm will tell you precisely where the high and low points are. Never try to blunt the highs or bolster the lows at this point because a wave pattern is both normal and desirable. Complete your Working Agenda now.

Sales Meetings That Work

Working Agenda

(Solution-Delivering Meeting)

Message: ______________________________

1. Objectives of the meeting: ______________________________
2. Who will attend: ______________________________
3. General format: ____ Assembly: ____ Break-out: _____
   Classroom: ____ Small group: _____
4. Location(s): ______________________________
5. Policies, methods, and skills to be changed as a result of this meeting: ____________
   ____
   ____
6. Benefits of the program:
7. Synergistic scheduling of necessary topics/presentations:

PROGRAM — Day One, Date: ____________________

Topic*	Speaker/Authority	Clock	Tools needed
a. ______	______	______	______
b. ______	______	______	______
c. ______	______	______	______
(Coffee break)			
d. ______	______	______	______
e. ______	______	______	______
(Lunch)			
f. ______	______	______	______
g. ______	______	______	______
(Coffee break)			

h. ____________ ________________ ________________ _____________

PROGRAM — Day Two, Date: ____________________

(Etc.)

8. Future meetings or programs to result:

*NOTE: Treat training sequences as a "topic" and describe below if necessary.

15

Coordinating on paper for control

Although your program is already taking shape in terms of both topics and speakers, it still exists mostly in your head and on a few sheets of paper.

Your next major step in executing the design is enlisting the aid of others as committee members; but in order to make any binding assignments, you will probably need the advance approval of top management. To get that, you will probably have to provide a justification for the meeting; estimate how much of whose time you will need and when; and demonstrate that you can direct those people in the production and execution process. The material in this chapter will help you to accomplish all that.

What you are really doing, then, is gathering all your thoughts and notes into a *communicable* form. That's your main objective, and you can accomplish it in any way you choose. But if you are facing your first major meeting, you might want the type of guidance provided by the form and diagrams that follow.

Committee assignments coordinator. Before deciding *whom* you will recommend to do *what* on your committees, read quickly through the whole of Chapter 16 to get a feeling for the problems and possibilities of combining various functions. Then use that sense to come back to this unit and prepare a tentative list of personnel, using the following Committee Assignments Coordinator.

Meeting justification. With your convention committee selected, you're ready to approach top management for authority to proceed.

Your overall purpose is to give management a full understanding of the purposes and potentials of the pending meeting, as you have come to understand them through study and paperwork. Your report, whether oral or written, should be no more detailed than management requires. It could be as simple as a brief summary letter covering copies of your profiles and guides, already completed.

If you believe the meeting is borderline or cannot pay its way (refer to the Work Sheet), make that specific comment. Ask for top management views on additional benefits of which you might not be aware; if none is advanced, ask them to decide whether you should proceed or cancel.

Do not *guarantee* the success of any future meeting. Until staff is committed and until actual production bids are in hand and covered by appropriations, you cannot be certain the event will actually occur at a quality level that can fulfill the needs and plan.

Your secondary purpose is to establish the degree of responsibility you will be shouldering and to seek authority in the same degree. Will you *manage* the meeting in the sense conveyed in this book, or will you assist as coordinator? If the responsibilities and authorities don't match, say so; if your authority isn't heightened or matched, defer all decisions to the chief. The problem at hand is then politics, not meetings; and that problem must be solved before production can proceed efficiently.

Gather all the profiles and guides you've completed to this point and review them. Then construct a presentation, using the accompanying Meeting Justification Guide.

Sales Meetings That Work

Committee Assignments Coordinator

Message: ______________________________

Date(s): ____________________ Location(s): ____________

Scheduled program hours: ________ Weeks remaining: ____________

Meeting Manager: ______________________________

Assistant Meeting Manager/Coordinator: ____________________

CONVENTION SUBCOMMITTEES

	Needed? (Check)	Responsibilities	Chairman and Committeemen	Coordinating Time (weeks)*
1.	________	Facilities inspection	________	________
2.	________	Facilities contracts	________	________
3.	________	Agenda and diagrams	________	________
4.	________	Budgets	________	________
5.	________	Tools and support materials	________	________
6.	________	Local help	________	________
7.	________	Speakers and support materials	________	________
8.	________	Menus and parties/entertainment	________	________
9.	________	Transportation	________	________
10.	________	Welcoming & registration	________	________
11.	________	Rehearsals;agenda x 3	________	________
12.	________	Spouses programs	________	________

When approved, this personnel roster establishes your convention committee (the chairmen named) and their subcommittees (all others). If you feel your chairmen might prefer to select their own assistants, add those names later.

*NOTE: Total estimated time *in weeks* must at least equal the related running time *in hours* of the respective program segments. For inspections and non-agenda items, estimate by travel days.

Sales Meetings That Work

Meeting Justification Guide

Message:

---

1. Write a brief summary memo enclosing copies of all (or those most pertinent) forms among these:
   a. Message Profile (Chapter 10)
   b. Audience Profile (Chapter 10)
   c. Consultant Evaluator (Chapter 10)
   d. Something-for-Nothing Evaluator (Chapter 10)
   e. Locations Comparison Sheet (Chapter 11)
   f. Work Sheet (Chapter 11)
   g. Objectives Profile (Chapter 12)
   h. Preliminary Agenda — Solution delivering: Problem identifying: Problem solving (Chapter 12)
   i. Training Profile (Chapter 13)
   j. Working Agenda — Solution Delivering (Chapter 14)
   k. Committee Assignments Coordinator (Chapter 15)
2. State whether or not, in your opinion, the anticipated meeting can pay its way. If doubtful, ask whether other executives see other benefits, preferably quantitatively.
3. If benefits appear to be clearly greater than costs, request authority to proceed with facility inspections, production bids for tools and services, and basic convention committee organization. If benefits are not clear and executives cannot offer others, request an executive decision about whether to proceed as above or cancel the meeting.
4. If questions about procedures and controls arise, explain the process using the following Activity Correlator and explain production control using the following PERT Diagram.
5. If all systems are on go, then GO!

Activity correlator. In the chapters on visual learning, you came to appreciate the value of the big picture when offered early in the learning sequence. Because the convention industry is so confused and confusing, you cannot expect your associates and committee members to understand exactly how to place their individual efforts in the grand undertaking. Even the terminology used in various trade publications and associations varies; and people often mean different things when they use similar words.

If you look beyond terminology to the underlying functions and activities, you'll discover that it's not particularly hard to understand what's happening.

As with every other activity in life, there's the *thinking* and the doing—here, the *planning* and *execution.* Much of the planning is on paper, of course, and everything you've done so far is part of that process. It will also include the inspection and selection of hotels, although that is physical activity that can glide directly into the arrangements phase, which in turn is part of the execution. Accept the fuzzy edges and the glides—they exist and won't bother you as long as you don't expect sharp delineations.

From the paper planning, one moves to the *design* or *creation* of the program components, including all the tools and take-home materials, the exhibits, distributor/retailer kits, and so on. At about the same time, you begin to separate the design elements into those that are *things* and those that are *events.* If you are expecting to use outside services, then you might, on general principle, plan to produce most of the things internally, and the events, externally.

Planning becomes *production* when contracts are let: *execution* begins. Because outside production assistance is relatively costly, most companies assign the on-stage meeting room events, visuals, and media to the producer of industrial stagecraft (along with the professional entertainment), and hold the respective convention subcommittees responsible for overseeing all the other events and group functions. Could it be more logical?

The ultimate phase of execution is, of course, the event actually in progress. The most common expression for this phase is "running the meeting," although that, too, is confusing because it can refer either to the overall coordination of all simultaneous events or to the chairing of a single conference among several. If you refer to the chief of all the production and execution activities as the *coordinator* and to the meeting chairmen as *chairmen* or *moderators,* that problem is licked

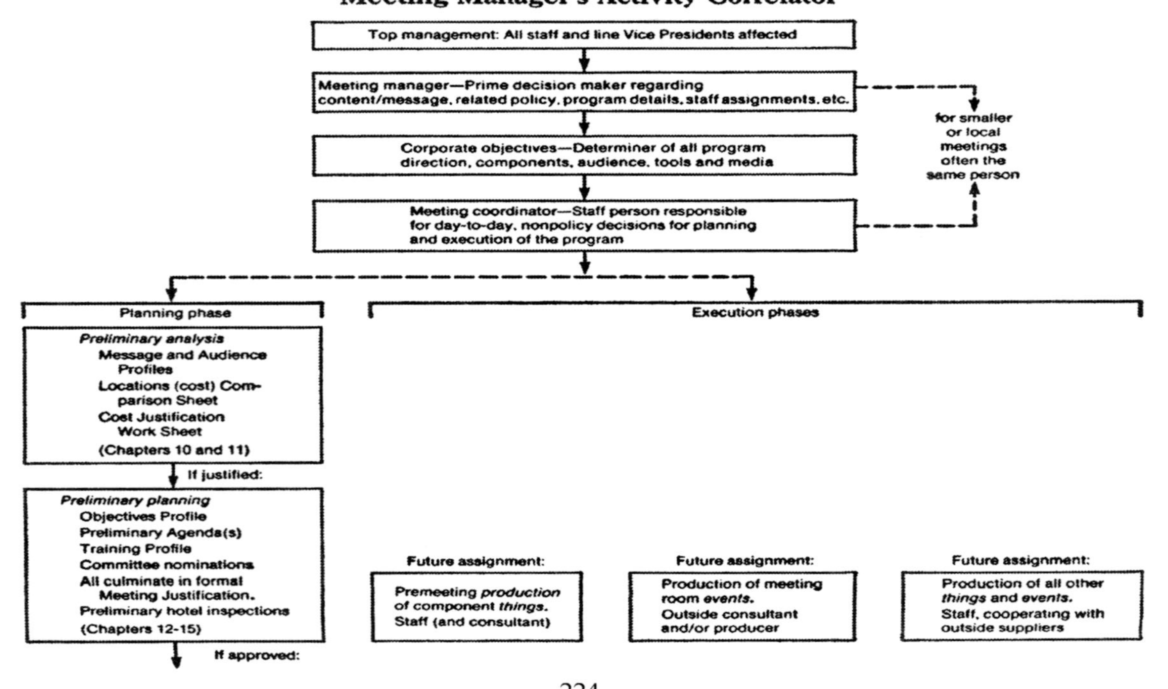
Sales Meetings That Work
Meeting Manager's Activity Correlator
Top management: All staff and line Vice Presidents affected
Meeting manager—Prime decision maker regarding content/message, related policy, program details, staff assignments, etc.
Corporate objectives—Determiner of all program direction, components, audience, tools and media
Meeting coordinator—Staff person responsible for day-to-day, nonpolicy decisions for planning and execution of the program
for smaller or local meetings often the same person
Planning phase
Execution phases
Preliminary analysis
Message and Audience Profiles
Locations (cost) Comparison Sheet
Cost Justification Work Sheet
(Chapters 10 and 11)
If justified:
Preliminary planning
Objectives Profile
Preliminary Agenda(s)
Training Profile
Committee nominations
All culminate in formal Meeting Justification.
Preliminary hotel inspections
(Chapters 12-15)
If approved:
Future assignment:
Premeeting production of component things.
Staff (and consultant)
Future assignment:
Production of meeting room events.
Outside consultant and/or producer
Future assignment:
Production of all other things and events.
Staff, cooperating with outside suppliers

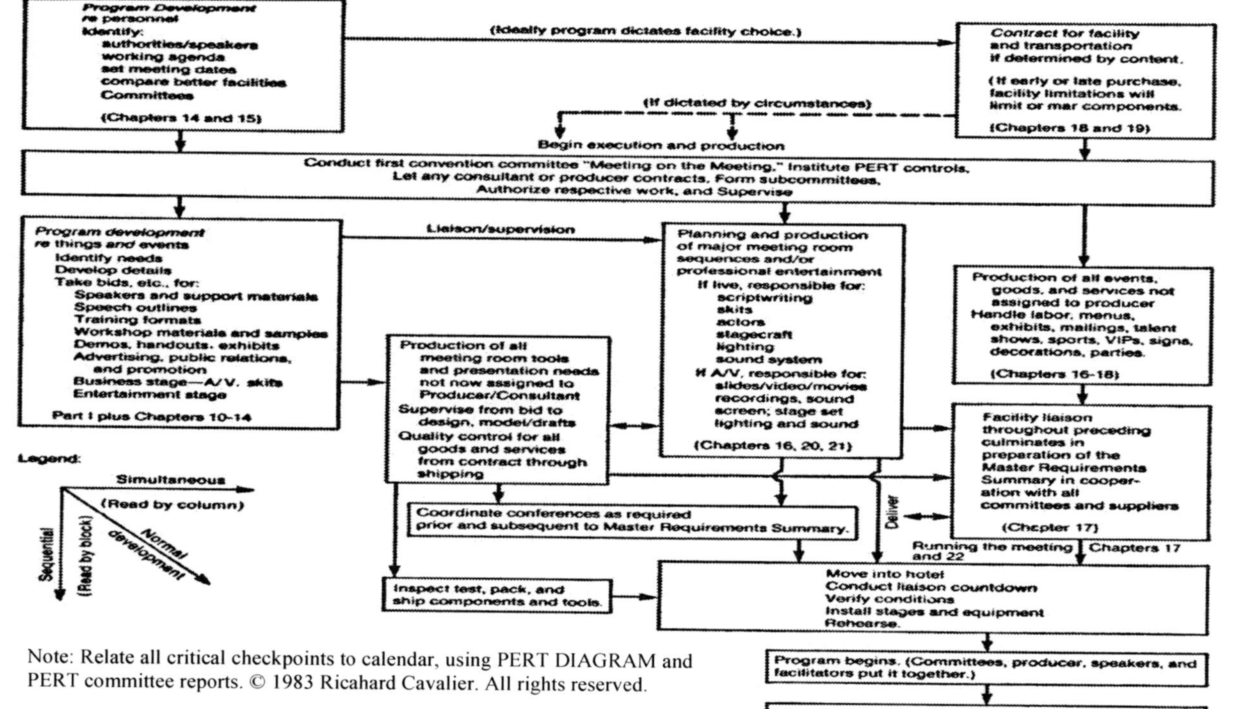

Note: Relate all critical checkpoints to calendar, using PERT DIAGRAM and PERT committee reports.

before it begins. The *facilitator* who assists the chairman has only that title, and the facilitator still should blend into the wallpaper.

The fact that all the activities surrounding and culminating in the major meeting or convention have logical relationships does not mean that beginners on your committees can automatically visualize the relationships between themselves and other members.

To aid you in plotting and explaining the duties of the various committees and their members, we have created the accompanying Activities Correlator. It's the first graphic in the convention industry to represent and relate all the potential activities of a major convention by function. On it you can spot all assistants for their benefit and yours. But you can also spot any potential supplier who attempts to dazzle you with jargon or generalities.

Take time now to review the accompanying Activity Correlator and get a feeling for the convention landscape. Do that before continuing to read.

The graphic might be far more ambitious than the program you've been outlining, but it's valid. And it will remain valid as a general reference for every meeting you will ever plan.

Yet we don't advise that you take even this diagram "as is." Create your own activity correlator, and include on it only those events and assignments which will compose your program. It might take as much as an hour of your time, but it will avoid confusing committee members who see "unassigned" entries on our master diagram.

Keep in mind that the Activity Correlator deals in *type* of function, not its timing. To assign a calendar relationship for the delivery of the goods and services with which each subcommittee will be charged, refer to the next unit, and to its Meeting/Convention Control (PERT) Diagram.

PERT analysis and diagrams. The logic of reasoning out all the indispensable steps of any process in reverse sequence is a common-sense approach that was formalized and codified in 1958 by consultants and suppliers working with the U.S. Navy on development of the Polaris System. By 1966 nearly a hundred variants had been identified.

The original was called Problem Evaluation and Review Technique (PERT), and it treated its planned resources and objectives in terms of optimistic, pessimistic, and probable conditions within each of the events, activities, and constraints that had a bearing on the whole. Those estimates of conditions were then convertible to calendar target dates.

PERT is ideal for exploring unknown new relationships of interim steps themselves known or unknown. That defines a meeting succinctly. As a paper simulation, a PERT diagram is costly in relative time for a small project; but the time requirements increases remain small even when the meeting complexity jumps substantially. So the larger the meeting, the better *bargain* PERT becomes.

If original estimates of time were significantly wrong, the PERT diagram's target dates would be wrong too; but that's a failure of the preparer, not the tool. Given reasonably accurate time estimates, PERT is a superior control tool. There is no substitute for a PERT-like schematic of a first-time meeting using any new format—or of any convention, which is invariably like no other before it

For subsequent meetings on identical formats, the PERT Diagram can be converted into one of its derivatives, the Critical Path Analysis. For repeats, the creative and production work will have been completed, and only the running of the event remains. The critical path is the longest period of time required for one complete cycle of the product or service under creation (the repeat event, such as a new-hire training program). CP is used to predetermine bottlenecks and eliminate them. For an excellent technical appraisal of the CP concept in quantified terms, see

"Plans, Projects, Programmes," in *Mathematics in Management,* by Albert Battersby (Baltimore: Penguin Books, 1966).

Despite the fact that PERT and CP methods have been used and widely discussed in business, none was published in the entire meetings/conventions industry until our 1973 book appeared. Numerous flow charts—misrepresented as PERT Diagrams—have appeared. While flow charts are extremely useful to their creator, they reflect his needs and circumstances and internal approval procedures, and are therefore virtually useless to any one else intact. They might provide a model for your intensive work regarding actual paper flow...if you need it. Apparently the editors who publish such flow charts don't understand their actual limitations.

By contrast, the PERT Diagram that follows is valid for each and every meeting or convention you will ever plan because it visually reminds you to convert every program element into a responsibility line with a calendar target date. You simply make new entries on the standard diagram form every time you begin planning a new meeting.

Your control of details is made visible and absolute. Not only does a conscientiously prepared PERT Diagram make outside assistance less necessary, but it makes clear that outside producers are one more potential problem area to be controlled!

Never make an arbitrary entry of dates on your diagram. The dates entered are still to be determined by the various subcommittees as they plan, investigate, and take bids on the various goods and services for which each is responsible. The manner in which they can report so as to aid the PERT process is established in the next chapter.

Review the accompanying PERT Diagram now. Notice that the major responsibility (subcommittee) crossbars convert all the categories of the Activity Correlator to individual lines of responsibility.

You can enter a date for any activity simply by marking an "X" under the appropriate "weeks prior" column—each of which will have a true calendar date according to the exact date scheduled for your meeting to begin.

The responsibility crossbars also correspond to the 12 functions of the Committee Assignments Coordinator, found earlier in this chapter, and to the special committee instructions, in the next chapter.

Plan to discuss the PERT control method with your convention committee. It's important that they understand how and why to construct the reverse-logic needs assessments and how to report them with time frames to you. A guide is provided in the next chapter.

We mentioned that the PERT Diagram is *time consuming* to make up, but that is not synonymous with *difficult*. Take the time. Your willingness to invest in understanding and control is your guarantee that you will indeed succeed in *managing* the event you are now setting in motion.

No matter how rushed you feel, make the time to coordinate all of the pertinent subcommittee PERT guides and reports onto an oversize graph chart, following our model. Plot each of the required assignment areas on separate horizontal bars representing the lines of responsibility. The vertical graph lines they intersect will represent calendar period—days, weeks, or months.

All the subpaths, representing separate activities essential to the main line of responsibility, feed into that main bar at the appropriate date; and all the responsibility bars feed into the central "convention arrow" at exactly that point in time when each must be delivered complete.

The shape and placement of the individual lines of responsibility are determined by delivery dates, not chance: the last-delivered items must appear at the outside of the diagram (that is, top or bottom) to eliminate crossovers and jumbled lines. As mentioned, this PERT Diagram is the only format which will lend itself, with minor variations, to every meeting or convention you will ever plan.

Sales Meetings That Work

Meeting/convention control (PERT) Diagram

Note: Hypothetical calendar; no attempt has been made to reflect actual time sequence in detail. To determine the calendar due dates for components of your meeting, refer to the *PERT Committee Guide & Report*, Chapter 15. Enter key dates on appropriate responsibility function bar below.

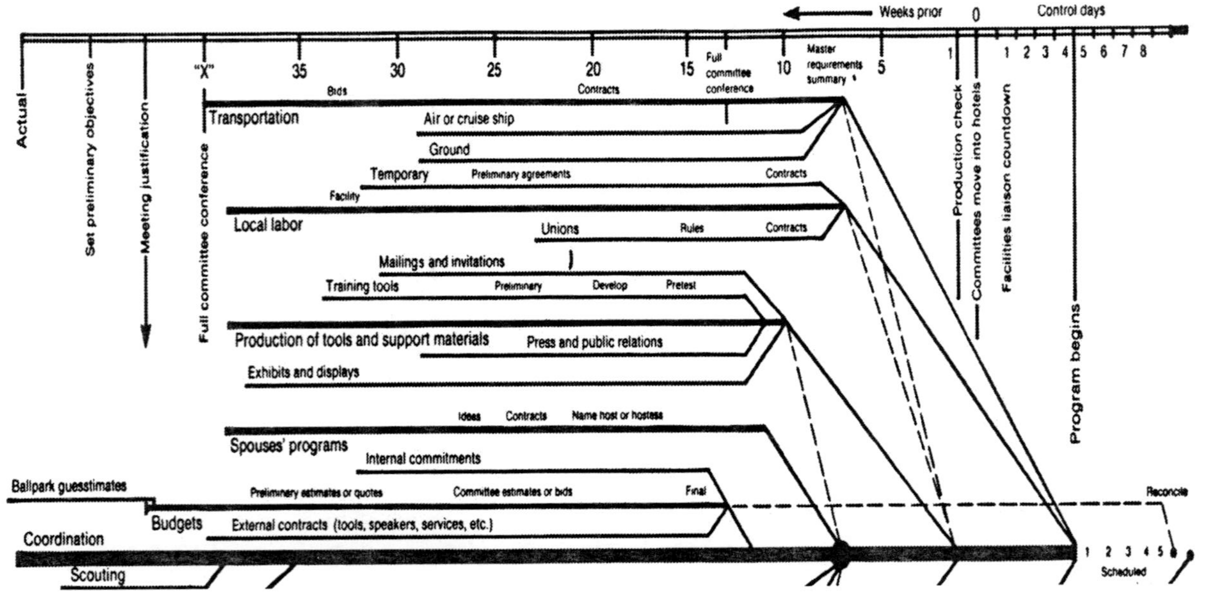

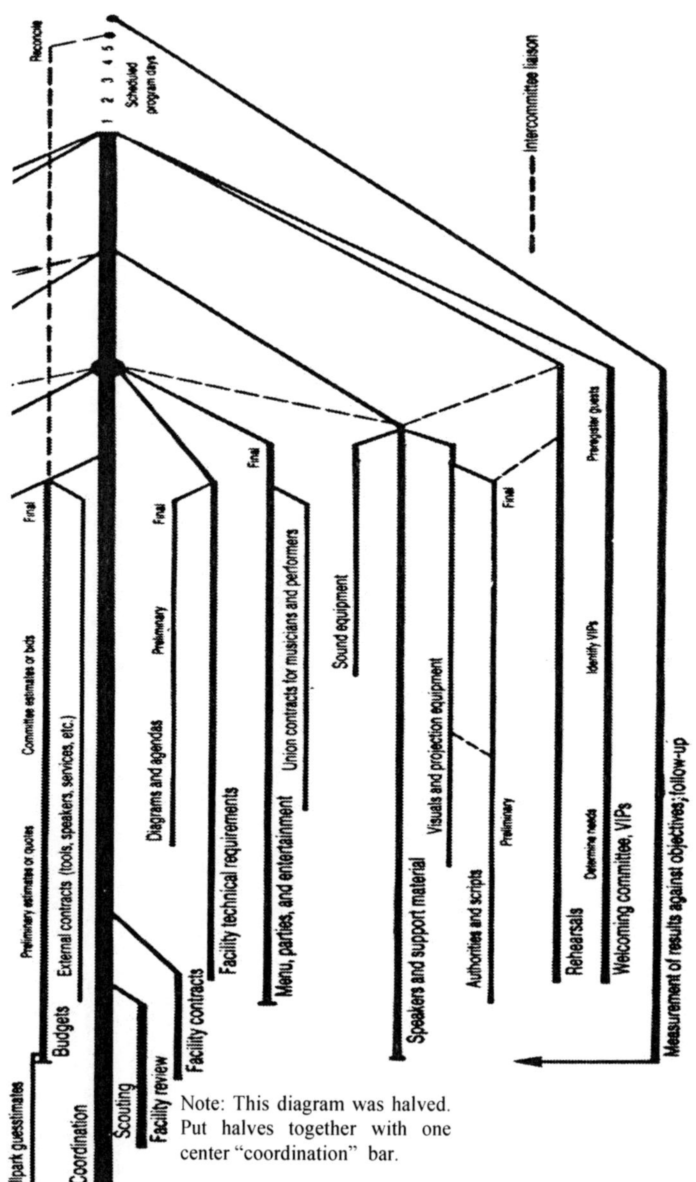

Note: This diagram was halved. Put halves together with one center "coordination" bar.

As soon as you begin to transfer information from your subcommittees' PERT Guides and Reports onto your master diagram, you will understand that the critical points and dates you make visible here eliminates the need to read through files repeatedly. You know at a glance how every subcommittee is faring; and that can be heightened by the use of a color code for checking off each point: green, go; yellow, caution; red, trouble. Control? *Fantastic* control!

16

Coordinating committees for control

If the meeting you're planning will be significantly more complex than a normal one-hour district sales meeting, you'll probably want or need to share the workload. While one person cannot be expected to carry his daily routine plus work alone to plan and produce a major meeting, giving the job to an uncoordinated group would be a worse alternative.

Someone must have an absolute understanding of the meeting concept during the entire period from initial idea until the wrap-up conference after the meeting or convention ends; he'll make the tough decisions, too. We have designated that man the *Meeting Manager.* He can be a supervisor exclusively, or can actually participate in the planning, coordinating and producing. That same degree of understanding must be shared by the person who will do the day-to-day work; he's the prime assistant, the *meeting coordinator.* The coordinator can be a staff member or a hired outsider. Even when the Meeting Manager participates, he must be backed up by at least one other person who Knows All; the company and project need that security.

Decisions must be made by the coordinator and/or the Meeting Manager because only they will have the overall understanding of the program. They might seek the advice of the single committee chief in charge of the function in question; but the convention committee as a whole will have uneven viewpoints and should *not* vote policy.

How should your committee be made up? As it must. Although 12 lines of responsibility are fully outlined in the Committee Assignments Coordinator and the PERT Diagram, not all will apply to every meeting. And even when all 12 apply, you need not appoint 12 different committee chairmen because some of the responsibilities can be combined—and some should be.

With your Working Agenda in hand, count the number of scheduled hours, including parties or banquets with entertainment. That number of program hours converts directly into the minimum number of man-weeks of time required to coordinate that program. Yes, one week per program hour! Now, given the calendar date of the meeting, and given the committee members' regular job commitments, how many men will be needed to deliver at least the stated number of man-weeks of time in the remaining calendar weeks? That's just arithmetic.

For instance, a seven-hour meeting will require seven work weeks of somebody's time, which can be shared; if only three calendar weeks remain until the meeting, at least three men must work nearly full time (3 men X 3 weeks) to execute it. If those men cannot devote full time, then increase the number of men assigned. As the number of men increases, so does time loss as a result of duplicated effort and interim conferences; so allow proportionately more hours of total committed time.

If only four men, for example, will share responsibility for all 12 categories, group the responsibilities logically. One man will find speakers and their support needs and their rehearsals (two categories) a full, logically related assignment. Another can easily handle menus and parties, local transport, room registrations and welcoming, and spouses' programs (four categories). Whoever selects the final facility should oversee contracts (conversion of agreements into specific services and clock schedules for room set-ups, and so on); because that affects the visuals and other on-stage events, the same person should be in charge of production of events, even if assisted from outside.

Whoever will be blamed if costs overrun budgets should be the guardian of the budget, and he should sit on each subcommittee which will be spending significant amounts of money. That will include hotel contracts, production of things and events, transportation, and menus and parties. With such interlock, overruns won't happen.

That logical structuring leaves only floor diagrams for the public rooms; hotel/motel liaison; and the hiring of local labor. These should be assigned to personnel in your company's same-city office, if possible; otherwise to the coordinator himself, who is most likely to be in the host city frequently and in contact with all other committees constantly. Eliminate duplicate trips by various committees whenever personal inspection is not necessary to an understanding of what can be accomplished.

Logical grouping of responsibilities does not automatically equalize the time commitments. Use the week-per-hour ratio where it applies and guesstimate the rest. The degree of detail work is your best guide to time needs. If it can't be estimated early in the process, appoint only the committee chief; let him investigate and then ask for help. Whatever the division of the workload, be sure each man understands exactly what is expected of him conceptually.

If you try to list all the things each should do, *(a)* you'll be wrong or inadequate in most details; *(b)* he'll look to you for step-by-step, hand-holding care throughout; *(c)* you'll take the blame for anything done incorrectly; *(d)* they'll all walk like zombies through the list without thinking one inch either side of the printing; *(e)* you'll waste more time than if you did the job yourself; and *(f)* understanding nothing, they'll be unable to explore and recommend alternatives or to assist you unsupervised while the event is in motion (see Chapter 22).

If you panic and hand out ready-made checklists, you will accomplish most of the negative things above without gaining anything more than a good looking, fast—but false—start.

As explained in Part I, checklists deal in bogus substance. They have three severe drawbacks. First, by trying to be all things to all people, they serve no one well. A general checklist reflects no agenda, no facility, and no timetable. Speed of lighting changes, for instance, can overwhelm stage lighting controls which might otherwise pass the "checklist" checkoff with sparks to spare.

Second, by being available, checklists lull their users into a false sense of security: either that completing the list completes the task or that checking a box indicates finished work. Nothing is ever finished until delivered in the meeting room; complete to date is the most you can hope for, or attest to, at any interim period.

Third, by existing, the standardized checklist implies that the committee and coordinating functions are simply a matter of checking off squares rather than of understanding every single element of program as it's added to the program!

Control is achieved only by understanding, and that understanding is achieved only by reasoning back from the final desired effect through all the interim indispensable steps in reverse sequence. That's the PERT method.

For example, if a speaker will use generated graph visuals, then the room must be darkened; do exit signs flare? Windows must have light-tight shades or draperies; light switches must be accessible. Artwork, ordered on a subpath; equipment, ordered; electric cable required: minimum of 500-watt, multiplug A/C circuit; circuit separate from room lights; therefore a control center for all switching; therefore a lighting control man assigned—union? Several speakers? Hire a projectionist; calculate total electrical load and distribute on several circuits for safety; reading light; more equipment and therefore a formal projection platform, set-up time, and formal rehearsals. Rehearse where and when? If the exact, visualized talk must be seen, it probably needs to be done in the meeting room—when can facility accommodate? At a rehearsal ratio of triple scheduled delivery time per talk, does adequate time exist between rehearsal and event? If not, what can be done? And so on.

Notice that only one small detail has been handled—that of one speaker's in-session visual support needs, with provision for other speakers. The job of coordinating the entire program will consist of creating exactly this type of analysis for every presentation or tool or event scheduled. There's no other way!

If, in this reverse-planning method you discover any program item which is either so complex that its pieces must be enumerated or one in which the pieces cannot be ready before the main event begins, then you might want to create your own checklist. *Then* a checklist is valid. Then it can help. Then and only then can you trust it to reflect your needs and serve your purposes because it fulfills and protects your plan perfectly!

Obviously, your convention committee and their subcommittees will need help in getting started. Committee chairmen should read any of the material in this book which pertains to them. Then they should be prepared to apply the following PERT Committee Guide and Report to each significant element in their assigned lines of responsibility.

Each subcommittee chairman will be asking his subcommittees to report to him on a series of summaries developed this way; and each subcommittee chairman will report to you, as the convention coordinator or Meeting Manager, in your operating title as chairman of the convention committee.

The PERT Committee Guide and Report will be self-explanatory once you present the underlying concepts, as this book has done for you. Once it's assigned, be sure to enforce the preparation and reporting of every program element being controlled by the form.

These completed forms are your basis for entering crucial checkpoints and dates on your PERT Diagram.

Take time now to review the accompanying PERT Committee Guide and Report.

Sales Meetings That Work

PERT Committee Guide and Report

(Make one for each facet of each of 12 Subcommittees)

Message (or Meeting Title): ______________________ Date: ____________

Committee Responsibility: ______________________________

Chairman: ______________________ Staff: ______________________

1. Responsibilities:
2. Description of key end-service or product:
3. Date required: ________________ Calendar time available: ______ weeks*
4. Indispensable prior steps, contributing to Item 2 above, which must be completed; list in reverse (dependency) order:

Critical prior step (Reverse order)	Elapsed time in days Best Worst Probably	Calendar Safe Target
____________	____________	____________
____________	____________	____________
____________	____________	____________
____________	____________	____________
____________	____________	____________

(Continue until basic first step has been identified and dated).

Total time required: weeks*

5. *Bottlenecks identified or apparent need for rush work:
6. Indicate critical checkpoints and safe target dates for transfer to the master "Meeting/Convention Control PERT Diagram:"
7. Initial Budget Estimate: $________ Probable Final Cost: $________________

NOTE: PERT represents timed logic. Any illogical sequences create potential problems. If any step in Item (4) above requires a complex feeder service or goods, construct a separate subpath on a duplicate Guide form and cross-reference via Item (2), the sub-committee responsibility. Once completed in its entirety, the Guide can be photocopied each report day. Each committee chairman should initial and date his report and circle in code colors the appropriate step then in progress. Applying management-by-exception criteria, request that only problems and *all problems* be commented upon in a brief covering memo.

CHAIRING THE FIRST MEETING ON THE MEETING

Once you've made all the evaluations necessary to complete your Meeting Justification and have mastered the reverse-order logic of PERT, you're prepared to meet your convention committee.

Here are some of the things you want to do in the first meeting you call:

1. Talk over the meeting's objectives and potentials.
2. Outline decisions made to date, if any, regarding dates and locations, etc. Distribute the Working Agenda.
3. Outline the anticipated next steps.
4. Convert those steps into committee assignments and name the respective subcommittee chairmen.
5. Demonstrate how their new lines of responsibility can be located and plotted on your own PERT Diagram, or on the book's version, if you'll need most functions.
6. Ask for immediate questions and comments on responsibilities or apparent improvements in assignments, methods, and so on. If anyone has special interests and can arrange an acceptable switch with someone else, encourage it
7. Establish periodic reporting via PERT Committee Guide & Report. Tell *who* will make final decisions.
8. *Avoid* discussing single subcommittee problems with the full committee. Discuss after adjournment; don't ignore any!
9. Get names of chairmen's choices for assistants and schedule initial subcommittee meeting. The number of participants will determine whether one or more meetings would be best.

The substantial amount of work already done will be evident. So that members of the convention committee do not feel they are being used as legmen, stress the countless details on choice and production that still remain. For instance, the probable speakers have been listed, but their scripts and visuals are yet to be prepared. Although you have scheduled a party, its theme and entertainment are yet to be chosen. The only thing the committee has been deprived of is the opportunity to take the program willy-nilly after viewpointless committee votes, which are usually more political than rational.

Discuss the overall concept of the program fully in the first meeting so everyone has the same initial understanding. Include the already-rejected alternatives, if any, and give the reasons. To let your subcommittees work up blind alleys is to court resentment.

For the subsequent subcommittee meetings, if conducted separately, let each committee chairman chair his own meeting. It's important to establish his position as chief; otherwise you'll find subcommittee members coming to you with details for which you have no context, causing frustration and lost time for all three parties.

Be prepared to give the subcommittees some amount of tips and direction in the initial organizing meeting(s). To help you to get ready to oversee them, we've provided some guidelines; take what applies and add your own thoughts. If the subcommittees will be gathered in one big meeting, consider handing out written notes on each of the lines of responsibility. It saves time and fights boredom in those who have no use for the esoteric details.

Guidelines for subcommittees

1. Facilities inspection and selection. It's almost impossible to be too careful about the facilities selected for a meeting. Whether you're using an all-in-one convention center or a combination of hotel/motel plus an independent auditorium or (movie) theatre, the facilities have an effect on the program.

Preselecting potential sites to be inspected need not be a headache if you work smart. That means avoiding the travel industry publications that list all the facilities in the nation. Even the telephone Yellow Pages do that for any given city. What really matters is the *current availability* on or near your target meeting dates. The best place to get up-to-date information on availability is the convention bureau of the city selected. In smaller towns, see the local chamber of commerce.

These bureaus know from day to day which conventions are already booked in town and which hotels have them. The convention bureau or chamber play no favorites and will tell you every facility which has both the capacity you need and the open dates you seek. There is none of the bias and public relations favoritism that colors most published lists (often limited to advertisers). And there is no charge to you. That's service at the right price!

One you contact those available facilities, the convention office will offer to send you printed brochures. Accept them as a starting point, but keep in mind that they are always out of date—sometimes substantially, and occasionally, intentionally. Ask about specific inaccuracies or recent changes; and hold the materials suspect until personal inspection proves them absolutely accurate.

Facility selection and contracting are so important that a special unit is devoted to it. The subcommittee chairman (and maybe his assistants) must read it before shopping (see Chapter 18).

2. Facilities contracts. Promises, promises—But some facilities won't give you the time of day after signature if it's not stipulated in the contract. What's free with the contract and what's chargeable over room rates and food? How many complimentary rooms for how many paid (25 to 35 per comp is standard); but if suites are selected, how many "rooms" does each cost (two to five is the range; a 150 percent differential)? No matter how hard they try to discourage you, get all public space commitments in writing by room name or number and never give up your meeting room to another group after you move in! The corporation attorney must review the final contract offered; he should review the sample contract submitted by competing hotels/motels. All should be familiar with the Hotel/Association Facility Contract, developed by the American Society of Association Executives, Washington, D.C. (see Chapter 18).

3. Agenda and room diagrams. Assembling a written statement and diagrams of needs is the task of this group; once the needs are known (but at least six weeks in advance of a major event), send copies through the facility's convention manager to each department head and require written response. Never make a positive assumption on a no-reply basis; that is, "If I don't hear from you..." Nobody reads those letters (see Chapter 17).

4. Budgets. No one can afford much of what suppliers can suggest. Advance budget estimates based on prior experience, information from counterparts in other companies, and telephone inquiries will help you to be more knowledgeable in initial contacts.

The only thing true of all budgets is that they're never quite large enough to buy all the good things you can conceive of. If you concentrate on the essentials of your program (tools and speaker-support materials), you can go back later and order the flowers and fillers.

Hotel billings can be a problem, often because of either forgotten charges (gratuities added by percentage) or unauthorized charges by your staff. You'll have the greatest control over costs if most meals are catered group dinners and those costs, together with room charges, appear on your master account. All incidentals can be paid in cash and rebilled to the company if legitimate expenses.

Never require meeting participants to advance the cost of their own rooms and meals when checking out. Hotel stays are so expensive these days that the cost can exceed a week's pay and put an unjustified squeeze on the family budget. In these days of computer billings, even credit card charges are in the man's mailbox before he gets home—and company expense reimbursements are notoriously slow. Don't let money problems sabotage your program: negative attitudes generated here can hurt for years.

Bulk billings for meals and for house labor, and so on are the only open charges to be signed for; give the hotel/motel a *written* list of names of persons permitted to sign bills and warn that you *will not honor* any other signatures.

Overtime blows budgets. Unless it's dictated by the PERT analysis for the function, don't authorize it.

5. Production of tools and (nonspeaker) support materials. Essentially the input/output supervision of suppliers, this function can be handled only by PERT analysis and diagram. Add as many subpaths as necessary to the main responsibility line to reflect all the (non-speaker) projects, including tools, exhibits, printing, art and slides, new product mock-ups, and so on. Many *freebies* are available from associations or potential suppliers promoting a particular viewpoint. Some of these freebies are media spectaculars, and apart from the categorical criticisms aimed at maximedia, these can spend so much of your money on staging costs that it's cheaper to develop your own presentation or tools. (Refer to the Something-for-Nothing Evaluator for workable criteria.)

6. Local help. You're always wrong in a union dispute; and as the outsider you're usually wrong in disputes between any two suppliers in Miami Beach, resorts, and smaller cities simply because they must still live together later. Smaller cities and out-of-the-way locations are death on competition. Concessions are usually held by brothers-in-law, who don't need to be competent. If you don't find *exactly* what you need locally and at a fair price, buy it elsewhere and transport it. In these circumstances, overpricing is standard because it's expected that you'd rather pay than ship. Do you want to give your suppliers that hold on you?

If you have a complex meeting, here are some alternatives:

a. Assign local company staff to the respective committees and let them supervise and recommend; or
b. Assign one or more company employees (committee members, before or after the fact) to live there for a week or so to nail down details; or
c. Hire a professional coordinator of conventions. A local man would probably be cheaper than a nationally experienced coordinator, but the local man's credentials will be harder to verify because he's working among the people who'll rate him every day. The toughest taskmaster is not necessarily popular.

If you really want to hold your meeting in the given city, go back to the convention bureau or chamber of commerce and tell them your problems. If you do it before signing any contracts, you'll have bargaining power.

Many local temporary-help chains have clerk-typists on tap, and many of them will be glad to tell you how to run your meeting—which is the way everybody else does it. Sometimes that makes sense, but usually it's just easier for them because of habit. Be careful before you get into a sticky situation.

Modeling agencies will provide poised women for exhibit booth duty if you will invite your clients. Give the agency a good idea of the type of person you seek, and it will preselect a group whom you can interview in the agency office and choose from. If your budget won't cover the top-of-the-line, try the drama coach of the local university—students always need cash.

If you need speaking actors, contact the nearest office of Actor's Equity (union). Equity gives casting advice and assistance generously. For plays and skits, rates are inflexible. But for modeling/product presentation situations, the actors are free to work at modeling rates if they choose. If the hours are long there's a considerable difference, because overtime rules are stringent at Equity.

In some airport locations airline stewardesses have formed modeling agencies to bypass scheduling problems of off-duty personnel. The local convention bureau will know of them.

Unskilled or semiskilled labor should be ordered through the facility itself if possible: you have a better chance of obtaining crews that have worked there before.

As a general rule, local help tends to be slipshod because it deals perennially with one-time customers. But there are stubborn souls in almost every trade and location who won't compromise with what's fair. Ask pointed questions. Talk written guarantees and contract, and you'll soon discover who can be relied upon. And those will become your suppliers without question in years ahead.

7. Speakers and support materials. If the speakers and their preferences are already known, the preparation of specifications for bids is the logical next step. Unless a talk is already fully scripted and acceptable, prepare a PERT Guide for each speaker, working in collaboration with him so that he feels committed to its dates. Then hold him to the checkpoints and dates. When presentations are being written from scratch, ask for an outline before the first draft—it simplifies additions and changes. Review a verbatim first draft before sketching art; the producer will need to make substantial changes in most cases, unless his staff has prepared the script from your outline.

Given those precautions, production of visuals is seldom complicated. Someone in the company is already familiar with exhibits, printing, training, and so on and can help even if not on the committees.

As a positive control and safety factor, keep a ringbinder with the basic outline(s) and every script progression of every talk. Carry the final version of all scripts into the meeting event and read along. If you follow the proceedings closely, you will be prepared to handle any hitch that might develop. What is your

Plan B? That belongs in the ringbinder, too. (Assign pertinent material in Chapters 5, 6, and 14.)

8. Menus, parties, and entertainment. Every catering manager in the world has had his days at the kitchen stove, and many of them are proud that they can still whip up a mean soufflé. So although the hotel is prepared to hand you suggested menus, ask for something unusual if you want it. You are not obligated to repeat the menus of other companies. Keep two things in mind. First, menu prices are somewhat negotiable, permitting the trading away of soup in favor of a fancier dessert. Second, the catering office is a profit center, and the prices will reflect the number of "free" meeting rooms and services already agreed to by the convention office. There's nothing for nothing in a hotel!

The best way to fight what you feel are overpriced menus is to serve carved beef sandwiches and beer at lunch and threaten to turn the men loose on the town for dinner. The hotel doesn't want to lose the dinner service and will compromise.

In major resorts, food is usually included in the room rate; usually it's quite good, and often it's almost unlimited. It's downright nasty to take dieters to the New York Upstate Borscht Belt, where meals are a main attraction.

In resorts, most entertainment is provided; only rarely is there a charge. Moreover, the staff recreation director can keep spouses and after-hours learners busy with sports, games, and whatever. Consider an employee talent show if you suspect there's some talent around.

Don't spend for paid entertainers until you've checked your alternatives. (For major stage shows, see Chapter 21.)

9. Transportation. There are several categories of transportation to contend with: intercity, city-to-resort, and intracity daily movements.

Intercity movement rarely presents problems unless your total movement out of the host city exceeds available capacity at your departure times. Generally the inward travel times of your staff are staggered by their personal preferences.

Do not choose cities arbitrarily. Your best-buy locale is determined by special fares and the huge differences between short and long haul per-mile fares. The airlines serving the prospect cities can determine the least expensive city by computer analysis based on the exact locations of personnel. You're making a mistake if you don't ask for that analysis.

Probably everyone knows by now that cheaper fares can be had on the web than from some traditional retailers or even some established consolidators. Discount retailers sprang up long ago in competition to the traditional trade; and even the airlines are dumping on the travel agents these days. So it's open season on airfares. At this writing, the most talked about sources for cheap digs and flights change frequently. You know them. Although they claim only to sell individual tickets and vouchers, they have a lock on the cheapest room rates offered by given hotels. You shouldn't expect to get those same rates on your demand-schedule, but at least you will know in advance how low the facility is willing to go.

However, if such on-line houses actually have clout with the airlines, they should be able to block large groups in advance, too. Because there are problems with even some bonded travel agents, be aware and ask for references. Check them, too. In California, all sellers are now required to obtain an identification number and to use it in all advertising. Do you suppose that was done because the travel industry is pristine?

But because computer-based, full motion video conferencing is here, you no longer need to buy bulk transportation or hotels. For the first time you are free of the budgetary inescapables of the past. If you can give up the unproductive fancies of the past, you might even have room in your budget for measurably better, more productive programs. Now, how can that hurt your job?

Why does it matter?

According to a spokesman for the American Express Consulting Services Division, "corporations are going to continue to look for new and creative ways to take out costs." The costs he's discussing are the approximately two-thirds chunk that airlines (44%) and hotels (22%) take out of the overall average travel budget...committed before you've even said, "Good morning." Although business ticket expense increased over 50% between 1995 and 1999, corporate executives are supposed to be pleased that the newest projection are for "only" 2% to 3% for the millennium year. At the very least, that argues for letting all your participants make their own travel plans at advance-purchase rates because in the same period, rates for discretionary and 7-day advance travel remained flat.

President John Kennedy was quoted for saying "I don't get angry—I get even." Business travelers might want to adopt the same strategy regarding airline fares. Although bulk quantities and discounts for frequent use are standard pricing practice for American corporations, the airlines don't feel obligated to use it. Back in the 70s, the average airlines business ticket for the average trip was priced under $200; today it's about $800. In the mid-60s, when we made a vacation trip to London, Paris, Vienna, and Rome, the cost was slightly over $600; today it's probably less than 50% more in constant dollars—and inflation makes that into a fraction. The difference is in multiples of about eight. Considering that the cost of airline trips has fallen substantially in real purchasing price over the past few decades, business might see itself as being gouged by the airlines. In statistics, business travelers provide about 40% of the passenger load but 80% of the profit. Message?

On-demand tickets (the most expensive sort) are charged at premium prices because—well, what's your alternative? Special deals are given to folks who buy early but might fly fewer times in their lifetimes than business travelers do in a month. Especially in these days of computer tracking, any corporation should be able to guarantee the use of at least 50%-75% of last year's total expenditure and be guaranteed flight space for the whole period or be given a stated number of el-cheapo air miles. That's the way that department stores get bargains on their advertising—just guarantee to use a lot of newspaper pages, and it's cheaper! Today, when airlines ask "What's the alternative?" business has one: two-way, full-motion video conferencing. And it's cheap! And it will probably be on your PC soon.

At most that means never traveling again when travel can be avoided—and video conferencing advances now make that possible. Now tell me one more time why "You gotta meet face-to-face!"

Probably everyone knows by now that cheaper fares can be had on the web than from some traditional retailers or even some established consolidators. Discount retailers sprang up long ago in competition to the traditional trade; and even the airlines are dumping on the travel agents these days. So it's open season on airfares. At this writing, the most talked about sources for cheap digs and flights seem to change frequently. You know what they are today. Although they claim only to sell individual tickets and vouchers, nevertheless the discounters do list the lowest price at which the hotel is selling under duress. Don't expect that you will be offered distress prices on a demand schedule, but at least you will enter into negotiations already knowing what the lowest price is at each individual facility.

At most it means never traveling again when travel can be avoided—and video conferencing advances now make that possible. Now tell me one more time why "You gotta meet face-to-face!"

Country resorts usually have things under control, too. After all, they solve the problem for somebody regularly. A few have put in a small private landing strip, which permits small craft to ferry in executives; it's too expensive for a large group, which generally ends up on a bus. The resort knows who and how much and is sometimes willing to make arrangements in your name.

In positive attitudes generated, the small resort can be surpassed only by foreign travel. Foul weather can hurt; so check out the indoor sports and health spa facilities, just in case.

Intracity transportation needs vary with the group. Much-traveled executives often prefer to stay near the airport; first-time travelers want to see the city and will get downtown somehow, probably at your expense. So if you're using far-out facilities, schedule a sightseeing trip; the bus tour companies have dinner-tour packages that might not exceed open-night expenses if the group is on its own. But the free ride creates control which permits an early-to-bed curfew. If you're staying in the city, try the municipal transportation company for charter service; it's usually the cheapest and air-conditioning is standard now, at least for the charter business.

10. Welcoming and registration; VIPs. Why spend a lot of time and money to turn people on during the scheduled program while doing nothing at all to welcome them a few hours before? A handshake and directions to where the gang is holed up will say more about what you think of them as individuals than will the greatest dog-and-pony show on earth.

If your group size doesn't dominate the facility, create a watering hole in one of the reserved public rooms—booze or soft drinks and coffee. Guarantee the bartender's salary and don't push. Music?

Pre-registration is a nice gesture. When your people appear, they sign a pre-typed hotel registration form and are handed the corresponding key. Besides eliminating lines at the main registration counter, a pre-registration table gives you a running tally on who has arrived. It also gives you a tally on the VIPs who might be greeted with a basket of fruit or liquor bottle in their room.

Don't make the mistake of pampering VIPs. They are entitled to courtesy and assistance, but they are not entitled to facilities and privileges substantially different from those accorded your own participants. You will have headaches only if you create them. Do not offer pick-up at the airport unless it's demanded, since flight changes and weather problems mess up many arrangements. Few VIPs are difficult unless nervous hosts lead them to believe they're being badly treated. Human nature is predictable despite titles. The chairman of the board of one of our Fortune-200 companies customarily refuses suites. He takes average accommodations; while nobody mistakes him for one of the boys, neither has anyone ever complained. That's especially effective when the best-available facilities are not-so-great.

It's not necessary to do any particular thing. What really matters is that the effects of a warm reception will last throughout the meeting. You can't do yourself more good at less cost!

11. Rehearsals. Every amateur thinks he doesn't need a rehearsal; the professional demands one. No matter how it might be rationalized, refusing a rehearsal is ego-tripping. Kill it.

Schedule a rehearsal for everyone. See people individually, with only the speaker's own assistants and your subcommittee in the room. Schedule *the* meeting room whenever possible to avoid extra expense for multiple set-up and tear-down and to create comfort with the surroundings of the actual event to follow. This is the last place at which a speech coach could help; the job should have been done at the time the final script was completed.

Stagger the rehearsal times. Allow triple the amount of time that the actual presentation will take—it will all be used. More important, it will avoid wasting the time of others.

In professional theater, superstition says that a poor dress rehearsal means a great show. Maybe. But for amateurs, that's asking for trouble. Rehearse until it's right, even if you have to take the problem presentation aside for practice while the subsequently scheduled rehearsals go on. At first, a problem speaker is apt to be irritated; it's an ego reaction. Stay calm and insist. He'll eventually thank you for being inflexible about absolutely everything that matters.

12. Spouses' programs. Whether or not to encourage their attendance is one question, and whether or not to pay if they do come is another. Depending on the program structure and available rooms, spouses should be specifically invited, specifically refused, or permitted to attend at their own expense—all by advance arrangement. If there's space, and if the locale is a desirable resort area, try to work in a motivational program, with the spouse's trip to be won as an incentive.

If you invite spouses, create a business program for at least three hours every day. This is a great opportunity to tell the spouse what the company is about; how it sits in the competitive market place; why the company expects the employed spouse to travel regularly. Here's a ready audience to try new products on, to discuss student-loan plans and other company benefits which the employed spouse might have forgotten to mention.

If the spouse attends a full day of business programs, the total costs are tax deductible; but that schedule is too rough. Try the three-hour business day, and deduct half. Either the company or person must pay for the incentive portion, which is considered additional income to the person. It can be paid after-taxes by the company, or the nondeductible portion can be reported on the individual's IRS Form 1040. Be sure all employees know in advance whether they are incurring a tax obligation. Check with the corporation's comptroller and/or the IRS.

If spouses are invited, stipulate casual attire to avoid wholesale family bankruptcies. Yes, the spouses can (tax-deductibly) sit in on general assembly presentations. But keep them out of the workshops, where every distraction hurts.

Use common sense. It's amazing how well it works in meeting planning!

You won't need a committee to handle this, but this is the logical place to consider insurance matters. In past years, insurance was never much of a consideration. Most people would not have thought of suing an employer or business associate or association. Now, anything goes. Protect yourself, but don't go overboard—life is not risk-free, and you are not responsible for things that you can dream up but nevertheless would be outside your control.

There are a few basic things to consider. First, someone in your organization is already in charge of insurance—that person should assess your needs here. Keep in mind that most hotels have insurance for untoward events that happen on their property, and common carriers have insurance, too, although it's often limited. Second, all hotels in a given city are subject to the same city fire codes; when suburbs are contemplated, there could be some minor differences. Nevertheless, unless you suspect non-compliance in a given facility, it's a matter of tweedle-dee and tweedle-dum between any one hotel and all the rest.

Many associations and some publications have made a big fuss about insurance needs in the past decade. Little fuss is really justified, and all of it is an attempt to create ersatz problems that they can then "solve" for you. With so many legitimate and actual problems long ignored and still waiting on the sidelines, it's really a tawdry attempt to gain respectability and the look of expertise that they might not have been able to gain through worthwhile action.

Before panicking, consider alternatives to the cause of the liability. Avoidance vs. likelihood is the determiner. Can you do anything differently? Then relax. There's nothing you can do to outguess weird situations and dishonest people with only ordinary diligence and intelligence. Life is wall-to-wall risk. The law doesn't require you to baby-sit your attendees. Just don't create dumb hazards. Enuf sed.

WHAT'S AHEAD?

From the time you conclude the subcommittee meeting(s) until you're ready to submit the Master Requirements Summary to the site facility, your job is to apply and enforce the PERT Guides developed. Do it!

17

Bringing the pieces together

Whether you are functioning at this point as the decision-making Meeting Manager or the actively supervising convention coordinator, keeping your subcommittees on the track and on time will be your prime responsibility.

This does not mean that you cannot carry some direct line of responsibility yourself. Most Meeting Managers want control over the budget decisions, and most convention coordinators want to prepare the Master Requirements Summary personally in collaboration with the various subcommittee chairmen.

As in all other areas of successful management, keeping the sub-committees on the track means reviewing their PERT reports against your master PERT Diagram and your understanding of how the project should be shaping up. It also means refusing to take the responsibility for completing any particular aspect of the subcommittee's work. If you take on a few details from each subcommittee, you will soon be so bogged down in trivia that you will begin to lose sight of the big picture.

On the other hand, you should not deprive any subcommittee of your counsel and best ideas. They should see you as an ally, not as an adversary standing between their ideas and top management After your first Meeting on the Meeting, you can guide them toward the following succession of activities. Each subcommittee should:

1. Confer separately to outline individual areas of activity and responsibility. The Meeting Manager or coordinator

need not sit in on every subcommittee session after everyone is secure in the group's direction.

2. Confer as soon as possible with either the speakers or the suppliers of other tools, goods, and services.
3. Determine which responsibilities will be handled internally (and by whom!) and which externally. That includes the writing of notices, invitations, press releases, if any, and so on.
4. Note any developing discrepancies between the original PERT Guide(s) and current reality. If discrepancies occur, determine whether an original miscalculation or an unnoticed, unintended change in direction has occurred. If the latter, act!
5. When able, describe in writing the final approach agreed upon for all speakers, goods, and services—using the PERT Guide.
6. Immediately thereafter, with the likely needs of the developing program in mind, make a final inspection tour of the best-available hotels/motels and make the final selection. Contract.
7. Submit weekly (or other specified periodic) PERT reports to confirm that all projects are progressing in the proper stages with good quality and on time. Note and explain *only the exceptions.*
8. Reconfirm as soon as possible, but not until after production is underway—the workability of each project from every standpoint. List every technical requirement and note any known hotel/hall/auditorium limitations which could affect the list. Also list every other requirement from any source or supplier, including internal.
9. List the subcommittee member who will be responsible for each. of the requirements listed above.

Once the requirements lists begin to arrive from the subcommittees, you can begin to draw up your Master

Requirements Summary. It will include the needs of your outside producer, if you have one; and from the time he is hired, he should also be reporting to you on either your PERT Guide or his own version of it. Never let your producer(s) work in secrecy; and be sure you check on the progress of your project at each critical stage and date he has established. (For detailed assistance, see Chapters 20 and 21.) All things considered, your producer is paid staff, even if temporary, and he should be supervised as such.

MASTER REQUIREMENTS SUMMARY AND FINAL AGENDA

One of the reasons you work with your Working Agenda for so many weeks is that until you receive confirmation that all specifications *can* be met, you can't include them on the program with certainty. The other common reason is that some aspect of the program might require technical equipment or labor in excess of what you could foresee early in the planning stages; it might be necessary to shift one or two items of the agenda to accommodate the easier/cheaper alternative. The adjusted Working Agenda is the Final Agenda.

Your most productive plan of attack will see you making up a preliminary Master Requirements Summary (see accompanying format) against your Working Agenda; then examine both to see whether any discrepancies exist; if so, correct them. When both are in agreement, finalize the agenda and then the summary.

In most instances, by the time you are able to complete your Master Requirements Summary, your event is getting close. That means about two weeks away for a relatively small meeting; or about two months away for a major convention. Time is now critical, and perfect understanding with all suppliers and with the hotel/motel and/or auditorium/hall/theater is essential.

Sales Meetings That Work

Master Requirements Summary

(Make a separate sheet for each room each day)

Function Room: <u>(Main) (Secondary) (Exhibit Hall)</u>

DAY ONE: Morning (Date)

Ready NLT _________ A.M. for ________ A.M. start of program

Stage: (List everything to be provided by facility. Use as much space as necessary. Do not combine rooms on one sheet; do not combine days unless *identical* throughout.

Sound:

Lighting:

Seating:

Other:

(Diagram here, if needed)

LUNCH BREAK at __________A.M./P.M.

DAY ONE: Afternoon

Ready NLT _________ A.M. for ________ A.M. start of program

Stage:

Sound:

Lighting: (If identical, indicate)

Seating:

Other:

BREAK at ___________A.M./P.M

DAY ONE: Evening

Ready NLT _________ A.M. for ________ A.M. start of program

Etc.) (If dinner service followed by reset for meetings, indicate)

BREAK at ___________A.M./P.M

RESET (stage only) (entire room) NLT___P.M. for rehearsal

(Etc.)

Notes: Special preparations (or problems to be avoided):

In charge of room set-ups for (Company): ___________

The Master Requirements Summary becomes the addendum to contract for which provision has been made in the original contract with the facility (see Chapter 18).

The Summary should contain no surprises for the hotel or auditorium staff, since all requests are based on prior inspections, conversations, and promises. If an unexpected need surfaces, call attention to it specifically; and get a specific acknowledgment that it can/cannot be accommodated. If not, there's time to take corrective action.

Full use of the Master Requirements Summary is a two-step process. The first is to forward the written material to the facility(ies) for study by department heads; and the second is for the Summary to become the basic document in a liaison count-down session between your convention committee and theirs.

Forward your completed Summary (preferably with extra copies addressed to department heads) to the hotel/auditorium/hall convention manager and get a written acknowledgment of: *(a)* its receipt, and *(b)* their ability to perform as directed, or *(c)* detailed "unables," including the reasons; these, if any, reflect misunderstandings before they can become panics.

Immediately, provide written instructions covering any "unables" and flag those areas for special attention during the all-staff liaison meeting after moving into the facility.

By this time, because of the way the human brain functions, the Pert Guides and Diagram will have converted themselves into a very exacting mental picture of the entire program. It will not be necessary to review your files, although all pertinent files should be packed and carried to your headquarters room in the facility.

Your mental picture of the program will guide all future decisions—especially when the event is in progress—effortlessly and almost automatically. And that is what is known as having a business meeting or convention under control!

Take time now to review the accompanying Master Requirements Summary format. Remember that it is only a suggested format. Your actual format must be dictated by your needs. Make a separate sheet for each room and for each day—that is, four sheets if you are using two public rooms for two days each. Run-overs count as one sheet, of course, regardless of the number of pages.

The Master Requirements Summary is the only document you will produce which is more important than the PERT Diagram. Give it the time and thought it deserves.

THE LIAISON COUNT-DOWN

The single most important meeting you will ever hold regarding your meeting/convention event is the liaison conference with all hotel department heads and their convention manager just before the formal start of your program. Ideally, it will occur one or two days before the Program Day One.

It is essential that your company's Meeting Manager or coordinator—as the person with the most comprehensive view of the program—take charge of the liaison conference.

Introduce all company staff members, including your producer, if any; then ask the hotel convention manager to introduce his staff.

Point out which of the subcommittee members will work with which of the hotel's department heads, although many will know each other because of prior inspection trips.

From this point on, each person on both sides is responsible for all of his—and only his—areas of responsibility as covered in the contract and the Master Requirements Summary.

From the standpoint of efficiency, cover the least complex areas first—telephones, public restaurants, housekeeping—and release those supervisors immediately.

The electrician/soundman and the carpenter and head houseman will work together throughout your program and will benefit from sitting through each other's discussions. Treat them as a team.

Don't belabor the requested services. Start with the *stated* assumption that everything requested will be delivered exactly as summarized *unless* potential problems are discussed *right now*!

Concentrate on problems, if any; the Summary is too complex to permit a point-by-point discussion; so proceed page by page and require the hotel to give you either the problem seen or a verbalized "Can do!" For practical purposes, there should be no problems considering the prior written response to the original submission; but misunderstanding could surface even when the goods or services can be provided. Usually they won't have understood your purpose; and when that's stated, they might have a better way in mind. Hear the alternatives and decide. Discuss even slightly hazy areas. Be sure everyone is comfortable with every aspect of the program and summary before adjourning.

If everyone comes to the all-staff liaison meeting properly prepared—and there's no excuse not to—and if only exceptions and problems are discussed in detail, then an entire three-to five-day convention can be cleared with perfect understanding in only three hours' time.

You'll find that to be the most rewarding three-hour span you've spent on the entire coordination process to date, because you will go to sleep *certain* that your program will be *able* to happen exactly as planned.

Once the program begins, it's every man to his assigned task. You might ask working committee members to regroup at the end of each program day; work on exceptions, if any. Otherwise wrap up fast and let everyone get on with tomorrow's work.

As you can begin to appreciate even in your first reading, success is no accident. More important, no accident will be able to destroy your program structure! That's *management!*

18

Handling hotels

Quality facilities are important to your program if you are still site-committed. However, that quality should not be expressed as the advertising suggests—as the biggest/newest/flashiest/most extravagant place on earth. Rather, it must convey respect for the individuals participating.

In scientific terms, the hotel/motel becomes a major part of the surround; that is, everything in the participant's conscious and unconscious awareness of place, excluding people.

An unspoken message of attitudes reflected by the facility is received by your participants on arrival; it must be acceptable at minimum. Yet it's not necessary 'that the facility be fancy; the quality level that most participants would choose while on vacation is the proper starting point. Trade up to the degree warranted by the importance of your message.

Convention life would be far easier if innkeeping and the public space capabilities of each facility were well matched. But some very fine inns—offering good rooms, good service, and tasty food—have small meeting rooms or none at all. Other facilities in demand because of their abundant meeting space offer shabby service and shabby attitudes and cardboard food. Inspect; test.

Rooms, food, and staff service and attitudes are far more important than the public space in terms of the surround. Most urban areas have many auditoriums and theaters and college halls to aid your space needs; but nothing compensates for uncomfortable living.

Always treat your inn and convention hall as separate entities, even when they're under the same roof! Living conditions and hotel cooperation count for more than national trade name or bowing-and-scraping waiters when the chips are down.

Once you accept that wisdom, you're ready to decide on the general type of facility to be sought. For brief or very large meetings, the city or city-airport facility often wins. For personal contact and enough solitude to encourage serious study and discussions, the conference center or hidden-away resort are in front. For an incentive award, contest award, or celebration (anniversary, banner year, major new product, and so on), the big ski or sun resort is the place.

Keep in mind that some companies offer portable classrooms. These trailers can be rented for short or long periods and will accommodate the smaller groups usually preferred for training and other small-group purposes. With portables, you can have your meetings in the company parking lot and avoid most of the site and transportation problems of the "distant" meetings.

Some planners are cautious about Las Vegas, New York City, and San Francisco, contending that there's so much to do that not only do participants stay out late at night, but they also spend more money unintentionally than the family budget will stand. Family budget problems lead ultimately to new job interviews.

When you're ready to go shopping, where do you start? Not with the travel trade directories listing every facility in the nation. Those are used by travel agents and airline clerks on a daily basis to do a different kind of job. Those directories are of little value to you, since even the telephone Yellow Pages tell you every hotel/motel in a given city—and so what?

What really matters is the current availability of a facility that has the capacity and equipment you need. The best place to get up-to-date information on availability of multiple facilities is the local convention bureau; in small towns, it's the chamber of commerce that has the information.

No bureau or chamber? Then use the Mobil Travel Guides. Because they rate the facilities, they are valuable aids to you when scouting strange territory.

Knowing who else will be in town will also help you to decide whether or when to be there. There's not much sense in fighting a world's fair or even a county fair, because everything in town that week is geared to fast turnover of transients. Yes, some participants might like to attend, but that's a different discussion and makes their problem yours.

With the list of availables named by the convention bureau or chamber of commerce, phone the hotel/motel. Ask the operator for room rate information and check the rack rate (that rate quoted to individuals, sometimes unreserved) for single accommodations—you might get a range; jot it down; then get your call switched to the convention office and get down to business. Were you treated courteously and promptly early in the call? If so, say so; if not, keep alert to other negative indicators in the conversations that follow.

Without stating that you have already obtained the rack rate, ask the convention rate for your group size—there should be substantial percentage difference, climbing with size of group. There are also seasonal differences in tourist regions and resorts.

In addition, most city hotels are under booked on weekends and will offer substantial discounts if you use Friday and Saturday nights. Ask. Bargain—they expect it.

Hotels are among the most cost-conscious, supply-and-demand-oriented enterprises in the world. To their net price they add the commissions paid to any middlemen. That includes intra-corporate referrals via national-franchise IN-WATS telephone reservation service as well as the celebrated "independent hotel representative." Today, add www and e-mail to your options. Hotel reps are independent businessmen who will be paid several dollars per room per night for calling a few hotels in your name. If you're sleeping several hundred, that's an expensive telephone call. Besides, if he commits in your name they treat him as the source of business, and you get the facilities "as is."

From the hotels/motels you consider prospects, get the existing brochures plus a letter from them stating that they can accommodate your group of (count) rooms/beds on (inclusive dates) at (price) per room/bed. Get a specific date by which the "blocking" of space, if they offer it, must be confirmed or released. Generally space will not be blocked on the first casual inquiry but only after, on studying the brochures and visiting the site, you confirm continuing interest. However, customers are not so plentiful that your prospective facility will cancel you out without warning.

As a rule of thumb, assume that all printed materials you receive are to some extent out of date. Ask the facility about specific inaccuracies or recent changes; you might get some.

But most printed material is prepared in vast quantities at infrequent intervals; and so many things could have changed that it's unlikely you can work for long from printed matter.

Only by personal inspection can you be sure the facility can physically accommodate your meeting. Only by personal visit can you be sure you want those people to serve yours. There is no substitute for a personal visit in advance of contract!

As discussed in the preceding chapter, the ideal time to contract for the facility is after you have a good understanding of your production needs. However, if it's unavoidable to commit earlier than that, consider the maximum specifications of the last two or three similar meetings to be your minimum needs for this one. Anything short of that could force you to bend your entire meeting to unwelcome limitations.

Because physical facilities will make the difference between competing facilities of equal innkeeping quality, we have created a special Facility Comparison Guide which appears at the end of this chapter.

However, because misrepresentation of capabilities and services is so blatant in the convention industry, *apparent* capability does not always translate into *real* capability or service. Therefore it's necessary to consider some of the problem areas as well as the ways to understand and deal with those problems.

Would you buy a used car there?

On those infrequent occasions when a hotel manager concedes that hotels do indeed goof, the example is invariably represented as forgetting ashtrays or ice water—and we all agree that's not a catastrophe. The real problem is that few "honest errors" of the hotel/motel are either honest or errors.

The three common and cardinal sins of any offending facility are these:

1. To sell a function room to another group to use immediately prior to your contracted arrival date and setup time. This is accomplished by telling you the room would be unused and available free of charge—and by discouraging you from reserving it in writing. The convention sales office and the catering department are both profit centers, and those managers benefit from personal bonuses fattened by overlapping promises. The official explanation is "Whoops."
2. To sell a function room to another group after you have already moved into that room simply because you do not have a profit-producing function scheduled for that time. Ditto on dissuasion on your writing a provision for *exclusive use* once moved into the room. The official promise is, "We'll reset it perfectly at our own *house* expense. By *house,* they mean only their only labor crews...but how will those semiskilled laborers reset your screens and projectors perfectly? You'll be stuck with the cost of all complementary reset charges—as well as the headaches for the lost time and effort accommodating them. If they tear down your set-up without your permission, bill them for *all* costs and/or damages; deduct that from the final bill; and never go back. There's no compensation for unnecessary problems.

Sales Meetings That Work

Protective Contract Provisions

Note: Most facility standard contracts are modeled on the standard Hotel/Association Facility Contract of the American Society of Association Executives, Washington. Variations can be critical; compare. Within the context of your or their standard contract, add these essential self-protection concepts. No attempt has been made to draw legally acceptable phrases, which is best left to your company attorney.

1. It is understood and agreed that the following function rooms shall be reserved and held available for the exclusive use of (Company) between the times and dates listed, unless later released as hereinafter provided, and further agreed that time and exclusivity are of the essence:

Rooms reserved	Available		If released		
	Time	Date	Time	Date	Total cost
________	______	______	______	______	$______
________	______	______	______	______	______
________	______	______	______	______	______

2. It is understood that (Company) shall release any function room(s) which might not be used, and said release shall be delivered in writing not later than _____days prior to the dates reserved. Any reserved function rooms neither released nor constructively used will be subject to a daily rental of $ ________, if offered for use without charge above. Failure to provide the reserved facilities named at the times stated herein shall render the Hotel liable for direct and consequential damages, if any.

3. It is understood and agreed that the Hotel is engaged as a convention facility and therefore the Hotel staff services agreed upon are equal in importance to the Hotel physical properties reserved and/or provided. As a consequence, all requested services agreed upon in subsequent conferences shall be detailed in a written Master Requirements Summary not later than _____days prior to the dates reserved herein and shall become an integral part of this contract. Failure to provide the agreed services of first quality at the stated times shall render the Hotel liable for direct and consequential damages, if any. *First quality* shall be construed to mean that all supervisors and at least (75?) percent of semiskilled laborers shall be fully experienced in this hotel and that none shall arrive to begin set-ups for (Company's) first day of programming after being (10?) hours on the job in that workday or if the completion time scheduled shall keep them beyond (12?) hours on the job in that workday.
4. It is understood that the exact physical structure of the reserved function rooms can affect the plans of (Company) and it is hereby agreed that should any physical alterations be scheduled to begin in any of the reserved function rooms prior to the dates reserved herein, then the Hotel shall immediately notify (Company), and (Company) may, at its sole option and without penalty, elect to cancel this contract.

3. To permit hotel staff (including the hotel's own convention sales and service managers) to walk away from problems, especially those that hotel policies or employees have created. Since most corrective measures seem to be "against policy" or "not in your contract," you get some sympathy and no help, unless at extra cost. The official excuse is, "We don't seem to have a record of it."

Because all three of those abuses are routinely and knowingly perpetrated, they must be viewed as unethical practices. Write a full, tight contract. (See accompanying Protective Contract Provisions.)

DEALING WITH PERSONNEL

Those offending management policies and attitudes generate related personnel and service problems, such as:

A. Inadequate staffing and inadequate training of staff. Both result from narrow (usually absentee) management based solely on bottom-line figures, which incompetent managers still don't see as short sighted and destructive. Such hotels still see themselves as being in the booze-and-beds business, rather than in the people business. While some really don't understand your needs, others simply don't care.
B. Overworking of house labor. During peak periods, your assigned house crews might arrive on your project after having been on the job a dozen or more hours (up to 30, in our experience) without a break. They cannot perform to their own standards even if they want to. Include in your contract a provision that no laborer will begin work for you after 10 hours on the job; and none will begin work which cannot be completed before the twelfth hour

on the job. The hotel can hire additional labor; their crew chiefs can supervise, if required.

C. Switching of personnel. You might find yourself talking details with one group of convention-service supervisors but facing strangers during the actual event. Consider that avoidable and intolerable; guard against it in writing.

D. Personnel turnover. Anybody can quit any job at any time in any trade; to that normal hazard, the chains add frequent personnel transfers. Whatever the reason, when key personnel leave they take with them all details not committed to writing, as well as subjective understandings and ideas.

E. Faulty personnel attitudes. Hotels are a minimum-wage industry. The kitchen, laundry, supply room and maintenance/house laborers—and even the chambermaids—earn little or nothing above the legal minimum. Yet they are directed to serve the exacting demands of companies billed at a premium price.

In our largest cities, most—of these unseen service workers are minority groups. Because they don't feel an overwhelming conviction that one of them will be the next president of the hotel corporation, their enthusiasm might occasionally flag. Handling different people every day of every year calls for the utmost flexibility and infinite patience; and it also teaches staff that you will be gone soon and won't return for a year, if at all. When there's a choice between your having a headache and their having a headache, it's understandably yours. Extra performance is usually demanded of a person who had no part in the promises made and no share in the profit realized if he goes the extra mile. Think *attitudes* as you fill in the accompanying Hotel Personnel Directory.

Sales Meetings That Work

Hotel Personnel Directory

(Make one for each facility considered)

Facility name: ______________________ Phone: __________

Address: ______________________ City: __________

Facility Manager: ______________ Catering Manager: __________

Convention Sales Mgr: __________ Convention Service Mgr: __________

Hotel's convention coordinator assigned: ____________________

Exact chain of command above during our meeting/convention:

Service Department Heads (meet all on first trip!):

	Name: Chief/Assistant	Regular hours	Reports to	Phone extension	Attitude +,-
Electrician:	____/____	____	____	____	____
(Sound):	____/____	____	____	____	____
Carpenter:	____/____	____	____	____	____
Head Houseman	____/____	____	____	____	____
Front Desk:	____/____	____	____	____	____
Credit/Acctg:	____/____	____	____	____	____
Housekeeping:	____/____	____	____	____	____
Telephone Operator:	____/____	____	____	____	____
Bell Captain:	____/____	____	____	____	____
Security:	____/____	____	____	____	____
Elevator Starters:	____/____	____	____	____	____
Other:	____/____	____	____	____	____
(Resorts, cruise ships):	____/____	____	____	____	____

Social Director ________/________ __________ __________ _________ _______

Sports/Recreation: ________/________ __________ __________ _________ _______

Other: ________/________ __________ __________ _________ _______

Basic checkpoints: Will these supervisors be on duty then? If not, why not, and who will be? Are any newly hired personnel totally familiar with facilities? If not, who can assist? Do they listen to your needs and suggest better, faster, cheaper, or easier ways? Do you want to work with and depend on those individuals? Transfer appraisal to Facility Comparison Guide.

COMPARING PROMISES AND PREMISES

It should be evident that if you put everything in writing—and if you don't expect anything more—you'll be adequately served. Most facilities now honor their written contracts, in letter if not always in spirit. Consumer pressure did it.

Your obligation to yourself, therefore, is to become a savvy buyer as fast as possible. You can do that by determining exactly the type of facility you need; then by comparing the promises and premises of potential sites; then by measuring and checking all needed public space and equipment in a personal inspection tour; then by writing a contract binding space, dates, and prices with provision for a late service addendum. Let's take all those ideas in turn.

Considering the purposes and production requirements of your meeting or convention, decide which of the following facility orientations best serves your needs:

A. The inn. The emphasis is on personal living; prestige and decor are important elements in some; bars and restaurants set the tone.

B. The conference center. The emphasis is on group business; efficiency, quietness, and technical preparedness are their strengths; rooms, meals, and lounges are usually good but not elaborate. The true conference center is distinguished from all false claimants because the center cannot sleep more individuals than can be accommodated in its meeting rooms. Recommended.

C. The convention center. The emphasis is on simultaneous group activities; beware plastic food, people, and furniture. In Europe, the recommended facility—advanced, equipped, capable.

Misrepresentation is common: space alone does not constitute a "convention facility." Staff skills—services—make the difference! Unfortunately, many managers of major complexes proved themselves in the days when space and decor were the prime attractions. Those managers have never been required to understand the communications objectives of their clients; so they can't require it of their staff. If you let their bluff and arrogance intimidate you, you're buying trouble!

If you can't find everything you need in one facility, then combine several. Take any fine inn and shuttle your people to a good theater or college lecture room where all seats are equipped with desks. Buying perfection piecemeal takes longer, but isn't that better than buying mediocrity in one lump?

Your alternatives include movie theaters, small regional legitimate theaters (most of which need the money), church halls, high school gyms and auditoriums, as well as the public hall or clubroom. Just look around.

Don't be dazzled by decor. Beautiful but uncooperative facilities become a blight on your program. When the facility lets you understand in subtle ways that you're lucky it will let you in, you're in the wrong place.

Look for helpful attention. Eager but unendorsed facilities take on new stature as contenders for your business. Certain major hotels use the endorsement argument against neighboring facilities, with the result that some fine complexes have never served a major national company or association. The national-endorsement ploy is totally without merit. When any facility has successfully organized for, and competently served, a technically complex meeting, it has proved itself worthy of your consideration. If the competition didn't think so, they wouldn't use the ploy.

Keep an open mind on facilities. When you know *what* you should be saying, *where* you say it is of secondary importance.

LOOKING PAST THE TINSEL

Don't buy glittering generalities. When a sales person calls on you, he has been very carefully briefed on all the catchwords ("buzz words" in Washington) and throws them about with abandon. If the convention and catering managers you meet are suave and reassuring, so in their junior way are the salespersons who call on you. Salespersons know you want "prompt, efficient, courteous service," and can certainly swear that "a responsible convention staff is at your disposal."

They know everyone likes "impressive atmosphere at prices unbelievably low for what you get." Food service is impeccable," as they tell it, and the food itself is "superb." The "flow pattern" for the crowd is unchallengeable, and the entire hotel is aware of your need for "split-second timing and silence."

It sounds so idyllic you can almost forget that the sales person has never planned or coordinated a convention, probably hasn't attended many, and has gained what little familiarity he might have during the three weeks he was inside practicing on some poor Meeting Manager's agenda. And there just might be one of his counterparts waiting at the hotel to practice on *your* agenda.

Promises are as much a stock-in-trade in the hotel sales industry as they are in the political industry. Both groups spend a lot of time and money telling you they know exactly what you want before proceeding to do exactly as they choose. In both cases, your complaints come after the fact and fall on the most insensitive ears ever found.

When that spit-and-polish sales person comes in, ask him to spend a few minutes telling you some of the pertinent details about recent conventions in his facility. What were the special problems, and how did the hotel help to meet those problems? How did the sales person assist? Whom? Can you phone to verify? If the sales person can't answer meaningfully, accept his folder and send him home. There's nothing more he can do for you.

Hotels needn't teach all their sales people how to run a convention; but all sales persons and service staff should respect your viewpoint and needs, know how they originate, and realize how easily they can be damaged. Sales people shouldn't misrepresent. If they sell from folders and hearsay, admit it, and merely try to arouse your curiosity for the facility, their job is done. But when their quota forces them to sign you at all costs—what does an extra promise here or there really matter? Besides, no one at the hotel will ever know!

Whose opinions can you trust? Your own and your assigned committee members, once they're fully briefed. For space, if you need it, measure it. For equipment, if you need it, test it. You take any facility "as is" unless there's a provision in the contract for improvements or modifications.

The on-site shopping for a facility is the business version of a ritual courting dance. If you arrive at the hotel or motel as a prospective buyer, then you are greeted with light banter at the check-in desk; given the best room (or suite) in the house, usually complimentary; find the telephone operator answering almost before you pick up; swear a bellhop has been stationed outside your door; and get unbelievable room service—all before you meet the hotel's convention manager. He waves off your profuse thanks, of course, because you got nothing more than "regular service." Once in a while that's almost true.

If you really want to know how your people will be treated, check into a paid, reserved room without fanfare; specify a minimum or modest cost room, and start taking notes. All you suffer is the loss of free liquor or fruit basket. That's a bribe; and if it didn't work, it wouldn't be done.

When you've checked the reception service, bell service, and even room service, tour the restaurants and bars and other public space—get a real feel for the place. Then phone the hotel convention office—they'll probably find time to see you. If you don't like what you've just seen and experienced, and it seems incurable, check out; but sometimes you won't have a good alternative. So armed in advance with specific complaints, get the sales manager to offer corrective measures, and write them into the contract.

Once you've made contact with the convention office, you can meet the staff and analyze the public function rooms. While inspecting the physical plant, make a habit of seeing the Big Three of the labor force immediately; electrician/soundman, carpenter, head houseman. Without their cooperation, nothing will happen right. They also control all sound, stages, exhibit areas, and drapery and lighting and can give you a rundown of inventory as it matches your needs. Does each have ideas and suggestions to simplify the task? A really capable man can spell out the plant's main advantages and shortcomings faster than you can spell your name. All you have to do is ask.

Verify details on every aspect of every room, access area, and equipment you need. Take nothing for granted. Elevator sizes and door widths limit the size of constructions you can bring in. Electrical outlets: determine whether you can or cannot use small equipment once the overhead lights are turned out. Controls: where? Dimmer-boards: test all circuits.

It's best to hear the sound system in operation with a group in the room, because people change acoustics just by being there to absorb sound, if not ideas. Most hotels have acceptable sound systems, but few are excellent.

Is there a true stage with wings and hidden access? Must the temporary platform stage be located in a particular place because of electrical circuitry entry points? Does the hotel have the cable to move the current elsewhere?

Is professional stage lighting available? Connected to the dimmer-board? At what cost? Many hotels ask $5 per 500-watt flood or spotlight, and you need 20 or more to do a passable lighting job. Considering that you pay electricians directly and they re-rent the same lights for 1,000 hours per bulb, the hotel's profit is enormous. And unjustified.

In most cities, portable dimmerboards can be rented, along with professional lighting equipment, including fixed spotlights (called lekos or ellipsoidal spots) or lens-focused lamps (fresnels, pars). If there's to be movement on stage, use a follow spot, which is probably owned by the local stagehands union. To light huge areas, especially for ambient room color, use the two-foot hemispheric reflector lamps (scoops). Adequate lighting is essential to everything except rear-projected visuals; and if front-projection is used, then lighting patterns must be dim and strictly controlled.

If you need several breakout rooms, are they available? Refuse the airwall-divided "ballrooms" because they are not soundproof, unless a visual break is all that's required. Don't force several groups to hold workshop sessions at opposite ends of one big room unless you don't care whether they can concentrate. Better to empty the furniture from sleeping rooms and meet there. Baize-covered tables and extra floor lamps will make the rooms suitable for workshops of a dozen or so participants.

If the physical plant and related equipment seem adequate, take an extra half hour to walk through your Working Agenda. Go from the sleeping floors down the elevators to the main meeting room; back to the breakout rooms; then to the dining rooms; back to the meeting room(s). Back to the sleeping floors. Where are the bottlenecks, the rest rooms and telephones, the wrong turns which need signs? Are the restaurants so far as to waste time? Does that mean sandwiches served?

Handling sometimes excessive hotel noises near the meeting room(s)? Will kitchen noises interrupt sessions? This, too, is PERT planning.

Take nothing for granted. Keep potential problem situations in mind, of course; but often it's the small detail that actually escapes your notice that causes problems.

During the entire inspection process, make it possible for the hotel/ motel/auditorium staff to help you. State your end objective rather than its pieces: that is, say "cabaret atmosphere" rather than "candles and checkered tablecloths." The facility has fulfilled common requests many times and might be prepared with special background or theme elements, available at low cost. If the hotel must rent outside you will pay a fee above costs—so do the shopping yourself, if you can.

Above all, after you state your needs, listen to their suggestions. If they don't have any, maybe they're not interested; take the warning. If they have thoughtful suggestions, you might want to use some. If the suggestions are valid but unusable, say why. No one likes to be confronted with endless rejections.

Details matter! Keep notes on everything you inspect. A good starting point is the Facility Comparison Guide which follows. Use a single vertical column for each facility; you can easily compare several prospective facilities for every important aspect before you make your final choice and place a contract. The Guide begins in Chapter 18.

Almost never will the facilities you consider offer the same advantages and disadvantages in like ways. So you will usually be required to trade off one essential for one or more preferred elements. Weighting various evaluation categories by the numbers might help in a pinch; but you can start with your personal code marks in the essential/preferred column. Review the Facility Comparison Guide now.

Sales Meetings That Work

Facility Comparison Guide

		No. 1	No. 2	No. 3	No. 4
Facility	Name				
	Address				
	Telephone				
	Owner/Chain				
Convention	Convention sales manager				
Services	Convention service manager				
Staff	Banquet manager				
	Meal guarantees, hours/%				
Personnel attitudes	Supervisors				
	Reception				
	Telephones				
	House labor				
Class	Luxury/deluxe				
	First/standard				

Facility Comparison Guide (continued)

Facility Name		No. 1	No. 2	No. 3	No. 4
Capacity	Suites				
	Rooms, double				
	Rooms, twin				
	Beds, total				
Credit cards or terms	Cards accepted				
	Charge: Man/company				

Service facilities	Laundry; price, speed				
(count and quality)	Restaurants				
	Bars				
	Secretarial				
	Shops				
	Barbers				
	Hairdressers				
	Health club				
	Telex address				
Contract offered	ASAE standard				
	Their standard				
	Our specific				
	Service addendum via master requirements				
	summary				
Languages — if	Management				
appropriate	Front desk				
	Telephone operators				

Facility Comparison Guide (continued)

Facility Name		Rank following as essential or preferred	No. 1	No. 2	No. 3	No. 4
Direct access to main function room	Participants					
	Freight					
Registration area	Multiple phones					
	Electrical outlets					
	Size					
	Security					
Master function room (specify size or count, as appropriate)	Length					
	Width					
	Height					
	Stage, perm/platform					
	Lecterns/platform					
	Dimmerboard, circuits					
	Auditorium-style seats					

	Banquet-style seats					
	Cocktails, seated					
	standing					
	dancing					
	Schoolroom					
Obstructions (posts or chandeliers)	Yes/no					
	Number/location					
Partitions of master room	Number/type					
	Sizes: 1.					
	2.					
	3.					
Personal conveniences	Toilets					
	Telephones					
Control room (sound, lights)	Dimmer/switch					
	Sightline to stage					
	Intercom system					

Facility Comparison Guide (continued)

Facility Name		Rank	No. 1	No. 2	No. 3	No. 4
Secondary meeting rooms	Name					
	Length					
	Width					
	Height					
	Prox. to master					
	Name					
	Length					
	Width					
	Height					
	Prox. to master					
Personal conveniences	Toilets					
	Telephones					
Control rooms (sound lights)	Room:					
	Room:					

Equipment inventory	Microphones, lapel					
(total count)	Microphones, floor					
	Lecterns/microphone					
	Tape recorders/players					
	Spotlights, etc.					
Electrical supply	Master function room:					
(stipulate supply point)	Max supply, amps					
	Volts, cycles, AC/DC					
	Secondary room:					
	Maximum supply, amps					
	Volts, cycles, AC/DC					
	Secondary room:					
	Maximum supply, amps					
	Volts, cycles, AC/DC					

Facility Comparison Guide (continued)

Facility Name		Rank	No. 1	No. 2	No. 3	No. 4
Exhibit capacity	Floor load: lbs./sq. ft.					
	Direct entry					
	Electrical supply					
	Compressed air, water					
	Useable floor size					
Elevators (adequate?)	Guest: count, capacity					
	Freight: count, capacity					
	Service staff: count					
House labor service charges (note if unions and mini-mums)	Labor, per hr					
	Equipment					
	Printing/copies					
	Drapery					
	Signs					
Other equipment (rental?)	Video conferencing					

Other faculties (health, medical/ handicapped aids, sports, recreation, clubs, conditions — not already covered)						
Personal observations, opinions						
Values	Group rates					
	Complimentary rooms					
	Free services					
	Average meal cost/day					
	Phone charges					
	Other					

TALKING TURKEY

Once you've made your personal inspection, you know how well the given facility will serve your meeting. If you're disappointed with the first site, maybe it's poor or maybe you're expecting too much. That is, if you're paying for chicken, demand chicken; but don't expect pheasant; and don't accept turkey.

By the time you've toured your second prospect, you'll know which of those factors is operating; by your third tour, you'll be a pro and have confidence in your judgment For future meetings, all past inspections become valid experience, and you're never again in a quandary. Experience is one of your best allies.

But even after your first-ever inspection, you still must reserve the right to see other sites. Tell this facility's sales manager that you are interested but that you are committed to seeing one or two other places. He expects that

If physical plant and service are acceptable, you can talk prices. If there are incipient problems, outline them and see what can be done to eliminate them. Then go on to prices.

Associations often seek complimentary rooms so the cash expense of association staff is minimized; a ratio of one *comp* per 25 to 35 paid rooms is standard; the cost burden is thereby shifted to the members attending voluntarily.

However, the corporation will be paying for all costs; so assuming you know almost exactly how many persons you will be sleeping, convert the comp ratio to reduced room rates—about 4 percent below the association group rate.

Remembering that *breakage* on advance guarantees for meals (see Part I) is an industry-wide ethical problem, make arrangements now for any estimates you must deliver because of unpredictable circumstances (such as voluntary dealer/ distribution attendance, early departures, or spouses invited).

Waiters and foodstuff deliveries are at issue; and a change of menu can often eliminate a problem deadline. If you must guarantee in advance, hold to a 24-hour advance plus 5 percent up-or-down variation from the set number; that's fair to both. Some hotels routinely demand 48-hours and 3 percent up only and pretend it's the industry standard. Beware 72-hour demands.

It's also important to remember that in today's computer-crazy world, the cheapest rooms seem to be on the world wide web. An interesting idea is to get a quote from the appropriate office of the hotel(s) being considered regarding your group size and dates. Then check www generally or priceline.com and its competitors specifically to see whether anyone is getting it cheaper simply for knowing it's there. Whether you do or do not obtain a better price from the web, you will gain good insights into the forthrightness of your group of prospective site(s). This information is, of course, related to that in Chapter 16—it's all travel-friendly, and all non-contributory to your message.

Because of the freedom of the web, you will be able to scout the competition in a way and with an ease that seemed previously open only through the large convention exhibitions once used in order to command your attendance—in order to give you the same one-stop shopping that the web delivers now. That convention exhibition promoted advertising interests more than member interests, in our opinion. Brochures are brochures, even at exhibitions. You still need to view the hotel in advance.

With luck and the time-and money-saving potential of video conferencing, meetings mangers might even be able to concentrate on the messages in their meetings. And won't that be a welcome change!

Remembering that much trade literature warns against the routine padding of liquor bills, decide up front whether to pay by the drink (it's recommended if controlled by tickets) or by the bottle (if opened, whether or not used up) at an open bar. Pay for the bartender separately for total control; if he's paid separately, drinks should cost less per glass.

Estimate the number of hours of each type of labor needed for room set-ups and changes; who pays? Ask the per-hour cost of house crew chiefs and their workers, if chargeable; which are union controlled? If unions are involved, what's the minimum union *call* (the hours paid, whether or not worked)? Advance notice required? Penalties for overtime? If any of these apply, plan to keep a time sheet on all labor during the event itself.

Assuming that what you hear is acceptable, you're ready to talk about the *blocking* of specific public and sleeping rooms. In blocking the space, the sales manager is guaranteeing you its availability until the agreed-upon confirm/cancel date. Obviously you must inspect the alternative sites before that date and staff the budgeting requests; so don't cut yourself short. But plan to honor the date you agree to.

Discuss incidentals, too. What is the cost of the laundry service? Some prices are staggering. During a long meeting, that could become a considerable cost. Two-week training programs get into trouble this way.

Don't forget tipping. Some facilities tack on a mandatory 15 percent gratuity for house crews as well as waiters. Some tack a percentage onto the total bill to distribute to all employees. Even if you pay a mandatory gratuity, key employees still have a hand out, and it's difficult to refuse. If you pay gratuities to individuals, pay by check. Never give cash to one individual to distribute on your behalf because too often it never leaves the original pocket. One auditorium manager even kept an entire case of Scotch, delivered tagged with the names of intended recipients. Checks avoid suspicion and accusation.

Now you're down to specific contract provisions. Ask whether the facility uses the standard contract of the American Society of Association Executives (ASAE) or its own version. If the latter, ask to have the specific variations outlined and explained to you. If the ASAE standard is used, read through it together and insert the necessary information. Be certain that both parties have identical notations; a photocopy of the initialed master is best for comparison, but not legal. None of the industry's standard contracts mentions the standards and penalties outlined in our Protective Contract Provisions form. Discuss your needed clauses at this point. In a climate of malpractice, those clauses defend your rights as a purchaser of stipulated services and facilities. Insist that the sense of needed clauses be added to the standard version. If the hotel refuses, it's probably not without reason; pick up your materials and walk out. That could be one of the best decisions you've made to date in choosing facilities.

Given a more aware industry, most facilities will try to provide what they promise in writing. Therefore, you must provide for submission of the Master Requirements Summary as an expected addendum to the contract under negotiation. Set a target date for submission of the Summary and meet it.

If your chosen facility later performs marginally, never go back. If it flatly defaults, bring suit: that's what contracts are for. And if it succeeds—if it provides everything it promises—book it for years ahead, even if it costs a little more than the average. You're getting paid for results, not hazardous duty.

Copies of the *ASAE Hotel/Association Facility Contract* are available from the American Society of Association Executives, Washington, D.C.

19

Meetings abroad

Tremendous changes have taken place in the international travel market over the past four decades. As late as the early 60s, travel was inexpensive and pleasurable; although seasons were long entrenched (summer for most of Europe; our winter for all the sun spots), the crowds weren't so enormous. That was due in part to smaller aircraft and in part to a less organized travel industry. A first-class hotel and meals totaled $25 daily.

By 1970, organized tours were the rule, but prices were still cheap: it was less expensive for an American company to send its meeting participants to Spain (airfare included) than to a major American city for a major program of a week or more. Then came the oil embargo and the tripling of aviation fuel costs.

With the fall from grace of the American dollar, prices in other nations rocketed ahead of ours. By 1980, American cities were far down the list of expensive cities—headed by London and Paris and Rome and just about any other place people really long to see. Group travel abroad on a discretionary basis became prohibitively expensive. With the world-wide recession of the end of the century and the subsequent American super-economy, shifts continue to occur and need your full attention.

By the mid 1980s, hotels asked about $100 daily for sleeping rooms; at the millennium, no one is surprised to be asked for $200 or $300 per day—the same as in the US. The international hotel chains have internationalized costs, as well as they've homogenized minimal service. Luxury service—traditionally meaning personal attention—was a European or Japanese invention that we've scuttled.

Once deregulation got here, the airlines had no cartel protection; but herd instinct and reduced demand were allowed to keep prices high and seats empty, contrary to marketing principles for a *perishable* commodity (today's empty seat can't be sold tomorrow). Only the emergence of low-cost regional (later national) U.S. lines could reverse that cartel mind-set. If you're prepared to bargain, you can benefit. Deregulation—hooray!

Ditto for hotels and beds. But the airlines and hotels have joined forces and are offering reduced-rate packages through a variety of wholesale and retail outlets. The latter might include their neighborhood travel agent, although agents are being elbowed aside, these days, in favor of dot-com.

Deregulation has simplified your task because there are no more pricing tariffs which the airlines can enforce against you and in favor of friends—the basis of the criminal suit mentioned in Part I. Your ability to send a group abroad today is limited only by your ability and willingness to pay the price. There's no sure tax deduction, but you can pay expenses chargeable to salaries, as incentive. Probably the company should pay after taxes.

Price is the main factor. Because of the roller-coaster value of the dollar, it's difficult to predict the future costs of an event nearly a year or longer ahead. To get your name on the line, many hotels now guarantee to honor the cost quotation regardless of what happens to prices in the interim. That can be beneficial if prices go up; but if prices go down? A few sources protect you either way; check details carefully!

WHERE SHOULD YOU BEGIN?

At the National Tourist Office of the countries which interest you most. All tourist-conscious nations have an office in New York City, and all are eager to hear from you. You can find them in the alphabetical telephone directory, or often under the *adjective form* of the name of the country; that is, Austrian, French, Italian, Mexican, and so on. A few names are awkward in adjective form; if you have any problems, check the Yellow Pages under "Consulates." Many countries have tourist offices in all of our large metropolitan areas; and 800 telephone numbers and www sites make it easy to get information if the office isn't local in your town. One of the best, current, all-in-one-place locations is the Los Angeles *Times* Travel section, "Sourcebook." The most current issue at this writing is Sunday, April 16, 2000.

Only the National Tourist Office of each country can and will give you an impartial and internally-standardized ranking of all facilities; they can also tell you which facilities are available on your dates. The NTOs can put you in touch with convention centers (called congress halls in most places), as well as hotels. The two are separately run so that the governments which built the centers would not be competing with existing hotels.

You'll also get a list of foreign convention coordinators. It's essential that you do business with coordinators established on the home turf. Yes, you can hire an American firm, but because things are different everywhere abroad you are buying only legman service; your American coordinator will almost surely hire the same foreign coordinator you would—at added cost.

You can ask the NTOs for absolutely anything. They will be forthright in telling you whether it is an included or extra charge at the facilities recommended. Best of all, the NTOs are governmental entities—their service is free to you!

Of course the NTOs are each biased toward their own country and national airline; but that's a declared—and therefore ethical—bias. It's a pleasure to work with foreign NTOs. Too bad our own convention industry can't take the hint...NTO services and willingness to research problems go far beyond the help available even through our domestic city convention bureaus, which shunt you more quickly to private suppliers for answers once the matter of facility availability has been answered.

Discouraged? Don't be!

Of course it will be more difficult to pull all the pieces together from a great distance if company affiliates are not on hand to take over the task. On the other hand, the foreign trip buys so much goodwill and motivational change (review Chapter 8) for so little additional cost that it is a boon to the company. Whereas, in the early 70s, it was possible to meet in Madrid, for instance, for less than the cost of a New York conference (including foreign airfare), those days might be gone forever. But check out for the lesser-known cities.

All executives and facility managers of these facilities around the world speak English, so you almost have to invent a language barrier if you want to enjoy one. Besides, innkeeping was an art in most parts of the world before the United States was a nation; they understand *service* and serve with pride.

What type of facility should you choose—American chain or foreign owned? Favor an owner-managed facility everywhere—even here at home! When you buy a familiar chain name, you are often buying franchise management, which is sometimes held captive by the investors, and absentee landlords can distort and damage. Franchisees can change overnight, and the promises evaporate.

In some places—usually off the beaten tourist path—the American chain is the best facility in town. That happened because of the airlines' need to guarantee suitable rooms to the business people being ferried around the world. But in the major capitals of the world, you can enjoy luxury (based on personal service, not lavender furniture), which our small boutique hotels now imitate. Worldwide, the best management is vested in the site!

Tax provisions revisited. The Tax Reform Act of 1976 permitted all legitimate expenses of up to two foreign meetings per person per year to be deducted if they met basic criteria: *(a)* At least six business hours daily for full days claimed; three hours for half days claimed. *(b)* At least half of all days away devoted to business. *(c)* Participants attended at least two thirds of all scheduled business programs. *(d)* Per diem expenses claimed did not exceed the per-diem allowances permitted U.S. government employees in the same area. *(e)* Participants did not control the decision to travel abroad. Incentive travel (as a nondeductible, tax-paid category) is not restricted.

However, the IRS evidently couldn't live with such clear guidelines, and in 1981 the rules were changed. Current criteria are: *(a)* All rules above are retained. *(b)* All cruise ships are off limits (except Caribbean?). *(c)* You must prove (to your local IRS chief) that it is "as reasonable" to hold the meeting outside the United States as inside. *(d)* All 50 states, U.S. territories, Canada, Mexico, and Jamaica are treated as "domestic." Details in IRS Publication 463. Restrictions!

Legally, the exemption of three foreign countries is capricious and arbitrary; challenges are pending. At press time for 1983, House bills HR#3191 (to permit full deductions for all American flag cruise ships) and HR#6140 (to liberalize deductible destinations) were pending and could become law at any time. Get details in writing from IRS/local, now. When editing for this new Third Edition, we called Washington for confirmations and were misrouted several times and waited for paperwork explanations several times more—and still got the wrong stuff. Stay with it. Eventually even the IRS should know what the IRS is about.

It's important to recognize the IRS restrictions as an attempt to end rampant abuse. So many executives and professional groups have used voluntary foreign meetings and conventions as disguised vacations that voluntary attendance at a meeting abroad is now suspect. Some travel interests have provided phony agendas and/or phony meeting-attendance certificates to American clients for submission to the IRS. If you get caught, the travel supplier has no liability, but you are guilty of tax evasion.

What's at issue is IRS non-recognition of motivational elements of group foreign travel in a legitimate-meetings context. The "reasonableness" of motivational programming now depends on the personal opinions and prejudices of countless IRS examining agents—that situation is unfair and untenable in a national agency. One thing is clear: American companies have never been guilty of wasting money on perks for low-level employees. So a company that chooses a foreign setting for a meeting of non-executive personnel surely has a defensible business purpose in motivation. The IRS should honor that purpose.

If you construct a defensible program and convince your local IRS chief of its reasonableness, get a written opinion. While the IRS could disavow its own agents' decisions in case of audit, the fact of a prior written opinion obviates charges of fraudulent intent and could tip the hearing in your favor.

Once committed to the concept of motivational travel with meetings, where should you go? Choice of destination depends on both purposes and people. Are your people more interested in glamour locales or history? Nightlife or sports? Sun or museums? Fishing or skiing? Do you have subsidiaries or important suppliers with plants to be toured? In other words, can they use their free time (after the six business hours) in pursuits which they find interesting and valuable? And do you need any further justification?

Given those restrictions, it seems reasonable to suppose that you should choose a destination that offers a distillation of the country visited—don't take an isolated locale where you will meet only other Americans! If nearby towns and points of interest are within easy busing distance, that's a plus.

In essence we're probably recommending capital cities. But having seen between 40 and 50 countries and hundreds of their cities in all parts of the world over the years, we can assure you that the capitals have gathered everything the kings and emperors found important in their time. Only Washington, Brasilia, and Berne were short-changed.

Glamour and the fascinating are a large part of the travel mystique, of course; but the benefits include the enlargement of the general frame of reference not only of the individuals, but also of the company when broadened perspectives can work for it. If your organization is multi-national, foreign trips are an instructional element worth fighting for.

American foreign policy is based on alarmingly superficial and proprietary monetary motives: dollar diplomacy has never died; but the willingness of the press to analyze foreign policy independently of news handouts probably has. Therefore the problems and opportunities of the world market are significantly different from the Pollyanna-and-Hennypenny news team reports we get daily. The greater the number of observers who can travel, the better the company's chances of making decisions based on the real world.

The differences—and there are many—are based on culture and values. In general, educated people in other countries are more curious, more independent, more intellectually vigorous, and less trusting of clichés to see them through the day and life. They have less dependable telephone systems and more dependable transportation; less choice in consumer goods and more taste and quality evident in what's available. While we seek the *norm,* they seek the *unique.* They seem to spend less time inventorying life and more time enjoying it. In short, they can teach us something.

If, after considering all those pros and cons, you are still interested in going abroad with your group, then it's time to consider the specifics.

Time zones. Because a jet travels at nearly half the speed of the sun, a day is fatiguingly longer going west and exasperatingly shorter going east. The body just doesn't shift gears fast enough to avoid side effects. Therefore airlines encourage you to stop enroute during transpacific flights; that's why Hawaii is located there. Flight to South America can cross only one or two zones (easy) or a half dozen if you're crossing from California into

Brazil. It's a half dozen or more for most flights from here to Europe, too.

When crossing a half-dozen time zones going east, most flights depart in the evening, U.S. time, and arrive in midmorning, local time. On the eyeballs, the hour is 3 A.M., U.S. time; and unless the traveler takes an immediate nap of about four hours or so, he could be turned around for days. We recommend checking in before noon; sightseeing for a couple of hours; and then napping from mid-afternoon to the dinner hour. By the time their clock strikes midnight everyone will be tired enough to want to sleep and relaxed enough to do it. It's a virtually foolproof way of adjusting within one day. Coming home, the flights leave in midmorning, European time, and arrive in mid-afternoon, our time; rarely a problem.

Languages. Anyone who speaks a little of the language of the host country should practice; the natives enjoy that. Otherwise you might mimeograph a brief list of key words and phrases. Translate only basic things, such as *please*, *thank you*, *good morning*, and *hello*. And *Where is a toilet*? Don't overdo the phrasebook approach; there's no sense asking question if you can't understand the answer. Ask important questions in English, and they'll find somebody to help. All over the world, people insist on acting just like people.

Cruise ships. In a sense, the ships are the best of both worlds: a floating resort that remains constant throughout the voyage, and an itinerant transport that docks in key ports at several predetermined countries. Because the ships are totally self-contained, they have lounges and theaters and clubrooms and all the incidentals (photocopy machines, projectors, social and sports directors) to handle a meeting. Inspect and compare ships just as you would any hotel—it's relatively easy because the ships dock every week or two, depending on schedule; you can visit as often as necessary once you book. Quality varies widely not only from line to line, but also from cabin to suite.

Review the cruise menus and accept invitations to lunch. That's the best way to decide whether the kitchen makes the grade.

There are many advantages to shipboard conventions, not the least of which is an audience captive in a facility that won't be taking on last-minute ladies' teas enroute. On the other hand, a storm could make a lot of stomachs queasy (does your ship have a gyrostabilizer?); that's why many companies skip the New York-to-Miami portion of the trip in winter and fly everyone to Miami to embark. Exception to the rule: things in the Caribbean are possibly different at IRS.

Some disadvantages en route, too. You can't send a taxi back for forgotten file folders; you're stuck with the chef if you don't like him; quarters can feel cramped in inclement weather. Those huge transit halls are *not* meeting space; they're overflow for all passengers. While you can't have any room permanently, you can have virtually any room (including dining rooms) on any schedule convenient for both parties. The cabarets have all the lighting and sound equipment used by shipboard entertainers, and you can borrow all of it at no charge, paying only the rental cost of extras you need. Cruise ships can be a great buy!

At some time in the considerations, someone will mention that the ship could sink. It could. Also a plane carrying half your crew could fall on the hotel housing the other half. Also the next California earthquake.... You get the idea. As the rash of hotel disasters has proved, there's no avoiding disaster.

Travel Agent. Your local TA could be extremely helpful to you or he could be another problem; it depends on the person. About 9,000 agents exist in the United States and about half belong to one of two professional associations, the better known of which is the American Society of Travel Agents. Your TA makes money by either of two ways: (a) by specified commission on the tickets or tours he buys for you or *(b)* by unlimited markup on special travel packages he might assemble for you. With lower commissions paid by travel interests these days, most TAs are less interested in people who are just looking around. Expect the high end programs or expect to pay a fee for service; exceptions, if you find them, are fine. Part of the new attitude is due also to the www ticketing that's newly available on direct purchase. If only the problems are left to TAs, then the problem solving should cost the source.

If your agent has personal knowledge of the destination you favor, he/she can tell you what the best airfares are, including any promotional fares; what the going hotel rate is; and what the sightseeing tour situation is. He can book any or all, and you can both benefit. On the other hand, if he has not seen the area and is working from directories and printed folders, his advice is suspect; always determine the facts before proceeding.

Some people say that they can often discover fares on the web cheaper than some agents report. That might be true—but are they available group fares to/from multiple cities? And *Newsweek* for April 25, 2001, wrote extensively on "Air Hell: 7 Ways to Fix Flying." Why bother? Is that a good way to prepare your employees to concentrate on your meeting material?

If you get information from the foreign NTO, comparative prices from your agent, and coordination from a local firm, that's solid meeting management practice!

Customs and Carnets. All countries tax imports, and their customs agents work out their aggressions on their own returning citizens. Tourists are treated with kindness-even with delicacy if arrangement to clear groups is made in advance by the NTO. People and personal effects are easy.

However, meeting materials and product samples are usually intended to go in both directions; but some companies have created problems for themselves by giving away or selling the products instead of repatriating them as promised. That can be viewed as smuggling or fraud—take your pick.

To minimize problems while promoting business travel, the International Chamber of Commerce has developed a *carnet* (say car-NAY); it's French for "notebook." The carnet lists all the materials you will be carrying round trip and provides a fast, certified inventory at all stops; valid in more than 30 countries you're most likely to visit. You post a bond equal to 40 percent of the value of the goods in transit; if you return everything, your bond is reimbursed. Pay duties on anything left behind—and keep those lists separate but handy.

The only problem area is the handout material, which goes over in a carton and returns in the participants' luggage. Provide for that, even if it means buying printing and ringbinders abroad in order to eliminate the nuisance.

Carnets are issued only by the U.S. Council of the International Chamber of Commerce, 1212 Avenue of the Americas, New York, 10036; branch offices in major cities. Their fee is small compared to the savings in time and temper.

Food and menus. When fearing that the rest of the world might be willing to poison us, it's rather reassuring to remember that many of the quality restaurants of the United States pretend to be something other than American. Only steak houses admit to indigenous cooks. The kicky part of the reminder is, of course, the corollary fact that many French cooks and recipes originated in France; Italian in Italy, and so on. So what's the panic?

Yes, water is bad in most parts of the world; people drink bottled water, beer, and wine, apart from coffee and tea. But food seems to be more important abroad—in some places because good food is a tradition and in others because there's not enough to go around. The result: attention to what's available.

So the Belgian main dishes, French sauces, Swiss ice creams and chocolates, Viennese strudels and game, and the Italian veals and pastas are rewards for the appetite. The English have marvelous theater. Sophisticates relish Japanese sukiyaki and tempura; and Kobe and Argentine beef rivals that of Kansas City. Almost everywhere in the world except home you get fish from the water instead of the freezer.

Many countries have strange or spicy specialties—and you don't have to order them. Menus center on foods of international acceptance; so it's not a big job. Veals and roasts take many forms, but beef filet is usually termed a *tournedo,* and it's smaller than at home.

A good rule: let your first meals be relatively bland and familiar; but let their chef show off a little in your last days there—use the potential of the *foreign* tour!

Electricity. If Ben Franklin had minded his own business, foreign travel would be a lot simpler. But now we're stuck with incompatible systems, which require transformers, plug adapters, and all manner of computations. Voltage matters, of course; but the matter of cycles and phases determines whether adaptation is possible and how easy it will be. Electricians can compute rather easily (scientific laws are like that) once you provide the specifics. When possible, buy or rent in the local country using "Travel Industry Service Evaluator" in the local country. If that's not possible, carry your own equipment *including the transformers* necessary for the step up or down in the two systems.

Ships operate on direct current, for the most part. And the electrical system is usually that of the shipyard where built. Ships docking in the United States have converters and transformers, but not always in the numbers needed for an elaborate program. Furnish exact counts of all electrical and sound equipment needed well in advance so they can arrange to locate compatible equipment.

Feeling confident? Why not? Foreign travel has a lot to offer; and even if you work a little harder to set it up, the value of goodwill and the leveraging power of enthusiasm will repay you many times over.

Foreign facilities can be compared on the Facilities Comparison Guide, Chapter 18; costs, on the Locations Comparison Sheet, Chapter 11; and service offers on the Travel Industry Service Evaluator, adjacent.

Sales Meetings That Work

Travel Industry Service Evaluator

Meeting title:

____

City (Country): ______ Group size _______ Season __________

Agent, Airline, Coordinator, or Hotel:

____

If foreign, local representative:

____

Service offered is (freestanding) (part of a package) (package-maker). Describe:

1. If various services are presented as a package:
   a. Can the recommended airline take us from where we are to where we want to be — direct? (Yes) (No). If no, elaborate:
   b. Is the recommended hotel in the same city as the international airport? (Yes) (No). If not, what provisions must be made?
   c. Are the meeting facilities professional? (Yes) (No). Are they government or privately owned? Specify:
   d. Are meeting costs calculated (by equipment requested) (per person)?
   e. If the meeting facility is not adjacent to the hotel, is the cost of shuttle transportation included?
   f. Additional costs, if any:
2. Does this supplier's package offer only transport and related service? (Yes) (No).
   a. If yes, are its schedules favorable (Yes) (No).
   b. If no, is its added "convention" service limited to sightseeing or all-inclusive innkeeping (rooms and meals)? (Yes) (No).
   c. If yes, are facilities and prices (better than) (comparable to) (poorer than) those outlined by the national tourist office?
   d. If no, what advantages and services go beyond innkeeping? Specify:
   e. Are the recommended hotel facilities (adequate) (above average) (superior)? How do you know?
   f. Are the meeting facilities (adequate) (above average) (superior)? Fairly priced? (Yes) (No). How do you know?

3. Which transport-related services are offered? (Check)
    a. Ground service at home airport(s). Consider group coordinator, special baggage tags and handling, etc.
    b. Ground service and bus on arrival (transfer to hotel).
    c. Information and assistance with air freight and customs.
    d. Special inflight service and/or foodservice.
    e. Informative folders on destination for our advance mailings.
    f. Folders on included and optional sightseeing tours.
    g. Other:
4. If "convention service" is offered, are these bogus services highlighted?
    a. Special reservation desk in your hotel (they benefit).
    b. Referral to theatrical agents / producers / coordinators who hope to sell to you (see "Something-for-Nothing Evaluator").
    c. "Convention" tour packages identical to those offered to any other travel group.
    d. Staff "convention coordinators" who have never personally planned meetings or will not be assisting on-site.
    e. If any bogus "services" are offered, should this supplier be disqualified? (Yes) (No). Why?
5. Does this supplier offer valuable assistance with:
    a. Meeting coordination on site? (Yes) (No). Describe:
    b. Message support materials produced on-site? (Yes) (No). Describe:
    c. On-site liaison with hotel/facility using resident staff? (Yes) (No).
    d. If yes, will the same individuals assist in coordinating the event?
    e. Are all stipulated services above included in the cost quote? (Yes) (No). Extras:
    f. If this supplier must hire additional personnel in order to fulfill the terms of this package, what will be the relationship and the chain-of-command?
    g. If additional personnel must be engaged, how will the quality of the "outsiders" be guaranteed? Specify:
6. Has this supplier offered an honest appraisal of service limitations?
    a. If yes, summarize:
    b. If no, is knowing misrepresentation a possibility? (Yes) (No).
    c. If limited services will be "filled in" by *free* or *referral* services, complete both the Consultant Evaluator and the Something-for-Nothing Evaluator, Chapter 10.
    d. If borderline, should this supplier be invited to bid? (Yes) (No). Why?
7. Describe specific hotel/facility services as a "convention center" (distinct from innkeeping function of rooms and food):
8. Describe specific travel agent services beyond arrangement of tickets and hotels, if any:

9. If our target meeting date falls in the high season of either the transportation companies or facilities, can we save substantially by adjusting our date by several weeks? (Yes) (No).
10. If yes, did this supplier *volunteer* that information? If not, why not?
11. Have all the basic tour, sightseeing tour, and special airfares been mentioned/offered voluntarily? If not, why not?
12. Given all the opportunities to volunteer or evade information, does this supplier seem trustworthy and competent?
13. Cost per person at recommended hotel, all-inclusive innkeeping: $ __________
14. Overall cost of meeting/convention facility services: $ ____________
15. Grand total of costs — hotel/meals plus meeting facility plus extras plus necessary coordination assistance: $ _______________
16. Final decision:

20

The producer as business assistant

If you look upon your prospective theatrical producer or any professional coordinator of conventions as being kin to your advertising agency, you understand the gist of the relationship.

All three suppliers offer you a combination of creative talent and strictly mechanical service. All three are prepared to do many kinds of things for many different clients; all have a company viewpoint related to their industries and needs even though they must try to understand yours before they can serve you. How successfully they can divorce themselves from their (preferential, not professional) viewpoint and adopt yours is the critical issue.

Egos abound in any creative field—generally in an inverse proportion to the talent underlying them. To do a program which is grander or splashier or otherwise more magnetic for trade or media attention than its neighbors is an advantage for *them.* So all three are tempted to encourage the paying client to buy something that *they* have been wanting to try. Often that's *what's newest.* This is not to say that *old* is necessarily better, but that new should offer *better*.

Yet ad agencies are ultimately disciplined by client market share, by which their performance is usually measured numerically. Producers and other coordinators are rarely, if ever, measured, unless blamed for a flop; and flops are rare if industry definitions of success (applause) are the criteria used. But what does applause indicate about *learning*? Especially if unmeasured afterward?

Production or coordination assistance from either source can take on two forms: production of components and production of the event itself. If you are creating visual presentations or skits, you will probably need outside assistance, at least with the components. If those components are complex—or if you have no internal staff assistance—you might want that same producer to oversee the event. With skits and other theatrical ventures, in fact, they do not exist (except as ideas) until presented at the event at which they unfold.

The producer's presence is essential. By contrast, the professional coordinator does many things that company people could do themselves if they had the time. The programming skills can be quite well developed by everyone after the first couple of programs. That's the thesis of this book!

Because most producers and their staffs are skilled in stagecraft, they tend to emphasize and recommend it even when it is not proper. Many have no appreciation for the support tools required in the training room and might even recommend against those tools in favor of a bigger "show." Don't ask a producer's opinion on things not related to his anticipated assignment.

Do ask his opinion on alternative ways of doing the kinds of things normally expected of his trade—that's part of the bid process. Beware of estimates that keep sliding higher while the conversation is in progress.

Be alert to signals that the producer/coordinator does or does not comprehend the business context of your assignment. Because theater people deal with what's most popular and trendy, they also tend to learn the business catchwords floating around. They often use that foreign language for face credibility—the illusion of knowledge which has no direct relationship to true knowledge. If their face credibility banter gets past your barriers, then you might not press for details until too late.

In theater, as in all other fields, sales persons promote the items that they feel most comfortable with. If your producer/coordinator staff has not been trained in training techniques or in a company atmosphere, its members can talk about it but not understand it. Be alert to the difference. And in all conversations, whenever you feel things might be going astray, refer to the pertinent profiles and objectives forms already made up. Those forms will keep you on the right track despite the blandishments.

Because of the carefully nurtured aura of creativity and genius which surrounds the theater, it's easy to lose sight of the fact that creating the visual/dramatic presentation takes talent, but packing the cases and hauling everything to the meeting site takes grunt labor. They should be quoted separately.

Therefore, be sure that the cost quotations provide for both types of service. The writers and directors and actors will be paid at creative rates; all the rest should be billed at something more like the current rate for a person from a temporary-help agency: detail, not creativity, shapes these tasks.

Once the program design work has been done, theatrical production itself consists of the assembly of bits and pieces within a specified framework for a specified effect. That assembly skill is the prime service a producer can offer. He buys most of the talent outside when needed. Except for his staff proposal writer, most writers will probably be freelance. All actors will be.

Similarly, the executive director will be on staff but the director of your presentation will probably be free-lance. The boss himself/ herself is usually the executive producer, and the producer (business manager) of your project might be the executive producer or, more likely, the assistant or even the project director.

Knowing which of all the area's freelance talent is proper for your program is one of the creative services that the producer/ coordinator sells. If finding the best talent requires an audition, he/she will organize and conduct it. Sit in; state your opinion when it matters; don't interfere; buy talent, not pretty.

You must trust the judgment of your producer/coordinator in his field once he's hired—that's why you're hiring him. But you must use every means available to test that judgment in advance of hiring, which could require you to phone some of the clients who endorse his work and see whether there are similarities between their projects and yours.

When talking with the producer's references, always ask about budget. The exact dollars don't matter because you can't witness the program, but the cost overrun, if any, is important. Remember that hiking the budget is the ethical problem of this segment of the convention industry.

Apart from his creative work, the producer/coordinator is your legman. He can provide liaison with the selected facility (if he has worked for you before, ask him to assist in selection—he has to work there, too). He can also rent and supervise stage and projection equipment; supervise rehearsals; hire and supervise union labor; inventory materials; collate assignments lists; and prod the company committeemen with whom they must work. Most of these tasks are mechanical and should be paid for at a mechanical, not a creative, rate.

If you are buying training programs and related support tools, go to a producer who has a track record in that field or go to a training company. Although the training specialist might seem the logical first choice, many have old standby programs in the file which you might buy retreaded at high cost. The producer with experience in the field could be the more original source.

If you are buying the services of a producer for the first time, you might want to select two. Give one the business stage and give the other the entertainment (see the next chapter). They will compete (attempts at sabotage are not unknown), and after the first event you can choose the better partner for next year and many years ahead. A producer whom you trust and with whom you work well is an asset to keep around for a long time.

Once you decide on a source, get his outline of critical progress points and target dates and enter those on your PERT Diagram. Oversee your producer/coordinator just like any other committee. You're paying for the privilege. Don't accept ego.

There are alternatives to the producer/coordinator. If your company has produced a number of fairly complex programs in the past, you have skilled resources, and you might not need to assign substantial portions of your program to outsiders. Yet the details of the stage need close supervision before and during.

You might want to consider the services of a media specialist. He would analyze your needs (especially if the visuals and other stage-craft are repeats) and recommend the necessary equipment. He would then rent it, oversee its installation, supervise the screening during the events as well as the rehearsals, and pack and return the equipment.

Sometimes he will want to be paid directly; sometimes he will attempt to be paid extra by commission on the goods purchased because a few double dip. Once hired, he should function and report like a producer/coordinator.

Whoever you ultimately hire, you will find yourself mixing responsibilities between committees and outsiders. Be clear about who does what; be clear about who reports to whom. The exact mix depends only on needs—nothing is *normal* or *proper*. Budget restrictions will be the final criterion—and at the established time rates of one-week-per-hour for coordination and program-time-times-three for rehearsals, both sides should be able to estimate total hours rather closely.

Sales Meetings That Work

Coordination Bid Estimator

Meeting title: ___________ Location(s):__________ Dates: ________

1. Number of scheduled hours of business _____; social ______; overall ______.
2. Number of days over which schedule is spread: _____ days; _____ evenings.
3. Number of man-weeks of time estimated for total coordination (at least equal to the number of hours in Item 1 above): ___________Hrs.
4. Number of hours/weeks which staff can handle: ___________Hrs.
5. Discretionary difference in hours/weeks to be assigned to an outside coordinator/producer: ___________Hrs.
6. Of the discretionary time assignable, what portion is:
   a. Mechanical (lists, checking, canvassing, rentals, liaison)? ___________Hrs.
   b. Creative (program structure, scripts, design/art, stage)? ___________Hrs.
7. Coordination rates quoted on competitive bids by producers or consultants:

Firm name	Hours/week		Mechanical	Creative
a. _______	________	for	$___________	_________
b. _______	________		___________	_________
c. _______	________		___________	_________

8. Cost estimate for total assignable time:
   a. Lowest quote above would cost: $ ________ mechanical;
      $ _______ creative.
   b. Highest quote above would cost: $ ________ mechanical;
      $ ________ creative.
   c. Long-term contract (or guaranteed flat fee) would result in this discounted sum by these respective firms:

_____________	______	% discount for	________ Units/flat.
_____________	______		________
_____________	______		________

d. Does the discount/flat fee structure affect the previous high and low? (Yes) (No). If yes, new low bidder.

Coordination Bid Estimator (concluded)

9. By personal value judgment, do the low bids and best capabilities seem to coincide in any one of the bidding firms? (Yes) (No). If yes, specify by name. If no, then what is the best combination? Why?
10. Does the apparent bid-winner expect to be paid directly or by commission on purchases? If commissioned, how can we minimize the conflict of interest?
11. Available budget (does) (does not) provide an amount of money sufficient to cover 100% of discretionary time. Therefore:
    a. Buy in full form the best source;
    b. Cut paid-out coordination expense by assigning less time;
    c. Eliminate coordination service; buy consulting or media service only;
    d. Transfer funds form entertainment or other non-essential functions. Specify:
    e. Buy creative/coordination only for specified segments of program. Specify:
    f. Other:
12. Based on available budget for coordination, the revised estimate of cost for the best bid is: $_________ mechanical; $ ____________ creative; or $ __________ flat fee. This covers an estimated assignment of ____ hours of mechanical and ______ hours of creative time.
13. The coordinator selected (does) (does not) accept the resulting assignment (in total) (with these conditions):
14. Resolution of discrepancies, if any:

Yet production of component parts proceeds like any other tangible you might order, so the real decision lies in the collateral services, the coordination effort. That's the focus of the accompanying Coordination Bid Estimator. Producers of AV components are listed in Bowker's current AVMP (old title: *AudioVisual Market Place*). Since virtually every producer of industrial theater produces both business stage and entertainments, the list probably does enough double duty to help you.

PREPARING FOR TWO-WAY

FULL-MOTION Video Conferencing

1. State main message. Concentrate on it!
2. State subordinate message(s), if any. Other meeting needed?
3. First, state learning aids dictated by main message.
   a) Production time needed: Min weeks_____;
   max weeks_____.
   b) Consistent with current tentative schedule? If not, decide whether to change schedule or message; never cheat message demands.
4. Then inventory extant learning aids that might help. Re-use of the old at this point can be dangerous to new ideas.
5. Name/location of topic/subject matter experts/authorities for main message.
6. Number of participants for this program. (Over/under30).
7. Number of participants for last similar program.
8. Actual cost of central airfare/hotels last program: $_______. Similar this time? If not, estimate: $ ______.
9. List all needed topics that are NON-proprietary and so can risk interception; these can be broadcast. Include all of your identical information/assignments/not-necessarily-simultaneous elements for recipients.
10. List all needed topics that ARE proprietary or otherwise secret or sensitive and so must not be potentially compromised by broadcast. Treat any such topics via written or taped self-contained packages sent in advance to receiving sites. Include here only such items as can tolerate slight variation in their presentation, as from district managers used either as experts or proctors.
11. List all needed topics that cannot be slightly varied and/or absolutely must be delivered simultaneously to all. The latter are the only message elements that require a single central meeting.
12. If written/taped materials will become the effaced experts or authorities in each participating office, who will conduct/proctor at each location (by title, if necessary in initial planning stages)?
13. If physical product or other tools are required, how will these be provided? Estimated cost? $________.
14. Estimated cost for:
    a) one-time lease/rental if likely to be non-recurring project? $________.
    b) amortized one-time use if multiple-year lease or purchase? $ ________.
15. What additional knowledge/skills/training will the individual locations' presenters need prior to the program?
    a) easily transmitted or shipped in prior actions? Specify.

b) small in-person training session required? Specify.

16. Estimated cost for video conferencing and related special requirements, if any: $_______.
17. Estimated savings if video conferencing is substituted for site-and travel-dependent meeting: $_________.
18. Recommend use(s) for anticipated savings:
19. Long-term value of video conferencing capacity if available for entire company, permanently: $______.
20. Shall video conferencing be recommended to program's primary originators?

WHAT ABOUT VIDEO CONFERENCING?

Perspectives for the First Edition (unchanged):

Although it was done in the early 70s, video conferencing for most corporate meetings is considered brand new. There are relatively lower costs for broadcast, more assistance available, more knowhow extant, more certainty of the signal, more places to bring the signal down, if groups are involved.

Using video conferencing depends on whether you will use land-based transfer systems over a short distance (telephone lines or microwave towers) or use a satellite to reach the entire nation and/or span an ocean. Costs differ dramatically.

You pay for what you use. You pay for initial production charges and for transmission time on the *uplink* (that is, sending the signal out), and you pay for, the antenna reception and transmission (over phone lines) to the site you're using, or *downlink*. Many hotels, theaters, and auditoriums are equipped to receive satellite signals. You also pay for the broadcast time reserved.

Costs can run in multiples of tens of thousands of dollars. What makes it financially attractive is the opportunity to pay for the television linkage with the unused travel money. That reduces time off the job for participants and results in an eventual cost saving for the company even when the cash outlay is about the same.

Desktop video conferencing on internal networks is said to be here but quite unused.

When networking, sending the signal up to the satellite is the really costly part—and you need to be prepared to make the most of the air time. You will need to pre-tape any segments which cannot be left to chance or any elements which can't be brought into the studio. So you will probably use a producer. He will know how to go about getting you on the air.

Nothing is more important than a sense of proportion. It is perfectly possible both to broadcast and receive video from each location tied into your network. That's also horrendously costly. What's cost effective is to broadcast video only from the headquarters facility and link everyone via amplified telephone networking. With this arrangement everyone can see the speakers and their visual presentations (some prerecorded); and it's presumed that it isn't necessary for the speakers to see the responding sales people.

Controlling what goes onto the air is part of having a sense of proportion. When questions and feedback that *create* the true conference are allowed to encompass minute details which affect only the single respondent or single locale, everyone else gets bored at extremely high cost.

The U.S. Army proved the need to narrow the scope of the program. High-level brass were on hand for two days of linkage; some of the conversation degenerated into discussion of whether certain barracks needed new funds for roofing. Moreover, with that much time being wasted, participants were tempted to duck out of their respective receiving; but that was impossible, for any participant could be asked a question at any time. It was an exercise in frustration as much as of communication.

On the other hand, the Ford Motor Company video conferenced its 1982 meeting to 40 locales, saving substantially over the dollar costs of prior years' seven regional meetings. Costs were further amortized by repeating selected portions of the program twice: for field managers (with phone feedback) and the media (without feedback). Seven broadcast hours (partially prerecorded) paid off handsomely!

Both the army and Ford programs were coordinated and produced by private producers. To the consternation of the producing businessmen, public television has entered the arena. It is possible now to produce your program in the studios of your local (major metropolitan area) public television station and receive it in the studios of any of PTV's member stations. Public television feels that the lower cost of its network—by saving on hotel charges and or telephone cable routing to other sites—can be substantial. It can be, depending on the mobility of your various groups.

On the other hand, if you cannot use their studio facilities, then the costs are similar to those of the business sector because satellite leasing costs are highly competitive.

Throughout your planning, keep in mind that once you begin to broadcast via satellite, anyone with a dish antenna tuned to that satellite can receive your program. That includes your competitors. Therefore absolutely nothing of a restricted or confidential nature can be broadcast with assured privacy. Signal scrambling is fairly secure but not guaranteed. Trade-offs are likely.

And also keep in mind that a video conference is only a scattered assembly meeting: all the workshop and training sessions necessary to a complete, valid program must simply be conducted in the various locales. That calls for self-contained packages mailed to the field ahead of the broadcast date.

If you go by satellite, get your act together well in advance, because there's no time to improvise once you're on the air. All the same program parameters apply if you choose the newly expanded Picture Phone service of AT&T.

Perspectives for the Third Edition:

As we go to press for the new millennium, newer developments in the always-new field of electronics are no longer merely on the horizon—essentially they're here! Already, in past years, you could have rented two-way, full motion video conferencing to/with all equipped stations. Today, if your company has broadband connections, you can transmit digital pictures that will flow on regular digital data channels on purchased equipment available from limited sources now. So you can then video cast for the added price of a cellular phone call. It's not phenomenally expensive. Yet it can save mightily on your travel expenses; it sacrifices virtually nothing in proved communications.

Equipment already exists to connect any multiple sites for under $5,000 per site on owned equipment. At present, software and bandwidth rule. You can rent complete production service and major gear. For a list of about 1,000 video conferencing companies nation-wide, broken out in several ways (including city/state and their size), see www.referenceUSA.com. (Use SIC code 482206). For other help, you might contact the Society of Satellite Professionals International, in New York, NY. They know transmission.

By 2003, if one major manufacturer's projections are right, additional, and relatively inexpensive, equipment should be available to do much the same video conferencing job from your company site(s). Current target price is also expected to be about $5,000 per site—purchased! It's too early to tell whether the current dot.com crisis will affect their delivery dates significantly. Remember, you're probably contracted for years ahead for hotels; so the time is now to explore options!

There aren't a lot of books dealing with this topic—what publisher would want to fight the industry's official position? But you can find video conferencing history (the first corporate use in 1977 and first commercial use with Ronald Reagan for *Newsweek* in 1983) plus really useful material in a serious book for serious prospects: *Straight Talk About Video Conferencing*, by Jack Hilton and Peter Jacobi.

For immediate help with your understanding of the rudiments and the don't-forget basics, see *Effective Videoconferencing,* by Lynn Diamond and Stephanie Roberts. Only 100 pages done in workbook fashion (with diagrams and fill-ins), it offers much help while being devoid of gobbledegook. Keep in mind that technical matters as presented are probably no longer state-of-the-art because no book can be current beyond its submission date in a field as changeable as electronics. Yet the caveats are probably still valid and useful.

Already it's possible to travel both your message and your (and their) images together, rather than traveling your people!

The Japanese are already using cellular picture phones, but their system is still incompatible with ours.

In short, unless you're already in touch with today's providers of current service, you won't be video conferencing company meetings tomorrow. But it will soon be easy—and wise—to do-it-yourself on company-owned equipment. For a few thousand dollars per meeting site—and substantially less than past travel costs alone!

As detailed elsewhere, about 44% of the total corporate travel budget is taken by airline tickets, and 22% by hotel costs. What percent of that entire corporate travel budget is assigned to your meeting(s)? And how would you like to save about two-thirds of that off the top, to be used for training or other communications purposes? How many new programs would that enable?

Think what the cost savings can do for your budget. Think of the increased time that will be available for thinking because so much less time is spent on the unproductive event planning, site-related tasks that were once necessary and unavoidable in order to gain (needed?) simultaneity at a site-dependent conference. Good stuff like inventorying sites, planning travel for VIPs and maybe all attendees and even spouses, planning spouses' programs, menus, and massive entertainment needs for the crowd...and, as if you didn't have enough to do, dealing with lost packages and bulk shipments of meetings material, and fielding screams because travel today is not the joy that once it was. See *Newsweek's* issue of April 23, 2001, on "Air Hell." A brief time later, *Forbes* Magazine weighed in with a similar critique. Is that airline experience considered a preparation for your participants' concentration in your meetings? How bad must things be if the business press criticizes the service of potential advertisers? And why can't the meetings/conventions industry do the same? Shucks, if the travel-happy slogan says "You-gotta-have-face-to-face," who are you to think about it and make your own decision?

There's just one more simple point. If multiple providers of PC-based, full motion video conferencing might soon be available (if actually delivered; we've never seen a multi-site desktop unit demonstrated yet), which one provider will provide you with the best collateral service in order to *deserve* your business? The inexpensive two-way equipment due (both here now and due in competitive fashion) by 2003 should be sold and serviced by two divisions of the same large, well-known company—neither division of which is able to demonstrate at this writing and neither of which is already known for meetings management knowhow. How good are their instructions to you and your people for operating properly? Fancy stuff like split screens or picture-in-picture will depend on your (or their) software. Caveat emptor: are you pushed onto producers?

Previously, because of high cost per site and jerky "still photo" frames, although video conferencing groups easily could have been "assembled" under the old system, costs were high enough so that it was perhaps as economical and maybe surer to buy tickets and hotel space. But that's changing *radically*, via special site rental equipment, (and almost surely coming), via PC screens, possibly using the familiar computer in your and their offices. Putting in the enabling equipment will make contact and clear communications a matter of a few keystrokes, with multiple people able to talk in many different directions (two persons at a time, of course) at the same event. So the new capacity can be both company-wide and not necessarily group-dedicated. What are you willing to pay for?

Apart from the jerkiness, the big objection to old video conferencing has been currently-unfounded pronouncements about psychological factors: "You need the camaraderie of face-to-face." Not only is that slogan unproved, but it's ridiculous: even with a relatively small central meeting, not every attendee will meet every other attendee in any case. Nor will the bosses meet everyone. We believe that strangers can work together on intelligently-explained projects because we were in the Army once, and not all of us knew each other or all the generals. Nor did all the generals know all of us. That's still true, but the military does win wars!

But if the old saw (about face-to-face) is true, then telephones and www virtual romances will never get off the ground because they're only substitutes for being there. Virtual investment groups can't hope to succeed. Virtual real estate tours will bog down. Bob Hope and Seinfeld will probably remain little-known because they expected to become known to millions of fans via radio and TV and movies— all "mediated contact." Poor guys—most of their fans have never met them face-to-face and so can't be considered real. Ditto the Three Tenors, Pavarotti, Carrera, and Domingo, more recently. Who of Public Television's millions of viewers have seen the Italian or French concerts in person? How many in Los Angeles? Under fifteen thousand? Surely those tenors should expect to be forgotten. Or to remain unknown! Isn't it Julia *Who*? if you haven't met *Roberts*?

Unarguably, the current generation (if not those persons older and possessed of a fossilized intellect) will accept substantial amounts of mediation in communications. Remember that those Middle Eastern Guys "met" internationally on Ted Koppel's Nightline news show long before they met in Washington to sign some papers. They simply didn't know in advance that they *couldn't*. After all, didn't they need face-to-face? It was all on your home TV screen. Now similar contacts might soon be available on your office PC screen. Does content count, or do you think that a few inches in size make all the difference to communication via TV screens?

Clearly, something else *is* at issue: it's the old non-verbal communication, or NVC. Psychologists agree that NVC is quick, silent, and virtually infallible (see Chapter 7). It's almost instantaneous when we meet, of course, but it also continues throughout the meeting because of clues to private thoughts given by visible body language. Curiously, NVC is precisely what's missing from telephone conversation, and maybe that's why it's easier to prevaricate by telephone rather than in person.

It's true that long ago, some social scientists felt that one-way, extremely-small-screen video did not serve the purposes of NVC well, and some (if attached to their old memories) still say so. But today's PC screens are as large as most home video screens were then; and console sets can be larger-than-life. Both or all speakers now can see each other even larger than life; and now there is absolutely full motion (just like in the movies!).

Yet *on May 21, 2001, Newsweek* quoted a reader in "Letters," responding to an April 30 special report: " 'For all the wonders of wireless technology,' he mused, 'when sharing ideas, there is nothing that replaces the importance of body language in a face-to-face meeting.' " Notice, no scientific attribution to substantiate his personal prejudice. Perhaps because there isn't any.

Given two-way, full-motion images, the jerky "still photo" screens can no longer mask NVC. So the original (and decades-old) criticisms are not automatically valid today—and, to our knowledge, no current studies have ever been conducted.. You see actor body language in a movie, don't you? But the actors are only pretending, while you are internalizing whatever you see in order to form opinions and even identify with the characters. Yes, we seem to be losing personal contact in many arenas, but in a society that values money above all other measures of worth, why be surprised?

Full motion/two way video conferencing (of whatever technical origin) can now deliver full-motion video views of body language plus much emotional rapport (brain electrical emanations are at root and seem to some degree to be transmitted by electronic signals). If not, you wouldn't feel an emotional tug when your favorite actor or actress emotes on the screen. If you can get all that through the convenience of your own PC, then why be site-dependent for your meetings' success? Why chase yourself across the nation for relatively minor change announcements that don't need full body visibility in the first place? If you doubt it, think about accounting or screw-turning or "say this instead" variations on the original way: how much body language could you need? For (new) product presentations, if you can actually provide several demonstrator units for several locations, then you needn't have all the participants in the same room. Period. Elsewhere, we recounted the *Sales & Marketing Management* magazine findings that regional meetings were almost always the money-savers among site-dependent meetings alternatives. Remember, you must measure before you can claim success—so no more entertaining-but-worthless programs, please.

If you haven't been paying attention, know now that easy and inexpensive distance-learning is here! The Mexican Board of Education has been proving that for years! In San Antonio, in November, 1998, Senor Antonio Mesa Estrada stated that the Mexican Board of Education can deliver all their key programs everywhere in that country simultaneously via satellite, despite distance, terrain, or poverty. Match that, can you?

So when will sanity, reason, and common sense come to the American meetings business?

On the face of it, video conferencing appears to promise an all-points, even permanent improvement for everyone who can get to a PC—one that can link all regions and district offices for only a few thousand dollars' one-time cost plus air time. If so, gone is the "need" to travel company staff and outside dealers for everything. Dealers have probably never really wanted to spend their time at your central functions in the first place. Most other people have other things to do, too.

One caveat: Narrow casting is only the little brother to broadcast, and neither of them is absolutely secure from corporate spies or other hackers, who can get into almost anything. So it's necessary to conduct your most sensitive business either on paper-version packages sent in advance or by several meaningless partial transmissions by www, courrier, or other method at an earlier, unpredictable time. It's highly unlikely that anyone will catch all transmissions.

Daily rental vs. *long-lease* vs. *purchase* will become the only budget-related considerations. If you'll have only occasional use for virtual face-to-face, rent it. If you want freedom from the perhaps large, perhaps small (but absolutely certain), improvements of the future (or need to avoid a larger equipment investment now), you can lease. And if you're willing to do the arithmetic involved in amortizing the equipment purchase for this and future years, you can buy now and hold and upgrade as necessary.

Want a second opinion on buy vs. lease? The CEO of Sun Microsystems Company (which can be presumed to know something about electronic marvels) believes that by the year 2002, all computing will be done by the central network computers; and that both office and home computers will be replaced with what he describes as "small appliances." He believes that kids will think our PCs to be fossils. The founder of that company believes that the PC will survive, but in a simplified form. Of course Microsoft's president believes the PC will remain, but not in its present dominant state. However, Microsoft's tag no longer mentions PCs specifically—now it says "appliances." After the final legal finding, all bets are probably off. Gateway, however, is joining with other firms to develop non-PC appliances.

Michael Dell, of Dell Computer, thinks that's nonsense: as systems get faster, so will computers, he says, and computers are here to stay. Robert Glaser of Realnetworks believes computers will survive as about 50% of all net access appliances. And Steve Case of AOL believes that there will be a blurring of distinctions between today's TV, phone, computer, and stereo.

More to the point, Microsoft's President & CEO, Robert Ballmer, believes that the differences will be more pronounced in the next five years. He adds that MS (which partners with AT&T) is helping AT&T to tie telephones and computers. That argues for major efforts to make video conferencing an ordinary method via some new form of picture phone; and it also makes two major corporations (to our knowledge) to move toward making a reality of this long-promised possibility.

And who even wants to try to separate *posture* from *position* of any of these key players? So much for second opinion. What do you think is best for your organization? Run with it!

Many other known corporations are already forming consortia to offer non-travel meeting service at home. Apparently the Japanese already have cellular video telephones not compatible with our systems; and most of Europe is more highly un-wired and using more non-cable communications techniques.

At this writing, though, there are several other firms which long ago could have given you quasi-motion video conferencing. Some could do it with special equipment and their (rented or purchased) large screens for the meeting room. Others can do it now or soon with your PC screens and their (rented or purchased) browser-equipment-plus-telephone and cable. Be alert: one purported “manufacturer” who claimed to be able to narrow cast via PC did not in fact exist as a company, despite large ads placed in prestigious publications. That individual failure to perform is probably less significant than is the lack of notice taken by the meetings industry as a whole. False claims have probably never been challenged by the meetings industry, which is the weaker for it.

What all of this means to your purchase plans, we can’t know. Is it smart to buy *cheap* now or smart to buy *time* until later? That’s your choice, based on your anticipated needs. But don’t let the travel industry stampede you into eliminating smart alternatives to travel!

As described elsewhere in this book, the training industry is now recognizing that computers *per se* are not The Answer, just as meetings *per se* are not either. It’s still a question of medium-vs-message, as it was when we first made that observation more than a quarter century ago. Marshall McLuhan was wrong, but his being wrong made lots of money for some suppliers. Worse, the meetings industry’s Pollyanna Press and associations aided, more than challenged, those basic errors in *viewpoint.* Who needs that kind of “assistance”?

For the latest academic research, see Professor M. David Merrill on www.coe.usu.edu/it/id2/reclaim.html.

Two considerations will be of primary importance to you when considering video conferencing:

First, and most important to you, will be the needed ability to separate proprietary information into components that can be narrow cast safely—or sent alternatively. Your company viewpoint will be salient. On that basis, blind commitment to the site-dependent methods of the past will be only voluntary and short-sighted.

Second is the awareness that despite supplier screaming and shouting and foot stomping, video conferencing will create the beginning of the end for supplier-dominance (through advertising censorship of the press) for the entire meetings and conventions industry. Neither we nor anyone will insist that you never again meet in person for some *essential* purpose, but face-to-face now has a new meaning. Believe it or not, the future is largely behind glass.

Finally it will be possible to learn, via www and books such as this, that the problems you've been having with suppliers *while blaming yourself* are in fact standard problems experienced by most competent Meeting Managers. We proved that in a survey of association members taken in the past by the first incarnation of MPI. That survey has been buried after the initial printing.

The difference is that you can now talk with experienced counterparts that you might never have actually met. But by virtually "meeting" on the www, you can probably get suggestions and even answers direct from the source. No more self-serving static and outright interference with facts and trends by middlemen. To that end, this author (The Source for nearly all early meetings industry systematic know-how and specific how-to, between 1960 and 1985) will cooperate with any reputable interests in establishing a web site *for* users, dominated *by* users. Now let advertisers try to co-opt that! Who wants to start?

Ours has always been a consumerist attitude, but such honest viewpoint based on hands-on (often unhappy) experience, was DELETED by MPI (the first industry association for users) from its first professional handbook when reprinting two of three of our Chapter 18 forms. MPI eliminated our embarrassing consumerist criticisms that were seen as unfavorable to hotels—the money people at their annual meeting exhibits. Splashy exhibits tend to draw members. But you and your company don't need to draw "voluntary members" to most corporate meetings (except once annually). Nevertheless, our contributions to that First Professional Handbook were greater in number, space, and originality than those reprinted from any other single source. Apparently the association was trying to pass off our *non*-offering of DELETED consumerist materials in Chapter 18 as our agreement with their pro-supplier views. Can any organization that has acted with such duplicity even hope to lead an ethical industry?

How doubly disingenuous! Would you say "dishonest"? What? In an industry rife with dishonesty? What can the industry as a whole say? Suggestion: "We're shocked. Shocked!" (Claude Raines' character, law officer *Louis,* re: outlawed gambling in the classic Bogart movie *Casablanca,* spoken just before Louis took his gambling winnings).

As a result of all the past and current duplicity in the meetings field, you probably don't *need* an association anymore. If the associations could not offer much original know-how, and if the how-to materials they originally provided were demonstrably censored, what can you hope to gain? WWW.com can get you any information you might want to get more quickly and dependably than you can get it at annual meetings. If you need help, lean on the Federal government's own website, America's Learning Exchange (www.alx.org). Vendor listings are free; so there's no implied quality endorsement. But there are other options. Key among them is www.referenceUSA.com, which lists topics by SIC codes and can give you an unbelievable amount of information by topic or company or city/state or company size. Your public library probably has a connection even if your office doesn't. For video conferencing help on the web, use SIC code 482206.

And if the associations are really doing such a great job, why should there now be a half-dozen or more associations competing in the meetings field? For the first dozen years of professional coordination (originated by our then-employer; we were on staff) there were none. Why multiples now? Don't virtually all people learn more or less alike? Then why should we need multiple groups? Purpose is not a factor in application of like learning theories. Purpose might help to make instant cozy for networking—but networking is anti-merit in concept and might not really help. Subject matter *field* is important to linking like groups, but field is not a learning function. And if you believe that's not true, then you cannot give countless individual approaches via a central, in-person meeting, either. Emotional decisions won't cut it! Back to reason and rational thinking.

Obviously, it isn't simple: there's been a paradigm shift in your ability to deliver worthwhile instruction and other information. But there's no longer another independent *business* reason for the centralized party that masquerades as a business venture.

Without honesty about major problems with over-promising/under-performing suppliers, most association programs in the field will probably be flawed to some significant extent. That could cost you your job, but no one wants to talk about it. As stated previously, the typical, dismissing comments regard ice cubes and ash trays as examples. But function rooms torn apart and command centers moved with little warning are among the real-life problems. Ditto electricians who have been on duty for too long a time that day-plus-plus to give you needed time and thought and energy.

Despite a couple of hopeful starts, we have never joined any convention group association permanently and have never felt either the need or the moral compunction to remain once enticed by unkept promises. How many associations promote ethics these days? That failure to act against industry deceit and outright fraud caused at least one of our first (and subsequent) early quits. If you do not treat your employees ethically, you know that your company will have major problems. Dependably! Then, if you're a member, why not apply similar expectations to the various associations?

In the last analysis, why submit yourself to all the tribulations and horrors of the past from which previously there was no escape? You can't pass them downward, and you still don't get paid for enduring unnecessary frustrations. Beginning even before the millennium year, the world has been becoming a better place for Meetings Managers who think for themselves! Now think video conferencing!

To estimate costs and benefits among your options, use the Locations Comparison Sheet, in Chapter 11. It's the same concept: just treat narrow cast specifications as a "site" named *Electronics*. To maximize your advantage and potentials via video conferencing, use the brand new form preceding, page 318.

21

Showbiz for entertainment

Psychological relief through diversion of interest or entertainment is a legitimate part of any program which lasts a full day or longer. Occasionally the social mixer is desirable even when the preceding program is not particularly long. This might be particularly true of meetings with distributors and dealers.

If you need to buy entertainment, you have the choice of working direct, serving as your own producer, or dealing through a production studio. Generally, the simplicity or complexity of the program will determine your response.

For the simplest of needs—say a musical trio during the cocktail hour—you need only phone the local musicians union. Describe the nature of the music you want (jazz, rock, background, and so on), and the union will give you several names of combos to track down, with a chance to hear the group perform somewhere. Hear them first, if possible A few phone calls can get you a booking. In any event, they will be capable musicians appearing at the union rate (or slightly higher, if "known" in the area), but without added producer's fee. Sign a contract, and it's a sure thing.

If you want to do a theater night, cabaret show, or pop concert, you can often obtain a group discount on a block of tickets for a scheduled night. If your group is smaller than the seating capacity of their "house," that's the way to go. If your group is larger, possibly that troupe can appear in your own facility. Bargain.

There are significant problems attached to any attempt to move any troupe from its present house into another, not the least of which are backdrops, sound equipment, and the timing of their program. So don't tackle it lightly. On the other hand, one of our clients moved a show out of a house seating only a couple hundred and regaled a crowd of several thousand with a production far superior to the average banquet show.

The show's own producer will produce for you, too, and provide a list of his staging needs. Both you and he should meet well in advance with your facility to work out all details.

For needs that exceed these, your best bet is to work with a production studio. The executive producer will get you organized rather quickly once you tell him the size of your budget. That's a legitimate question, since available performers charge fees ranging from a few hundred to a few hundred thousands of dollars. Be direct; don't apologize. He can tell you what type of thing your budget will buy; if that doesn't suit you, lower your sights or raise your budget. It's good to shop around, because the price for entertainment is what the market will bear. Ordinarily, five different clients will pay five different prices for identical programs. To understand your options, you need to understand the way show biz operates.

Who should be your producer? Two types function in show business: the impresario and the industrial producer. The impresario creates programs for the public on a speculative basis in hopes of winning huge profits; he takes huge risks and often loses.

By contrast, the industrial producer takes no risk beyond the cost of his presentation to you. After that, if he is hired he has a guaranteed audience and a guaranteed profit. He is, therefore, a consultant to the exact degree that your advertising agency is: both deliver a creative product to your specifications.

But there is a difference. You can observe the progress of a print or broadcast campaign and make adjustments during the creative process. But with entertainment you are buying an event that cannot be viewed in advance.

So when you buy show biz you are buying your producer's taste and ability and reputation; you can supervise his mechanical processes, but not the event. So when you choose, you must be sure.

The superior producer is the one who can take your budget, whatever its limitations or largesse, and create an entertainment program which by comparison with standard productions makes your own show a real treat and buy. He does that with imagination and flair—his own personal creative contribution.

His imagination is exercised in his choice of entertainers and/or themes for the program—say a banquet show. His knowledge of the performers' material and his feel for the compatibility of their styles and pacing are the essence of his value as your consultant. When you locate a person who understands and respects your viewpoint, listen to him. Present your objections, if any, and hear his counter proposals, but never second-guess him: you really don't know show biz, even if you were the star of your high school talent show.

The shady operator will betray himself early in the visit. He suggests performers beyond your budget; offers "commissions" or "dates" with the girls (both bribes with intent to blackmail). If you bite you'll find yourself with an extremely expensive and uncontrollable producer ever after. It could mean your job.

So look for the ethical producer. Treat him as a business partner; and once he proves what he can do, stick with him everywhere in the nation. An extra phone call or airfare won't break you. Blind buying might.

Talk fees up front. He's in business; he has overhead; he must charge some minimum amount if he is to take on your project—that's just for suggesting several alternate programs, but without *booking* the performers. Many producers will suggest programs by theme or format on speculation, with a list of stars who would be proper for that particular show. That's file material out of their past experience—it's probably not billable. Beware the producer who says he can get "any" of a list of well-known stars. Nobody can promise.

It is traditional in entertainment for the stars to sign only 30-day cancel-able contracts. That permits them to commit to more lucrative engagements—movies, TV series, and so on—that might be offered after your lone event. So signing a contract is no guarantee that the star will actually appear, and a reputable producer will be sure you understand that.

Furthermore, the trade traditionally puts acts on *hold* when the producer's client says yes but must staff the contract and cut a deposit check. Some of these commitments fall through, and so the star's agent often takes several holds. The marginal producer often accepts a second or third hold (not a ghost of a chance); but the shyster is legally free to bind you permanently. He will send somebody in place of the proposed star, but it might be a dog act. Legally he will have fulfilled his contract.

Notice, we aren't mentioning *ethics.* The only show biz ethic is *get the money.* To *lie, cheat, and steal* seems common, because so little is provable. You *must* investigate.

Get references. Check them out. And ask around, too, because nobody will tell you what his flops are. Don't be embarrassed to call your counterpart in other companies or your company's advertising manager. Your ad agency buys talent too, and they know which producers are reputable. Best, your ad agency gains nothing by misleading you, and they know it. The more willing various companies are to talk show biz with each other, the sooner the malpractice will end.

Once you've selected a producer and agreed on a workable budget range, he will ask you to choose among four key types of programs: the variety show, the book show, the revue, and the Big Band. The personality and preferences of your audience are the determining factors—you should lead here.

The variety show is a combination of independent performers, each doing an 8-to 12-minute routine that is their specialty; the featured entertainer will play for 30 to 45 minutes; your show will last about an hour or more. Your band will play for dancing before and after the show to fill the three-hour union minimum call. The band, but not the performers, are paid for a rehearsal, if needed, a couple of hours before the doors open for dinner.

Theme decor ("Night in Paris," for example) is common with these shows; you can choose two acts (a comic and a singer, usually) or up to four or five. United Attractions of Chicago (our former employer, now defunct) probably originated this theme-show genre in the 1950s. Have fun, but don't make a circus of it!

The book show is becoming uncommon these days because of the high cost of scripting and producing a respectable show. Moreover, because people are over-entertained by television, their expectations are higher than most budgets can meet. Unless you absolutely can't do without a full script, look to the semi-book show. This is simply a narrator's script that strings together the ideas or facts that you want to communicate (common at company anniversary time or the retirement of valued employee). The advantage is that the performers, except for the narrator, are not rehearsed; they do their variety acts but the script creates the illusion of integration and cohesion. You get much of the effect and little of the expense of the full book show.

The revue can be either a string of humorous skits or a full-fledged girlie show, such as Las Vegas features. Since the skits would be available as "theater," we'll talk about the girls. These shows are wondrous spectacles, cost thousands of dollars to stage each night after investments of upward from a million dollars just to get them off the ground, and are beyond your reach unless you can take your group to the hotel showroom where they are appearing.

Outside Las Vegas the revues are smaller and less ambitious. With less elaborate scenery and mechanical elements, the revue might be moveable. Because of the size and union interests, you should be assisted by a producer.

The Big Band was the paramount form of name entertainment in the 40s. Anyone who could hear the Glenn Miller, Jimmy or Tommy Dorsey, Harry James, or Guy Lombardo bands just didn't miss the event. While the leaders are now gone or retired, their musical libraries are alive and well; the charts are the same; so the sound is the same. Since each band contains its own show (usually a comic and a vocalist group), it's complete with a single contract. And it's promote-able in today's nostalgia mood.

Once you've decided, the producer can suggest and place holds on performers. Once you're agreed, expect him to ask for a deposit. His total input of time will be only 10 to 20 hours per show; but he will deliver that time over a long period and will need to make some expenditures in cash during that time.

Back to the fee. He is entitled to ask whatever he chooses as an executive producer, limited only by your resistance. But if his charge is within the range of other consulting concerns, he's being fair. For the talent he buys and for the equipment and staff he sends over to make the event happen, he will bill costs plus overhead/profit. Whether all of this is rolled into one price quotation is up to you; but the nature of the assembly operation is clear, and you should be sure to separate the creative from the mechanical services, just as with the business stage (review the preceding chapter, if necessary).

The more expensive the show or star, usually the more easily the project comes together. The pros are prepared; the talent still proving itself is sometimes still practicing to be great. Some make it and some don't. That's the wonder of show biz. Get a handle on costs early, using the Show Biz Cost Estimator, adjacent.

BUDGETING FOR ENTERTAINMENT

Even though the immediate benefit of any entertainment is in the nature of goodwill, for which precise cost-effective measures are usually overlooked, you must establish a reasonable limit for the budget.

If the meeting very clearly pays its way, then the difference between the required support materials and the permissible overall budget is available for entertainment and other diversions.

If the meeting is borderline in cost/benefit analysis, then the attitude is likely to be *spend as little as possible.* In either case, you will find that the dinner-theater (there) or the banquet-and-show (in your facility) tend to deliver the biggest bang for the buck.

There are many reasons. First, a group dinner tends to be an enjoyable event even without a lot of trimmings. Second, if you must serve dinner in any case, then a small additional investment in upgraded menu and music pays dividends because every dollar over minimum tends to show. Third, once people are in a good mood, they can be entertained by anything from a sing-along pianist to a folk group or trio to a full show. The appropriateness of the entertainers, rather than the cost, seems to be the key.

If you choose an elaborate event it becomes promote-able, especially to women, who like to dress up and go out to dinner. If voluntary attendance of spouses is contemplated, a dinner-dance will bring them out. If early attendance is voluntary, a cocktail party fancy enough to be promote-able will get them in early. The uses of entertainment *as entertainment* are many.

In almost every instance, there are attendant costs besides those of the performers. If you will have only a trio or piano player, the facility will usually provide a platform stage and one microphone without additional charge; they might throw in a couple of fixed spotlights.

Yes, a stage is always necessary. It can be at the end of the room or in the middle of the floor. It can be in the balcony, or it can be just inside the door where people enter. What do you hope to accomplish with the music? Dancing or background or feature? That's a clue to where the group should be placed.

Sales Meetings That Work

Show Biz Cost Estimator

Meeting title: ___________ City: ____________ Date(s): ________

1. Group specs: Count: ______ Budget: $ _______ Cost per person $ _____________

2. Alternative forms of entertainment available in that city:
   a. Cabaret revue — *their facility.* (Yes) (No). Because (consider quality, house capacity, distance, prices, etc.):
   b. Cabaret revue — *our facility.* (Yes) (No). Because (consider cost, loss of settings, etc.):
   c. Dinner and theater combination there. (Yes) (No). Because:
   d. Special stage show. (Yes) (No). Because:
   e. Music for cocktails and dancing only. (Yes) (No). Because:
   f. Open (unscheduled) night for their choice of activities. (Yes) (No). Because:
   g. Group tickets purchased in advance for public event (sports, theatre, pop or classical music, etc.). (Yes) (No). Because:

3. If a special stage show is preferred or required:
   a. Basic production costs at facility:

Platform stage:	$__________
Lighting and sound equipment:	__________
Stage decor or drapery:	__________
Labor for work above:	__________
Union minimum for orchestra:	__________
Basics, subtotal:	$__________

   b. Discretionary production costs:

	Low: $	High: $
Star performer:	_______	_______
Supporting acts (all):	_______	_______
Room decor:	_______	_______
Orchestra rehearsal:	_______	_______
Producer's fee:	_______	_______

Options and contingencies:	______	______
Multimedia sequences:	______	______
Discretionary subtotal		$________
Anticipated grand total:		$________

4. Considering the cost per person in the anticipated grand total (plus provisions for possible overages) should any of the alternatives in Item 2 above be reconsidered? (Yes) (No). Because:
5. If so, which of the alternatives become(s) newly acceptable? Why?
6. Would local transportation be needed for any? (Yes) (No). Does that affect the new decision? How and Why?
7. Assuming that the cost of a star is the standard estimate, can savings be realized on:
   a. A star already contracted by a nightclub in town — to be seen there?
   b. A star already scheduled on tour in the area — to appear at our facility?
   c. A star already sponsored on TV by our company or a supplier? (Some will appear for-expenses-only for the sponsoring company; at reduced fee at sponsor's request for a third party.)
   d. A name band already scheduled into the area?
8. Resolution of discrepancies in any of the items above:
9. Final decision:

The stage provides a focal point. It allows the entertainers to be seen over the crowd even when they can't be heard over the hubbub. But if you do anything more than the minimum described, the stage also becomes a focal point for cost. At a small meeting the proportional cost vs audience size could be high.

Setting the stage. Because a formal stage or hydraulic lift stage is rare in modern hotels, risers with folding legs are often stacked several high to create a stage of useable size and height. For a small combo and small crowd, a platform of 24 inches high is adequate and 36 inches is ideal. For a major show and large crowd, 48 inches is absolute minimum and 54 inches is desirable. The square footage of stage floor will be determined by the size of the band and the nature of the performance.

Some hotels attempt to discourage you from going 54 inches high because they don't have enough platforms. If they admit that, it's a limitation you must work with; if they try to hide the facts, insist, and put them on the spot That will discourage future faking.

A platform stage built of stacked risers must of course be skirted; sometimes the hotel provides the skirting free, but often you pay the carpenter. Any stage hides equipment and break room for the musicians and performers—so there must be a backdrop (as a focal point for the audience) and curtained *wings.* You will pay for all that, sometimes by the running foot.

If you must pay separately for the drapery, consider renting a painted theatrical backdrop, from a theatrical rental company, of course. These are available in many scenes to promote themes at low additional cost over installation fees paid to the hotel, if any.

Lighting is essential. It's wise to have footlights, and one or two follow spotlights are essential to light any performers who will move about on stage. In any case, the appearance of a follow spot in a darkened room heightens the dramatic effect.

If you will encourage dancing, avoid placing the dance floor immediately in front of and contiguous to the stage. If you do that you create a vast desert in front of the performers. They lose their indispensable measure of audience feedback—called laughter and applause. Always place at least one row of tables between stage and dance floor, and a couple rows if you can. Besides encouraging the performers, you'll gain an extra row of ringside seats, always in demand.

You will also pay for house and union labor (including the stagehands union when you borrow follow spots); maybe for special sound equipment; and for the producer who holds all these pieces together. Still want a big show? Work out the following Banquet Show Bid Comparison Guide.

Sales Meetings That Work

Banquet Show Bid Comparison Guide

Meeting title: ____________________ City: ________________
Date(s):____________________
Name of Producer: ____
City:____________________

1. Dollar cost quoted: Low $ _________ High $ ___________; All inclusive (Yes) (No) for (variety show) (book show) (semi-book show) (Big Band*) (Revue).
2. Size of group: ____________________ Cost per person: $ ____________________
3. Which of these basics are included in this producer's presentation:

$__________	Platform stage	$____________	Hotel labor
__________	Lighting (fixed)	____________	Union labor
__________	Follow-spotlights	____________	Union musicians*
__________	Sound equipment	____________	Collapsible proscenium
__________	Stage décor/backdrop	____________	Dimmerboard
__________	Hotel drapery (cost not justified)	____________	Producer's fee

Subtotal, basics $ ____________________

4. Which of these discretionary items are included:

Starring performers suggested:

a.____________	Low $ ____________	High $________
b.____________	____________	____________
c.____________	____________	____________
d.____________	____________	____________

"Stars" Average: $ ________________

Thematic components:

Décor for (stage) (tables) (walls)	Low $ ________	High $ _________
Supporting acts suggested:	____________	____________
a.____________	____________	____________
b.____________	____________	____________
c.____________	____________	____________
d. Dance line:___girls	____________	____________

"Themes" Average: $ ______________

5. Necessary components not included within this producer's bid:

Facility costs:		Producer costs: Orchestra rehearsal	
________	$________	________	$________
________	________	________	________
________	________	________	________

"Extras" Average: $ ____________

6. Grand total of estimated costs; Items 3, 4, and 5, above:

Basics (or all inclusive)	$____________
Star	____________
Theme	____________
Extras	____________

*Union musician minimums not applicable to Big Band.

7. Are any of the recommended stars/performers already on hold? (Yes) (No). Specify which. When can they be placed on hold?
8. Does the contract provide that (Company) will be released without penalty if the producer is not immediately able to obtain a contract with one of the suggested stars? (Yes) (No). If not, why not?
9. If not, is misrepresentation of availabilities a possibility?
10. What type of contract will the producer offer us:
    a. Noncancellable (except for act of God).
    b. Option to eliminate canceling star; saving $ ____________
    c. Other: ______________________________
11. If the producer obtains a 30-day cancelable contract which is subsequently cancelled, what alternatives will be offered to us?
    a. Automatic substitution, guaranteed equal-or-better.
    b. Option to eliminate canceling star; saving $ ____________.
    c. Other: ______________________________

(Note: Provisions based on later cancellation of a signed contract should not penalize the producer, who cannot guarantee any star's actual appearance.)

12. Does this producer have a superior eputation in the trade? (Yes) (No).
    If so, is his bid competitive in price? (Yes) (No). Comment:
    Are his staging ideas fresh/unique? (Yes) (No).
    Did he "work to create something special/original for us?
    Have you personally seen one or more of his shows?
    Do his past clients recommend him? (Yes) (No). Why?
13. Before suggesting this program, did the producer ask intelligent questions about the company audience? (Yes) (No). Interpretation:

14. If this producer was neither recommended by a trusted advisor nor able to show us his actual shows in progress, on what is this bid based — only promises?
15. Should this bid be held for final consideration? (Yes) (No). Because:
16. Should this bid and producer be permanently rejected? (Yes) (No). Because:
17. If held for consideration, where does this bid rank among others?
    a. If more expensive, is the producer worth the extra cost?
    b. If more expensive, can this producer suggest ways to cut costs?
    c. If less expensive form a superior producer, can we use this same producer on the business side of this meeting/convention?
18. Final decision on this bid/producer.

22

Running the meeting

If you have conscientiously applied the sense of each analysis guide offered in this book, and if you have reviewed those justifications whenever questions arose, you can be confident that your message is protected.

What remains now is "only" the execution of the event itself, generally known as running the meeting. As mentioned, that term is applied indiscriminately to both the overall task of coordinating the simultaneous events and the chairing of the individual meeting or workshop segment.

If you will be chairing or facilitating a meeting you will want to draw on two key skills: agenda control and platform speaking. Parliamentary procedure is the accepted method for giving the audience free play of ideas within a context of order and progression. Although it is not essential that you follow these rules strictly, most executives have a fair understanding of parliamentary procedure and expect to see some evidence of it, especially when the matters of precedence and the germane could lead to disagreements. The standard reference is Robert's Rules of Order, available at any bookstore.

Platform or public speaking techniques cannot be learned from books; they must be practiced under a coach. Most colleges which have an adult education branch offer public speaking courses, and they are worth your time and dollars. These courses build both vocal quality and the ability to extemporize, that is, to organize your thoughts while on your feet in front of a group.

The combination of the chairman's ability to direct the discussion and the speaker's ability to argue and persuade are the elements of successful meeting leadership. Moreover, those same leadership skills, in various and subdued contexts, are the skills needed *to facilitate* a meeting (to keep the process moving but not to chair or lead). For two excellent references on meeting leadership, including facilitation, read Leland P. Bradford, *Making Meetings Work* (La Jolla, Calif.: University Associates, 1976) and Michael Doyle and David Straus, *How to Make Meetings Work* (New York: Wyden Books, 1976).

Keep in mind that meeting leadership and speech making are two totally different techniques; never confuse them in your meeting room. Speeches are one-way flows of information; but the leadership role is to heighten the interpersonal relationships, to weld individuals into a cohesive group acting in concert to achieve a desired goal. Only a leader can do that, for that's the essence of leadership.

Let's return to the other sense of running the meeting, that of coordinating simultaneous events in progress. That, too, is a leadership position, because rarely can you see to all details alone except in the smallest and simplest of conferences.

If you can rattle a typewriter with fair accuracy or play a musical instrument, you already understand the coordinator's role in running the meeting: getting all the fingers to do in unison and in time the specific tasks they learned separately and haltingly. In this case, the "fingers" are your committees.

Your convention committee and the subcommittees its members chair are fully prepared to supervise the presentation of the program elements each committee created or produced. If the company is acting as its own producer, the entire convention committee, however large or small, belongs at the meeting site. For particularly complex conventions, their subcommittee staffs might be needed, too.

The nice thing about your committee chiefs is that they can actually be in a half dozen places at one time; that's the sort of thing expected of the Meeting Manager/coordinator also. Trying to do everything alone is what causes exhaustion, ulcers, and frazzled nerves; that's decidedly uncool.

To coordinate with style, choose a place to be and let everyone know they can find you there if they need you. The best place to be is backstage at the most important event each hour or other point of change. When you're on the spot at the one that counts, you'll know exactly what's happening and be more relaxed for that knowledge. Yet because you're easily accessible to all your colleagues you can also manage their program sequences by exception. Follow this system faithfully, and events will never be outside your control.

Incidents will happen during any major meeting. Speakers can take sick or be stranded by bad weather. Projectors can jam, and light bulbs can burn out. The house lighting can fail or, as one skilled Meeting Manager relates, the rooftop swimming pool can pop a seam and rain on your parade. There's no end to the number of things that could go wrong. But those are mostly in the nature of natural disasters—unpredictable and unavoidable.

Control of the meeting or convention in the managerial context relates to those things within your control, and it has been the intent of this book to make you aware of all of them. Moreover, when the routines are under your control you are best prepared to deal with the disasters should one happen. Nothing we could not handle has happened to us in 35 years of professional planning, producing, and coordinating events. Why? Because the audience is not privy to what should have been—unless the roof falls in, anything that occurs will pass for what should have occurred. Make that roof or swimming pool. But you get the idea.

You've put that meeting together using proved techniques. The meeting will work. It will become a whole. It will exhibit cohesiveness and synergy because that is the nature of the beast. The piecemeal approach to individual areas of responsibility and potential problems is simply a micro analysis of the many parts that make up the whole.

We've taken the meeting apart in this text to demonstrate that there is no mystery in, and no insuperable problem posed by, any component. When you are prepared to control the meeting, it cannot take control of you. Neither can it cause you to deliver or lose control to persons whose interests are not compatible with your objectives.

When you put those parts together, your job is simplified by the functional (committee) approach even if you do most of the work alone; and the results are safeguarded by the PERT mechanism. Success is highly predictable because it operates as the effect of a given cause.

Because the meeting is an event, it never exists prior to the unfolding, cannot be viewed as a complete entity at any point during its unfolding, and can be described but not recaptured after it is finished. Therefore it really exists only in the mind of the Meeting Manager—validated by results.

It is the intangibility of the meeting which demands that its tangible elements be precise, compatible, balanced, and executed exactly as planned. And it is the dependability of synergism which assures you that the meeting whole will be greater than the sum of its parts.

Throughout the text, we have worked with absolutes (always, never, only, and so on). You might choose to compromise, but be aware that any compromise increases your risks. Take as few as possible. If for every meeting—regardless of size or cost—you think through all the pertinent items of meeting justification and protect your decisions with PERT, it is impossible that the meeting not succeed. Believe it. Then prove it to yourself.

Plan. Plan meticulously. Let that plan dominate the event. Then the event unfolds as predetermined and the meeting achieves its objectives. Then *you* achieve *your* objectives, and this text achieves *ours.* Good meetings!

23

Just Looking

"Never look back," said baseball great Satchel Paige, "because something might be gaining on you." "Those who forget the past," said philosopher George Santayana, "are condemned to repeat it."

Probably most Americans are inclined to agree with Satch. On the other hand, Santayana was probably right. Both of those viewpoints figure prominently into the current (and perennial) problems of the meetings/conventions industry, even though the Pollyanna Press won't discuss the latter—nor, for that matter, will the user-associations, whose first order of business such discussion should be. Well, life demands a little of each, plus.

As a consequence, we believe that we should discuss both of the viewpoints above. And although they seem to be mutually exclusive, we'll create a few paragraphs directed to both and hope to come up with a perspective that you can live with...if you choose to ignore the options you now have because of electronics.

The issue arises because of the decades-long domination of the meetings/conventions industry by key advertisers. Because of that domination, much important knowledge is not widely (if at all) disseminated, and embarrassing comments and critiques rarely or never see print. Of course it's necessary to apportion some blame to the editors of those trade publications who aren't skilled enough to recognize significant advancements and to others who cannot resist the venality that caters to their advertisers rather than to their readers.

While talk radio is running its collective mouth these days, none of the associations has taken to editorial observations or members' roundtable discussions of abundant problems. Lots of talk about *tips*. Nor for that matter has TV provided an industry mouth, although that's less to be expected. It's a problems-blackout. As a result it's virtually impossible for neophyte Meetings Managers to learn *on paper* how to avoid the pitfalls of the industry...and those are numerous...unless practitioners take *SMTW* to heart and act accordingly. Otherwise virtually everyone must make virtually the same mistakes previously made by all their colleagues—which, of course, translates into repeated but undeserved sales by the marginal suppliers. That helps to sell advertising, but it doesn't aid users—who are, presumably, the rationale for the publications.

Codification of the entire industry's methodology (much of it original with us) and the industry's first meetings control system originated with the publication of our first book, *Achieving Objectives in Meetings,* in 1973, following preliminary exposure of several of our Profiles. For historical purposes, we'll likely put it back into print, *although all of its business forms are contained in this volume.* And the industry has subsequently standardized on words and phrases that we first introduced into the industry. If you find those words in this book and also in the industry press, such terminology probably started with five years of our magazine columns and the first book, *Achieving Objectives in Meetings.* That original book title is now a standard phrase in the industry. Why, then, should users accept the terminology but not the systems and critiques of the hands-on originator's experience? For whose benefit the censorship, if not the industry's suppliers, rather than the users'?

Looking Around:

Timid or unethical meetings editors aside, advertising and criticism can co-exist. A major multiple example is contained in a single issue of Computer Currents magazine for July, 1999: a)

From Jeff Bertolucci: "The original version of [Brand Name A] couldn't locate my local PBS station. [Brand Name B's] version can, but it can't download data from it. Go figure." b) From Robert Luhn: "The next time you consider buying a Mac or a PC ignore the vendor's clever (or dumb) ads and look critically at what they make and how. Are you getting a real value?..." c) From Robert Lauriston: "[Brand Name A, Brand Name B, and Brand Name C] aren't particularly well integrated with [Brand Name D] suite or with each other." and "This is a complex database manager designed for professional programmers. [Manufacturer Name] does its customers a disservice by passing it off as suitable for average [Brand Name X] users."

That's *real* help in print! Why should it occur with computers but not with meetings management? And lest you think that the examples above are an aberration in one issue of one magazine, let's examine a different magazine in the same field:

In MicroTimes, from the issue of July 23, 1999, we noted five different writings giving opinions on issues of consequence in that field:

1) From editor Stephen Lawton: "Today everyone seems to be running top 10 lists, ranging from the ridiculous to the sublime. Don't get me wrong—I love David Letterman's Top 10s. What I can't stand are the lists in trade and business magazines that purport to be useful but aren't. Since these lists normally fill lots of space and offer little of value, how could I resist the challenge of actually providing useful information in what has now become one of the great American pastimes—spouting off about nothing?...OK, so this isn't rocket science. Sound advice doesn't have to be." Does that sound like kin to our "acres and acres of ads" or "cotton candy" in our Chapter 3, unchanged from 1983?

2) The same magazine; from Lawrence J. Magid: "[Manufacturer Name] loaned me a device and a [Brand Name] phone to use it with, but I'm not enamored of it.... You should consider one other technology for keeping track of your life. It's called paper. It might be out of fashion, but it still works." Yes, printed in an electronics technology magazine!
3) Ibid.; from Diedra-Ann Parrish: "If you attend industry trade shows and keep up on technology trends, you've probably heard a lot about project management software. But reading about it and making it work are worlds apart." See our "Comparing Promises and Premises" in our Chapter 18, retained with no line changes from 1983.
4) Ibid.; From Lewis Perdue: "'Many merchants don't know that they have choices [re: credit card terminals]: to buy the terminal, to lease it, or to forgo it entirely in favor of PC-based [products],' [Named Interviewee] says. She suspects some merchant-account providers deliberately keep customers in the dark because it is highly profitable to do so." Enuf sed about the practice of silence and disinformation, way back in our 1970s magazine publications.
5) Ibid.; From Peter Ruber: "IBM invented Fibre Channel technology in the late 1980 in two versions and released the specifications to the Institute of Electrical and Electronics Engineers (IEEE), a primary standards-making body for the computer industry. Sun and other players picked up the FC specifications in the early 90s and were instrumental in forming the Fibre Channel Arbitrary Loop committee (FCAL). The committee refined it for distributing computing environments." Are there any adopted standards whatsoever in the meetings industry apart from our suggested ones? There's both opportunity and need!

Yes, brand names printed! Not to belabor the point, but in the June, 1998, issue of Training magazine, page 36, a major subhead reads: "The Internet doesn't instruct. Learning styles are irrelevant. The 'Nintendo generation' learns the same way as the rest of us—and other heresies from instructional technology pioneer M. David Merrill." Sensible, these comments. And shades of our maxi-media comments, published in the early 70s. Is this not precisely the triumph of media over message that Merrill's complaining about?

Sensible, these comments. However, the US military has said approximately the same things with ISD (Instructional Systems Development) several decades earlier than Merrill, as did Dr. Joseph H. Kanner nearly four decades earlier than Merrill. It simply wasn't picked up widely in the trade papers until very recently. Why? Because with Merrill's comments, it obvious that today's Trainers and Meeting Managers face the same problems on a grander (read "more expensive") scale as in decades previously. Fortunately help is still here, via the websites. One is governmental, called America's Learning Exchange (www. Alx.org). Remember, vendor listings here are free and guarantee nothing. But that's the norm in all meeting managementAnother is www.referenceUSA.com, which can offer about 1,000 listings of video conferencing provider companies by break-outs of size and location—*caveat emptor*!

Reconsidering the issue of medium vs message via Merrill: What's wrong with editorial awareness that such regression in knowledge can be allowed to go unnoticed for years throughout an industry as committed to general learning and specific training as the training discipline should be? And why should it have taken anyone so long to re-recognize the obvious? This is an incontrovertible example of the meetings industry's treating one of its clear failures of understanding as a "new" topic worthy of discussion today. Is that intellectually honest?

Media are message-delivery mechanisms, just like human presenters. Period. What does the presenter or mechanism *know* about your message? Now consider how much that gentle concern about message content is minimized by the meetings industry, which has a possibly lesser but significant interest in learning and instruction through meetings as does the training industry. Do conventions have no purpose other than to exist? When will these two separate industries (training and meeting/conventions) realize that they are part of the same *group communications* field? Isn't all the information in both planned for dissemination, preferably with understanding and feedback?

There's been a serious blurring in journalism these days between editorial text and advertising sales support—witness the fiasco at the *Los Angeles Times* when it shared advertising revenue for an issue with an advertiser without informing the public or staff up-front. When that happens, the public is always the loser. This was a scandal even among staff and other journalists and publishers. Let's stress it: shame in an industry so committed to lowest common denominator that it deals regularly in car chases and "if it bleeds it leads." How does that compare to the BBC news version of the world? And why can't even that degree of indignation at ethical gaffes be found in the meetings and conventions industry?

TV anchor Dan Shorr pronounced on a Charlie Rose program in May, 2001, that TV news is caught up in the bottom lines of the conglomerates.

As another instance, we found the following item in *Training* in a special advertising supplement. "These kids have been watching television and computer screens and playing video games almost since birth," notes Thomas Smythe, sociologist. "They have learned to process information differently because of that. They use the Internet instead of the library, a CD-ROM instead of a book." Likely fact (has anyone measured his claim?): Kids input information from different sources differently (possibly), but they *process* it identically. Doesn't the editor read the Mr. Merrill he prints? We won't argue that editors should censor dumb stuff, but might they not report gaffes to the advertiser for correction before printing? But the underlying comment does argue for the growing acceptance of mediation in general, as in two-way, full-motion video conferencing. Why isn't that covered widely? Or would the travel industry object? Please don't do another *McLuhan,* Mr Smythe.

If you have any doubt about whether people will accept mediation, think back on Natalie Cole's album singing "with her father," Nat King Cole. It added new dollar value to old catalogs and boosted Natalie's career. Now Liza Minelli is doing it with Judy Garland's records and memory. And Fred Astaire is dancing with a vacuum cleaner. There's only one downside to the duets and dance ads: they never happened in actuality. It all happened with mixers in the studio, and everyone knows that. So the extent to which people will accept mediation in the meeting room cannot be projected from pre-media experience. Acceptance just happens. Try it. The young will.

Training magazine also ran an editorial article that asked whether anything new had occurred in the past fifteen years before February, 1999. The answer is apparently not. (There are new advances in understanding of the *areas* of the brain affected by certain activities but no more new knowledge about *process*.) Consequently the educational-knowledge summaries delivered by this book's first edition (1983 and repeated in this edition) can be considered to be still valid.

Fred Nickolson, head of strategic planning at Educational Testing Service, Princeton, NJ, stated specifically in that issue: "Regarding our understanding of adult learning, it's not that we haven't made progress in the last 15 years but that we haven't made much progress in *thousands* of years...The only definition of learning provided in that [unreferenced, then-recently published pedagogical] textbook was a statement to the effect that learning is whatever it is that tests measure. Scary, isn't it?"

The same magazine then printed a complaint by a consultant, who said that ISD is "too cumbersome" and followed up with a volume dedicated to that issue Yes, ISD is demanding and does not permit any shortcuts. But shortcuts lead to missed evaluations and therefore errors. Why take shortcuts? And when consultants look for shortcuts, should you beware? Consider us a great believer in ISD. Working in training before formal ISD existed, we developed methods so similar to many basic ISD methods that endorsement is inevitable. If ISD has worked well in four different versions for decades for the military and in countless versions for corporate America, your only question should be, "Is my version complete?" There's no accounting for what that quoted consultant learned and still remembers. So don't you be dissuaded from using one of the finest tools for message protection that has ever been invented!

It's very "in" these days to criticize Instructional Systems Development (ISD) for its cumbersome nature. It is that. However, if it's applied inadequately or where it does not belong, that is the fault of the practitioner, not the system. If you use a hammer instead of a screw driver, it is not the fault of the tools when the screw can't be turned. Use common sense. It's in short supply in the related industries, but it usually works.

Much attention is given to the rapid turn-around possible with having job incumbents train their successors or others, often the new hires. If "mimic me" will work, use it. But that's probably the key system used by and since the caveman and will surely work again. Does it need meetings/training industry endorsement?

Others say that ISD is useless in contemporary business, where there is no precedent for much of the work that must be done. Maybe not. However, problem solving is needed first...and then the planned solution can and should be taught according to ISD principles.

Best to guard against accidental (or intentional) exclusions of important points on repetition by creating an outline or actual script for the teachers to follow each and every time. One of our clients proved that to himself when he gave us an audio tape of a session he had delivered and said that we should find a certain item. It was not there, even though it was included in his taping of a different session, then in his hand. And it was important to the whole, in his estimation. Goofs happen. Try to minimize them. He became a believer in fixed outlines!

And we don't accept the position that any company can or should provide boxed development programs for subjective areas of employee development—that's a new twist on the encounter programs of decades ago; and those were snake oil remedies that often created unrecognized damage!

Even if message-protection doesn't seem to matter to the meetings industry organizations and publications, it still should still matter much to you. Your job depends on it as much as any meeting participant's does—and probably more. Use common sense. If your incipient automotive genius needs help, does he need to change a spark plug or build a car single-handed? Work for the needed skill, obtained wherever the skill is available—that's the prior history of the world.

Also in *Training* magazine (February, 1999) you can find an article entitled "Is There a Learning Curve in this [training] Industry?" As the young say, "Duh?" Just because trainers are dealing with *other* peoples' job performances and personal lives, should that require special skills? Does learning take time? That need for skills has been disguised by the stampede of good sales persons into home office jobs via training posts. Unfortunately, great sales persons do not necessarily make great teachers...that's why there are so few truly competent trainers out there, by percentage. Lacking skills, they "try this" or buy the latest fad program blindly and wonder why it doesn't work. Consider that there are probably a hundred thousand small and mid-sized companies that need, but do not have, a competent training manager. The incompetent and insecure trainers are always among the first to buy promises and fads and worthless new developments, including ersatz new technologies and fancy charts. You can read more about this in Merrill, et al: www.coe.usu.edu/it/id2/reclaim.html.

There are also about a million small companies that employ workers, but apparently these don't matter to publishers. Countless people work there and are too often poorly trained there. These small and some mid-sized companies are essentially ignored because they don't have an impressive budget. After all, small business provides only about half of all jobs in the US. Tough sales—why bother?

Why put so much emphasis on *Training* Magazine? As stated earlier, we believe that meetings and training are facets of the same field of *group communications*. But to acknowledge that, all the industry magazines much first eschew their current focus on narrow "controlled circulation," which focus just happens to benefit their advertisers. You're *a fish in a barrel* if you qualify for controlled circulation—or did you think that it really meant that you'd finally *arrived*?

One can draw a number of conclusions besides those brief comments made above, but two will suffice here.

First, a great service can be done by the true experts for the less-skilled in the industry if the experts can share their skills and knowledge about what *doesn't* work, as well as what does. That argues for honesty in user organizations and publications.

Second, if an industry whose product output is as complex as that of the computer/electronics industry can set standards within ten years of its founding, why couldn't the convention industry associations manage that within their triple time spans of operation? We called for standards and ethics in our address to the 10th Anniversary Convention of MPI, back in 1982, and were given the Tony Award for the best presentation of the convention. But standards and ethics were not enacted then...and not, to our knowledge, to this time. Who benefits? Surely not you, the user!

Several years ago, in a letter to all alternative meetings industry association CEOs, we suggested that the various groups combine forces, whether or not retaining individual memberships in special interest areas. Years later, nothing. Even if the associations gain in their membership, nevertheless the members lose in clout.

Private interests' *goods* that conflict with other persons' private or public interest *goods* are not unknown in other fields.

After all, in New York City, Boss Tweed's Tamany Hall gang controlled surface transportation and so delayed the New York subway system construction for about twenty years after the first working pilot tunnel was built. For whatever their reasons, contemporary persons are trying to delay the outstandingly clean and pleasant subway system's expansion in Los Angeles. These subways are the backbone of mobility in both gridlock cities (yes, we've lived in both cities), and private interests might carry the day short-term in LA, too. And LA as a whole really can't spare the time for delay. But what goes around comes around, as the saying goes. Subways (or monorails) will probably win ultimately. They have long been backbone systems in Chicago, Washington DC, and maybe even San Francisco. And for unrelated reasons, the meetings/ conventions industry is about to have its comeuppance, too, simply because of progress via electronics. Having eschewed *content* as a valued component, the meetings industry as currently composed has nothing of value to offer Meeting Managers who no longer need the circus atmosphere associated with large central meetings of any kind. Because of video conferencing, message content can finally predominate! Association needs to attract volunteer attendees among members does not automatically translate into corporate need. Associations are the wrong models for companies!

Do yourself a favor: *think* about your upcoming meeting. Determine well in advance its purpose and message. If you don't have a purpose, camaraderie won't cut it—that's too expensive and too disappointing, even if everyone claps. "The medium is the message" won't cut it, either. Ask Mr. Merrill. Ask the military. Ask Dr. Kanner. These people have asked basic questions and provided basic answers that you can (and should) use. All quotes of these experts are consistent with this book, whether spoken before or after its original publication. Unscrupulous individuals and organizations will try to trade on a misreading of those thinkers at every opportunity. Don't make the process easy for them.

Parting shots: You can enjoy looking at complex charts that purport to tell you what size print to use to read clearly at blank screen size and blank distance. Terrific. They forget to remind you that the eye is a lens. Anything that you can read with the unaided 20/20 eye at any distance can also be read at a far distance IF the same multiple is used for item image, screen size, and viewing distance. Simple—and you don't have to pay "experts." That includes the wall-sized blowup of a postage stamp.

Also, you've probably heard about putting important materials in the "top left corner" of your screen. Well, not really. Top left was determined by subjects who stared at a dot in the center of the test screen. When eye focus is shifted to read that "top left corner" material, instantly there's a new "top left corner," and it's off screen. Such bogus expertise is waiting for you around every corner, and you'll probably be sorry if you buy it. If you think about it, such information is not really new.

Consider that in theatre, for generations and maybe hundreds of years, stage-right has been considered the advantaged position. Especially up-stage right (far back). Stage-right is the actors' own right when facing the audience—and analogous to an upper-left position on the screen or in a book, if viewed horizontally. Amazing what bogus "experts" can discover to part you from your money. But it's probably even more amazing that so many Meetings Managers can be sold so little for so much money.

Looking Back:

The industry must admit that failed programs are not simply negligible money losses to the user-member organizations nor *merely* prestige or job losses to the Meetings Manager—they actually represent the loss of opportunity to all parties...including the participants who never learn what was intended because they're being entertained instead by "business" presentations.

Because meetings deal with a person's job performance, the meetings are dealing with individual careers and family lives...yet the emphasis has been too much on the color of the draperies and the temperature of hors d'oeuvres. We first stated those criticisms in the 1982 address mentioned above, when we won the MPI Tony Award. But nothing much changed except their me-too training built in part on the bones of censorship of our materials. Is that "professional"? Or worthwhile? But MPI voice-records all convention addresses, including ours, and those are available for sale. Contact the MPI in Dallas, Texas (the successor group is now called Meeting Professionals International), and ask to have a copy sent to you. Many recorded talks are available; they're not expensive but can be very enlightening—pro and con—if you can learn by omission!

Now follows a wider reprise of our objections: Since correction would benefit all Meetings Managers, don't consider that foregoing in this chapter to be simply a Bill of Attainder against an industry fraught with uncorrected shortcomings and a general lack of ethics:

Our first presentation to MPI, early in its life, was made at the request of its then-chief, Marion Kershner, who had been our company's client (and our personal responsibility) while at his different management organization. The award was won that year by Dr. Eden Ryl for her new and innovative film on motivation: the acceptance of personal responsibility. We had written the training guide for that first film, "You Pack Your Own Chute," in its initial distribution, back in the 1970s. "Chute" was first treated to national publicity via *Sales Management* (now *Sales & Marketing Mangement*) magazine, which is considered by the trade to be "outside" the industry. If that's true, how did *SM* help to launch Dr Ryl's film inside the group communications industry?

If that's true, how did "Chute" succeed at all? The film didn't use the clichés of teamwork or wrong way/right way. It dealt forthrightly with the serious issue of taking personal responsibility for our lives. Teams can't do that for individuals. No "needed" laughs were scripted. And in the process, "Chute" became the single highest-selling motivational film of all time! When will the clichés be dumped?

At this writing, over twenty-five years later, the film is subject to complaints, mostly from competitors, that the film is "out of date." Yes, clothes, hairstyles, and dates do change—give the critics their due for such astuteness...but is personal responsibility still an issue in life? Do clothes and hairstyles and one then-current reference affect this (or any) film's intrinsic message? Why do the competitors simply complain? Why don't they just quietly make a better film? *Or don't they know how?* We've talked and had lunch with Eden Ryl several times recently. She's doing just fine, thanks, and so were her several other films, which have now been temporarily withdrawn, possibly in anticipation of other directions for them. Have you heard about them? They're old, if that's all that matters to you.... But, then, people still watch Charlie Chaplin films, don't they? The clothing styles are old in those films, too.

We critiqued industrial film construction back in 1983, too. See our Chapter 5, above. Why don't the meetings/conventions industry associations help their user-members to evaluate films on a *content* basis?

Industry Critiques via Actual Happenings:

Also, the world's first seminar on incentive travel was created in the mid-70s by New York University's School of Continuing Education. We chaired that conference. As chairman, we required all discussions to acknowledge the known averages of trip costs, whether or not some presenter-suppliers chose to promote higher charges. Most did promote high end, and it made the point clearly. From the lectern we quote then-published norms. Paid programs owe their participants more than access for suppliers. Why don't the industry associations take on the task of riding herd on rampant costs? Notice, in Chapter 16, that

American Express Consulting office has listed averages—and they're related to a travel firm! Price hikes can be expected from suppliers, but silence (and refusal to identify cheaters) from the users' own associations need not be tolerated. What else do they offer that's worth paying for?

Also in the mid-70s, when *Sales & Marketing Management* magazine sponsored its first and groundbreaking seminar on meetings, of course we participated as its meetings management columnist. Key to the magazine's presentation was its then-new Survey of Selling Costs that gave average rates for key hotels nationwide. That survey showed that large central meetings are always more expensive than regional or district meetings (the latter choice depending on amounts/costs of any new presentation or other demonstration equipment needed at each locale).

That published survey probably helped to keep hotel rates down. Key to our presentation was the logic that if central meetings were always the most expensive, then regional and district meetings should be more in use whenever *simultaneity* of presentation was not of paramount importance. The hotels picked up on it by creating new meeting spaces smaller than their older ballrooms and/or by buying and rehabbing nearby old movie theatres as "new" meeting facilities (previously recommended by us to be your alternative facility). The industry associations and press appear still to be thinking it through. Keep in mind that *S&MM* magazine is considered to be "outside" the meetings/conventions trade; its sister publication in the industry wants to control the "inside" ads. If *S&MM* readers hold meetings, then how is *S&MM* "outside"?

Exception: About a decade later, mid-70s, a meetings industry magazine printed an article about Mobil Oil's 1960s foray into non-simultaneous shows (not previously unknown) so that Mobil's own executives could meet all of their dealers in smaller, relaxed, resort surroundings. The plan was phenomenally successful in results and in oil industry awards received. Did we forget to mention that our company (and we personally) were the consulting coordinators for Mobil Oil during those mid-60s meetings? Mobil also used various instructional "games" (not discussed by the magazine, which was too much hung up on non-simultaneous meetings, only ten years later.)

Strangely, the industry as a whole doesn't happen to think that saving you money is relevant. So it's now left to two-way, full-motion video conferencing to create a workable bypass to all the past prevarications and rip-offs that have been fixtures in the trade...ever since we created the then-formless "industry's" first published systematic how-to forms in the predecessor to this book, *Achieving Objectives in Meetings, 1973*. Does that smack of criticism? Feature that. And from an authority, too. Do you suppose or suspect that something might be amiss in the industry?

But there are occasional attempts to "help"—that is, to print things that should pass for help. For instance, in the early 60s, one of our national-association clients wrote of having used bits of theatre methods to punch up its announcements from the stage. But the headline at the magazine read: "Association Now Turns to Broadway" and promoted years of fun but useless Broadway borrowings. Oh, yeah, we ghost-wrote that client's article; so we understand the mess created thereafter because of the distortions.

In the mid-70s, a convention industry magazine printed an article by an "expert" columnist who felt that the terms clinic, conference, debates, and forums, etc., were expressions of how long those meetings lasted—and, incredibly, gave day-limits. As the material repeated in our Chapter 12 (previously established back in our mid-70s articles and in the 1973 book and the 1983 edition of this book, too), those designations have roots in performance function and parts of speech. Terms are confused and denigrated by such "experts" who don't recognize those major differences.

In the same vein, several magazines have published paper flow charts and *mis*labeled them PERT Diagrams. We first brought PERT Diagrams to the meetings/conventions industry (See our Chapter 15) in the early 70s, via Crain's *A&SP* magazine. PERT is timed logic; paper flow is irrelevant to meetings management. A flow chart is essentially an office-management tool, reflecting actuality in a single organization. The mislabeling, of course was the editor's attempt to parrot what he didn't truly understand: a timed, generic production control mechanism. PERT Diagrams will work for everybody because each person sets the final target dates for himself/herself against relatively inflexible functions. But flow charts are a record of processing order in a single organization, and the borrowed versions are essentially worthless to every other company, except possibly as a visual model to adjust and maybe imitate when illustrating local paper flow. The flow forms are complex, and they do look nice and complex in print. But they're worthless in your meetings management. And isn't that a marvelous help?

Finally, the grand rip-off! We once identified fee-for-service as one mark of the consultant free from *conflict of interest*; and so the entire industry of "consultants" started charging fees or publicizing their charging. Well, somebody has to pay the consultant; so expect a fee. However, the salient point is *freedom from bias and conflict of interest.* They forgot to mention it. Unless that's stated in the contract, your "consultant" will be free to profit from any direction, including those that might not be favorable to you, such as double dipping. The associations have never challenged this outrageous practice, nor have the magazines.

Soon after our *Achieving Objectives in Meetings* was published, in 1973, a convention industry magazine sponsored a discussion among a few persons considered to be advanced in the field. The magazine didn't realize that at least one of the advanced participants had called for a rush, pre-conference delivery of our book—because AOM had already been recognized as the real advance. The trade magazines never mentioned that embarrassing book until reviewed by MPI six years later. One magazine sponsored how-to meetings taught by a woman employed by a (now-defunct) San Diego conventions firm. She taught largely out of our book, unacknowledged by the magazine, of course, because we don't exist. We became a non-person, Russian Cold War style. But we still signed her copy of our book—which was heavily annotated and highlighted in yellow.

The entire industry uses the Message Profile and the Audience Profile we created in the early 60s (uncredited) for an aggregate ringbinder text claimed (but not copyright certificated) by our then-employer. We have the first copyright certificate issued by the Library of Congress for those items because the false claimants could not swear to having originated them. You have to watch yourself in this industry!

Those early forms have been imitated and reproduced ad nauseam—but never improved. Have the imitators no personal expertise that would permit their improvement on borrowed work? Similarly we *created* the phrase "achieving objectives in meetings" as the title of our first book and it has since become a commonly-used phrase in the trade. So the industry surely was aware of our work and writings.

Finally, the biggie: When creating its first Professional Handbook ringbinder for member training in the mid-80s (more than a dozen years after MPI was formed), MPI asked for permission to photocopy three chapters from the first version of this book. Two chapters were reprinted in full. The third—still Chapter 18 and still highly consumerist—was stripped of all consumerism: DELETING ALL TEXT that we intended for helping you. Two essential forms were reprinted, but separated—is *system* terrible or just undesirable? Our demanding legal-protections suggestion form never was reprinted, either. It challenges some common (for many decades) supplier techniques.

Several years ago, when we first discovered the unauthorized editing of our Chapter 18 material, we objected to MPI and billed. A local lawyer asked for specifics, including our copyright forms; which we provided. Silence! However, since the statute of limitations on claims had expired, we (the author!) would have had to prove recent-discovery. How to prove that? So MPI has refused to respond since that time. Legal? Yes. Ethical? Well ethics was never an especially strong point in the meetings industry. MPI apparently began by trading on the attendance list of Jay Lurye, our former co-worker, who had, in the previous year, sponsored the very first World Meeting Planners Conference, in Chicago. Not a new idea from MPI. Incipient-MPI apparently crossed the street with his lists of potential members. And the rest is sad history.

Given the Napster legal decisions in late July, 2000, regarding protection of intellectual property and copyright, the courts are still favoring copyright rather than "freedom of speech" piracy. The primacy of copyright was previously unchallenged; so MPI cannot absolve itself unilaterally to favor of its "open platform." Ethical observers probably never thought so, even in the mid-80s.

So cheating this writer, who had already tried to help (by participating in two MPI conferences and writing definitive observations re: meal guarantees for their publication, see Appendix A), apparently is negligible in their scheme of things. Maybe that's why so many other associations have sprung up in this field after that time. What are Meetings Managers looking for that they're having so much trouble finding? But the other associations don't seem to recognize that they are merely splintering user purchasing power (which should translate into reform power) but in return are nevertheless adding nothing new to the methodology thereby. And that favors the *status quo* advertisers and exhibitors.

Will they ever accept our suggestion to combine efforts? Don't hold your breath—just check out video conferencing potential and avoid these types of non-contributory problems.

Before continuing, it's probably best to mention just a few horror stories relative to all of this, lest it seem that our past writings are the entire or even major basis of criticism:

A hotel worker who received our advance shipment of meeting material locked it in a closet to be sure it would be safe. Thanks. However, he neglected to tell anyone and subsequently took the meeting-day as a day off. Numerous phone calls and running around by all staff preceded the finding. Delaying the meeting, naturally. All of this in order to "simplify" our arrival! Lack of interior control is a sad reality at many hotels today. So you need to double-check everything. Then pray.

At another hotel the Catering Manager in charge of meetings (that should tell you something) forgot to tell his night crew that our work crew would be arriving for prior evening set-up. When told, on arrival, we were expected to "understand." We insisted that he be phoned, rather than waste our night and consequently delay the morning meeting; so he was called. But he later refused to explain or apologize and also refused to speak to our staff for the remainder of the several-day event. Everything had to be done through intermediaries. Understand that, almost throughout the meetings/conventions industry, hotel executives are important and customers are not.

At several other hotels, which had previously dissuaded various of our clients from *demanding in writing* the exclusive use of needed function rooms, the hotel insisted on tearing out our entire carefully-placed rear-screen projection set-ups because the function rooms had not been *demanded exclusively* in writing...and the hotel now had revenue offers. Legally, in fine print, they had the right. So our client required them to hire a visuals consultant to oversee the work both before and after and to restore everything to original condition. The hotel paid because the client refused—it was not the client's tear-out. If it were the clients' errors, those might have been understandable change requests, though still not acceptable. With a multiple-day meeting already in progress, it's absolutely inexcusable! Be sure your contracts are explicit!

At another meeting, a supposed "expert" was sent by a guest speaker to arrange that speaker's unusual photo slides setup. The expert didn't know what projection throw-distances he needed and was asking to have the stage reset to he's-not-sure-what dimensions. The hotel was willing to change—after all, our client was paying! We refused and provided the minor information to the "expert" and hotel. You can get "help" from almost anyone and might be fooled if it only barely exceeds your own knowledge, but will it be useable when you get it?

Another hotel had a breakdown in its only ballroom's air conditioning system on a Sunday, the day before our client's first business meeting; but they did not contract for repairs until Monday because they did not want to incur overtime expenses. After all, only 800 people would be affected! Our client refused to approve a delay, and reluctantly the repairs were made. Why should there ever have been a question? Our meeting was contracted months in advance to open on that Monday. With travelers attending from across the nation, no less.

What's important to this entire recitation is that our personal publications in years 1970-1977 occurred during the formative years of the meetings/conventions industry as an entity. Our experience dates from about a dozen years prior to MPI's formation. The publication years ranged from two years before MPI's start to much of a decade after MPI's beginning. Check the copyright on everything you see in print today, and you will know when you have found The Source. There was very little published how-to and absolutely nothing like a message-protection system before our 1973 book. Our years of concern ended with the deletion of our consumerist materials by MPI. If the industry had no concern for its own best interests, it seemed not our place to insist. It *seemed.* But the industry *has not delivered anything better* to date, despite abundant opportunity. *Better* probably isn't needed. So our disappearance from the spotlight cannot be seen as their progress. That's why we feel constrained to mention today's new form of progress: the potential salvation from hucksterism offered by two-way, full-motion video conferencing.

New as of this writing is the web site of the American Hotel & Motel Association, which will give you quick access to over

11,000 facilities. This web site lessens the dependency of hotel properties on exhibitions such as the association conventions and might be the opening gun in a divorce, ala the travel industry's travel agents.

Looking Ahead:

We've already covered the big news in Chapter 20: two-way, full-motion video conferencing—at big savings in time, money, and temper. Possibly even on PC relatively soon. Fast, sure, and very inexpensive in the latter form—and for both you can miss all the fun required for site-dependent events (See Chapter 16).

Many people claim to have reservations about VC because that might suggest thoughtfulness on their part. But if people really meant what they say (or say what they mean), why are New Year Resolutions in such disrepute? The sole remaining legitimate reservation is probably the old saw about person-to-person, and "Will two-way, full-motion video really do it" for you? That's an understandable question if you're investing multi-millions of your own money—then press the flesh. Politicians think that works, although persons never-pressed also vote for them. But, as we suggested before, how much flesh-pressing do you need in order to show your participants how to turn a screw driver or solve a math problem or demonstrate a minor device? The problem is that too many national central meetings do too little of provable value—and too many Meetings Managers go along for the ride because they're afraid to talk *sense* to top management, whose business *good sense* should be!

Everything presented above should contribute to your understanding of all the trials and tribulations, headaches and heartaches that can be ELIMINATED if you eliminate the site-dependent portion of your meetings. Not only will you regain your sanity, but your company will save BIG on costs of the large central meeting, which feeds on its own size. Yes, *Sales & Marketing Management* magazine can help you to prove that for the current year. And yes, you can discover the savior-producers-manufacturers of video conferencing equipment with a little inquiry. As stated, see www.referenceUSA.com.

Keep in mind that *Business Week* Magazine has already printed a special advertising issue regarding video conferencing, in Fall, 1998. It was not overly-well supported by the travel industry, as you can understand. As of this writing, the anticipated next issue was in limbo and appeared as only a few pages for November 26, 2001. And since the *Business Week* experience with video conferencing exactly parallels its experience with the Meetings & Conferences special ad issue from the mid-70s (which we wrote secretly for its first two—and only—years), it's clear that something is operating besides simple disagreement with our personal ideas. It appears that the travel industry advertisers who essentially control the meetings/conventions Pollyanna Press are simply not willing to support a competitive journal *that they can't control!*

Then, combining the experiences of Business Week, superficial criticisms of Dr. Eden Ryl's films, and our own brush with industry censorship, you can begin to see the dimensions of the industry's Dirty Little Secret.

This does not pretend that the balance of the American press is pristine. Think only about the sex scandals in any government, or the Elian Gonzalez tear jerking vs law, or the Los Angeles *Times'* unannounced revenue-sharing with one of its advertisers in a special insert, or the press orgy about Monica. However, the flaws of such press actions were challenged at the time; and with discovery, the *Times* episode brought apologies from all the perpetrators. The convention industry press apparently keeps the profits instead.

This chapter should contain a fairly comprehensive description of the types of ills that beset the meetings/conventions industry. But lest this book end with impotent complaints against organizations that might (nevertheless and still) refuse to act in the best interests of users, we propose your easy individual action: easy to understand; easy to implement.

By means of the "Caveat Emptor" form at the end of this chapter, we propose to foster worthwhile action through capability already in the hands of each computer user who is a reader/user of this book, individually and immediately.

Full discovery of site information from your peers via www is already possible. Use it. As of the advent of the www, readers and users now have the means, as well as the need, to research their potential actual meeting sites to a degree never before possible...because now they can get the truth from their own counterparts, rather than from middlemen.

Having specific information about specific sites being considered, every reader/user—you—can make the most knowledge-able decisions ever.

Poll your colleagues in the meetings management field on any pending commitments that you feel are essential to your program. If you're not sure how to start, use our form intact. Or adjust it however much you wish. Permission is hereby given. MPI apparently doesn't think it needs permissions—they opt for encouraging "open platform," which seems an invitation to theft of intellectual property because that phrase has no legal status or prior meaning. Any future violations of author rights could be met with severe legal action from numerous authors.

Responses to your www inquiries could be honest and direct...or they could be unsigned, glowing epistles from the sales offices at the sites you're researching. So as a matter of safety and security, be suspicious of (or disregard) all memos received unsigned or those for which no re-contact is permitted or invited. For practicality, work only with responses signed by reachable persons at known (or verifiable) companies and addresses.

So do look back for precedent. Do look ahead for likely directions. But in the meanwhile, don't forget to look around. And if you don't like what you see, do something about it:

a) Demand honest critiques from the publications you might still read and take everything printed now with a grain of salt; and
b) Look to two-way, full-motion video conferencing. It will likely be a *lifesaver!*

There are probably three main reasons that we recommend checking on hotels when we're also recommending video conferencing to eliminate the hotel hassle:

First, you'll probably need to show top management how you've calculated the figures you'll be presenting in order to sell video conferencing as an intelligent alternative to sites. And the figures presented should not simply be blue sky.

Second, it's a fact of life these days that Meetings Managers must contract for hotel space several years in advance if the group is large or if the program might be especially important. Years in advance, it's hard either to know numbers or to even to cancel if importance wanes. By contrast, it's no problem whatsoever to cancel video conferencing meetings—all it takes is an e-mail to all— or a phone call or www, if you need to compare notes with the canceled persons. Even if canceled, participants are already in their own offices. Nearly four decades ago, we first recommended (in the survey report preceding the ringbinder) that if you don't have a reason for a meeting, don't have it. The field repeats our comment but doesn't believe it.

Third, if you must do business with a previously-contracted site, then it's best to do so when already armed with knowledge of that site's strengths and weaknesses. If you discover something really horrendous in advance, you might want to cancel outright. If large groups can cancel states and sites as a women's lib or gay lib or flag lib statement, why can't you? If you discover a wonderful strength, then you might want to build that element into your agenda for that program.

CAVEAT EMPTOR

(GENERAL OUTGOING WEB ADDRESS)

____

Please help!

Anyone who has information (either especially pro or con) regarding any of the following properties can aid a fellow Meetings Manager to make a fair deal on a good meeting facility.

Facilities being considered now:

Name______________________________
City ______________________________
State _______________

Name______________________________
City______________________________
State _______________

Name______________________________
City ______________________________
State _______________

1) Was/were the designated facility(ies) in actuality what they seemed to be in folders and/or other descriptions, including your personal conversations with staff?

2) Were the attitudes of the facility service staff equal to or better than that described by personal discussion with other staff in advance? Service with a smile throughout? Were staff "fresh" in the mornings or already overworked?

3) Do you believe that the pricing structure was both competent and fair...and as described in advance? Delivered to agreed terms and agreed budgets?

4) Were you subjected in any way to bait-and-switch tactics or what you felt were unwarranted upcharges or hidden fees?

5) How recently (year 19____/200__) did you use that facility? For ____ meeting days? _____ Advance commitment?

Additional comments, if any:

6) Would you return there for another meeting (if no advance commitment now)?

7) Are you willing to be contacted for details? (Yes) (No).
If yes: First name

____.
Tel No: ______________
Other ______________________________
Best time ________________
Day ____________________________

Thanks a million. Reply to (Your name, if...)
Company _____________________________
Dept or Title ____________
at www or e-mail _________________
Tel No (identifies) _____________

IMPORTANT NOTE: Private communications are not generally subject to libel claims **IF** the information is true and provable **OR** if it's not widely publicized by the writer. I promise not to publicize your comments. Have your say in confidence. I'll respect it...for a more ethical industry!

For any reason or for all three, it's worth your time to check. But in the last analysis, the tools to be more secure in your choices are in your hands now. That's new! Besides, what happens between you and any responding colleague or counterpart is your personal and private business. Private communication is not libel. Provable items, no matter how egregious, are not libel if proved. Good or bad, no one need ever know! Again, good meetings to you.

Appendix

Having seen our original article on breakage (hotel meals guaranteed to be paid but not served), some older Meetings Managers thought it would be interesting to see at least a few lines used as a reminder for younger Meetings Managers. So:

In September 1979, the MPI (then, Meeting Planners International, now known as Meeting Professionals International) printed, in their MPI Newsdata newletter, the brief original house organ) our long article regarding meal guarantees, excerpted below. The chief executive officer of the MPI, the late Marion Kershner, himself phoned all mentioned persons to confirm the quotes given. Kershner was shocked because some trade magazines had been spewing some hotels' official line—that the 48-hour advance guarantees were now (meaning then) the "standard" and that 72-hours was gaining acceptance. That's not what we had believed earlier, and it was not what we discovered on investigation.

Read the following brief excerpt and wonder about credibility of the media in this industry:

COMPETITION BRAKES
GUARANTEE TREND

"Despite increasing pressure by hotels toward longer advance periods for meal guarantees, the 24-hour advance period is not yet dead. Even the emerging new "standard" 48-hour advance period is not firm; and not a single facility contacted was willing to acknowledge or endorse a 72-hour period as policy. Standard Rule for meetings managers: negotiate or take the risks.

"A spot check of perhaps 20 major convention facilities across the country indicates a uniformly restrictive change in hotel policies toward variation in setups on those meals guaranteed. Whereas all hotels were once prepared to serve 10% up or down from the guaranteed count, today most allow 5% up-only; some, 3% up-only. Guarantees for hors d'oeuvres are generally non-variable."

Because money and policy quotes change rapidly, there's no sense in repeating outdated stuff here regarding the actual numbers then given. What's important is the publications' own relationship to their readers. Suffice it to say that no major hotel contacted was willing to claim a 72-hour policy. There are two severe consumerist quotes also included from a couple of executives of independent member-associations, including a now past president of MPI. Maybe MPI will tell you why they promote consumerism so little (if at all) these days.

The list of hotels quoted included the Fountainebleau in Miami Beach; the Sheraton Boston; the Mayflower in Washington, DC; the McCormick Inn, the Hilton Palmer House, the Drake, the Holiday Inn Mart Plaza, the Hyatt Regency and the Regency O'Hare Airport—all in Chicago; the Mark Hopkins and the St. Francis in San Francisco; and the MGM Grand in Las Vegas. Because some of these facilities are legendary, we expect that the newer Meetings Managers might not recognize them. Is there anything there that you older Meetings Managers would not consider for quality? Yet, they didn't agree with the industry and its Pollyanna Press.

So who was helping whom to push up prices and increase Meetings Managers' headaches? Although corporate managers know that everyone will be taking meals with the group, association managers rarely know in advance exactly who will and who won't, unless tickets are sold. Even then it's sometimes guesswork because many participants' decisions are made at the last minute. So all long-advance periods are undesirable. Hotels say that deliveries by their provisioners are less frequent these days and that waiter unions are more stringent—so longer advance periods are necessary. If and when that's true in given cases, it's valid. Both sides have a point, but arbitrary policies are not the answer. If you can't win a concession on such a small (if profitable to them) point before contract, what do you suppose might happen later, in a crunch? Negotiate a satisfactory guarantee period or walk away...forever.

A related issue: in 1999, the Ojai (CA) Valley Inn & Spa advertised for a conferences and catering manager. In a shameless newspaper employment ad they stipulated "Working knowledge of food and beverage and ability to produce creative and revenue driven menus." Does that say "what the traffic will bear" to you?

What's really going on in the meetings and conventions *market*? Is that any substitute for what *should* be going on in the *industry*? We can't answer those questions for you because we've never understood the answers the trade and its press gave. But reading these criticisms against the uncritical material in the industry's Pollyanna Press should make the point for you.

Work hard to protect your message—the message is the reason for the meeting! Work hard to protect your company. Work hard to protect your budget and job. They're all at risk when you plan a meeting outside your company walls! The good news is that with the advent of full motion video conferencing, possibly computer-based, you don't need to go outside your company walls anymore. No more meal guarantees. Ever. And you don't need to incur all the fun of analyzing hotel offers or ticketing and reticketing for VIP's and maybe all participants, or lost baggage and meeting supplies, or canceled flights, or undependable producers and visuals suppliers and temperamental speakers. If there should happen to be a video contact outage on any given day (as happens occasionally on international news shows) you can do the program the next day with little wasted time today because most participants are already in their own towns or offices. Besides, if you present less material each day on more (scattered?) days, maybe your participants will even have time to think about some of it. Shakespeare said it first: "Tis a consummation devoutly to be wished."

Bibliography

Note: Titles cited tend to be seminal works especially notable in the context in which mentioned. Some authors have written other books worthy of attention, as have still other authors unnamed.

Battersby, Albert. *Mathematics in Management.* Harmondsworth, England, and Baltimore, Md.: Penguin Books, 1966.

Beqiraj, Mehmet. *Peasantry in Revolution.* Ithaca, N.Y.: Cornell University Center for International Studies, fifth monograph, 1966.

Blumenthal, Arthur L. *Language and Psychology: Historical Aspects of Psycholinguistics.* New York: John Wiley & Sons, 1970.

Bormann, Ernest *G. Discussion and Group Methods.* New York: Harper & Row, 1969.

Bourne, L. E., Jr. "Learning and Utilization of Conceptual Rules." In *Concepts and the Structure of Memory,* ed. B. Kleinmetz. New York: John Wiley & Sons, 1967.

Bradford, Leland P. *Making Meetings Work.* La Jolla, Calif: University Associates, 1976.

Bransford, John D. *Human Cognition: Learning, Understanding, and Remembering.* Belmont, Calif.: Wadsworth, 1979.

_______, and Nancy McCarrell. "A Sketch of a Cognitive Approach to Comprehension." *In Cognition and the*

Symbolic Processes, ed. Walter Weimar and David Palermo. Hillsdale, N.J.: Lawrence Erlbaum, 1974.

Brehm, Jack W. *Theory of Psychological Reactance*. New York: Academic Press, 1966.

Broadbent, D. E. *Perception and Communication.* New York: Pergamon Press, 1958.

Brown, James W., and James W. Thornton, eds. *New Media in Higher Education.* Washington, D.C.: National Education Association, 1963.

Buhler, Charlotte. *Psychology in Contemporary Life.* (Munich, 1962). New York: Hawthorne, 1968.

_______ and Fred Massarik, eds. *Course of Human Life: a Study of Goals in the Humanistic Perspective.* New York: Springer, 1968.

Buhler, Karl. Tatsachen und Probleme zu einer Psychologie der Denkenorgang; III:*Uueber Gedenkenerinnerungen.* Arch Ed. Ges. Psych., 1908. Accessible only through references.

Cantril, Hadley. *The Human Dimension: Experience in Policy Research.* New Brunswick, N.J.: Rutgers University Press, 1967.

_______,*Pattern of Human Concerns.* New Brunswick, N.J.: Rutgers University Press, 1966.

_______,*Gauging Public Opinion.* Princeton, N.J.: Princeton University Press, 1947.

Cavalier, Richard. *Achieving Objectives in Meetings.* New York: Corporate Movement, 1973.

_______, *Sales Meetings That Work.* Homewood, IL: Dow Jones-Irwin, 1983; Third Ed, Bloomington, IN: 1st Books, 2001.

_______, *Practical Word Power*. Dundee, IL: Delta Systems Co., 1989; Second Ed, Campbell, CA: iUniverse.com, 2000.

_______, *Managing Through Training*. Bloomington, IN: 1st Books,2001.

_______, *Common Sense ISD*, Bloomington, IN: 1st Books, 2001.

Chomsky, Noam. *Syntactic Structures.* The Hague: Mouton, 1957.

_______,*Aspects of the Theory of Syntax.* Cambridge, Mass.: MIT Press, 1965.

_______, and Morris Halle. *The Sound Pattern of English.* New York: Harper & Row, 1968.

Cohn, Arthur H. *Attitude Change and Social Influence.* New York: Basic Books, 1964.

Corsini, Raymond J.; Malcolm E. Shaw; and Robert R. Blake. *Roleplaying in Business and Industry*. New York: Free Press, 1961.

Dale, Edgar. *Audio-Visual Methods in Teaching*. New York: Holt Rinehart & Winston, 1969.

Daw, Charles W. and Edward A. Dornan. *One To One: Resources for Conference-Centered Writing*. New York, N.Y.:Harper Collins Publisher, 1992

Dember, William N., and Joel S. Warm. *The Psychology of Perception.* 2d ed. New York: Holt, Rinehart & Winston, 1979.

Diamond, Lynn and Stephanie Roberts. *Effective Videoconferencing: Techniques for Better Business Meetings.*Menlo Park, CA: Crisp Publications, 1996.

Dodd, David H., and Raymond M. White, Jr. *Cognition: Mental Structures and Processes.* Boston: Allyn & Bacon, 1980.

Doob, Leonard W. *Public Opinion and Propaganda.* 2d ed. Hamden, Conn.: Shoe String Press, 1966.

Doyle, Michael, and David Straus. *How to Make Meetings Work.* New York: Wyden, 1976.

Eliot, John, ed. *Human Development and Cognitive Processes.* New York: Holt, Rinehart & Winston, 1971.

Frankl, Viktor E. *Man's Search for Meaning: an Introduction to Logotherapy.* Boston: Beacon Press, 1962.

_______ *The Will to Meaning.* New York: World, 1969.

Franks, Jeffery J. "Toward Understanding Understanding." *In Cognition and the Symbolic Processes*, ed. Walter Weimar and David Palermo. Hillsdale, N.J.: Lawrence Erlbaum, 1974.

Gazzaniga, Michael, and Roger Sperry. "The Split Brain in Man." *Scientific American* 217, no.2 (August 1967), pp.24-29.

Herzberg, Frederick. *Motivation to Work.* New York: John Wiley & Sons, 1959.

_______, *Work and the Nature of Man.* New York: World, 1966.

Hilton, Jack, and Peter Jacobi. *Straight Talk about Video Conferencing.* NY: Prentice Hall, 1986

Hosford, Philip L. *An Instructional Theory: A Beginning.* Inglewood Cliffs, NJ: McGraw-Hill, 1973.

Hovland, Carl; Aurthur Lumsdaine; and Fred Sheffield. *Experiment on Mass Communication.* Princeton, NJ.: Princeton University Press, 1949.

Human Resources Research Organization; U.S. Army. *Comparison of Techniques for Guiding Performance During Training.* Washington, D.C.: U.S. Department of Commerce, 1971. (Document #AD-730655)

Hall, Edward T. *The Silent Language.* New York, N.Y.: Doubleday & Co., 1959.

Iacocca, Lee. *An Autobiography.* New York, N.Y.: Bantam Books, 1984.

Janis, I. L., and B. T. King. "The Influence of Role Playing on Opinion Change." In *Communication and Persuasion,* ed. C. I. Hovland; I. L. Janis; and H. H. Kelley. New Haven, Conn.: Yale University Press, 1953.

Kanner, Joseph H., and Alvin J. Rosenstein. *Television in Army Training: Color vs. Black/White*. Audio-Visual Communication Review 8, no.6 (1960). Available from University Microfilms International, Ann Arbor, Mich. (Document #C-1466)

Knowles, Malcolm. "Adult Education." In *The New Media and Education,* ed. Peter Rossi and Bruce Biddle. Chicago, Aldine, 1966.

_______.*The Adult Learner: a Neglected Species.* Houston: Gulf Publishing, 1978.

_______. *Modern Practice of Adult Education: Andragogy vs. Pedragogy. Chicago: Follett Publishing, 1980.*

MacKenzie, Brian D. Behaviourism and the Limits of Scientific Method. (International Library of Philosophical and Scientific Method.) Atlantic Highlands, N.J.: Humanities Press, 1977.

McLuhan, Marshall. *Understanding Media.* New York: McGraw-Hill, 1964.

Mager, Robert F. *Preparing Instructional Objectives* (Programmed). 2d ed. Palo Alto, Calif.: Fearon, 1962.

Margerison, Charles J. *Managerial Problem Solving.* London: McGraw-Hill, 1974.

Maslow, Abraham H. *New Knowledge in Human Values.* New York: Harper & Row, 1959.

_______, *Eupsychian Management.* Homewood, Ill.: Irwin-Dorsey, 1965.

_______, *Toward a Psychology of Being.* New York; Van Nostrand Reinhold, 1968.

_______,*Farther Reaches of Human Nature.* New York: Viking Press, 1971.

Massaro, Dominick W. "Auditory Information Processing." In *Handbook of Learning and Cognitive Processes: IV, Attention and Memory,* ed. W. K. Estes. Hillsdale, N.J.: Lawrence Erlbaum, 1976.

Melton, A. W. "Implications of Short-Term Memory for a General Theory of Memory." *Journal of Verbal Learning and Verbal Behavior* 2, pp.1-21.

_______, and J. M. Irwin. "The Influence of Degree of Interpolated Learning on Retroactive Inhibition and the Overt Transfer of Specific Responses." *American Journal of Psychology* 53 (1940), pp.173-203.

_______ and Edwin Martin, eds. *Coding Processes in Human Memory.* New York: John Wiley & Sons, 1972.

Merrill, M. David. *Wake Up! (And Reclaim Instructional Design). In* Training magazine, June 1998.

_______, et al. "Reclaiming Instructional Design." www.coe.usu.edu/it/id2/reclaim.html.

Miller, G. A. "The Magical Number Seven Plus or Minus Two: Some Limits on Our Capacity for Processing Information.." *In Psychological Review* 63 (1956), pp.81-97.

_______, *The Psychology of Communication.* New York: Basic Books, 1967.

Newsweek. "Air Hell." New York: April 23, 2001.

_______, "Letters: Wireless vs. Body Language." New York: May 21, 2001.

Peppers, Don. *Life's a Pitch; Then You Buy.* New York: Doubleday/Currency, 1995.

Pisoni, David B., and James H. Sawusch. "Some Stages in Processing in Speech Perception." In *Structure and Process in Speech Perception*, ed. A. Cohn and S. G. Nooteboom.. New York: Springer, 1975.

Robert, Henry M., et al. *Robert's Rules of Order.* Glenview, Ill.: Scott-Foresman, 1970.

Rogers, Carl. "A Note on the Nature of Man." *Journal of Counselling Psychology* 4 (1957), pp.199-203.

______, and B. F. Skinner. "Some Issues Concerning the Control of Human Behavior." *Science* 124 (1956), pp. 1057-65.

Rose, Homer C. *The Development and Supervision of Training Programs.* Chicago: American Technical Society, 1964.

Rosenberg, M; C. Hovland; et al. *Attitude Organization and Change*. New Haven, Conn.: Yale University Press, 1960.

Skinner, B. F. *Walden Two*. New York: Macmillan, 1948.

________, *Science and Human Behavior.* New York: Macmillan, 1953.

________, *Beyond Freedom and Dignity*. New York: Alfred A.. Knopf 1971.

Smith, M. Brewster. *Humanizing Social Psychology*. San Francisco: Jossey Bass, 1974.

Sutich, Anthony J., and Miles A. Vich, eds. *Readings in Humanistic Psychology*. New York: Free Press, 1969. (Monographs by 24 humanistic psychologists; superior overview.)

Watson, John B. *Behaviorism*. New York: People's Institute, 1924.

Waugh, N. C., and D. A. Norman. "Primary Memory." *Psychological Review* 72 (1965), pp.89-104.

Weibe, G. "Some Implications of Separating Opinions from Attitudes." *Public Opinion Quarterly* 17 (1953).

Weick, Karl E. "Monograph." In *Attitude, Ego Involvement and Change,* ed. Carolyn W. Sherif and Musafer Sherif. New York: John Wiley & Sons, 1967.

_______, *Social Psychology of Organizing.* Reading, Mass.: Addison-Wesley Publishing, 1979.

Wicklund, H. A. and Jack W. Brehm. *Perspectives on Cognitive Dissonance.* New York: Halsted & Wiley, 1976.

Wundt, Wilhelm. *Outlines of Psychology.* Leipzig: Engelmann, 1897. (Contributions to the History of Psychology series; reproduction of 1916 ed.)Translated by E. L. Schaub. Frederick, Md.: University Publications of America, 1980.

Index of Forms

Index

About the Author

RICHARD CAVALIER has designed, written. produced, and or run countless meetings and conventions of every size, type. and complexity for both corporations and associations on a national and international level.

In the early 1960s he began using techniques then considered innovative and advanced—closed-circuit TV, multimedia, sociodrama in the meeting room, and exhibit games. His sales promotion and sales training techniques have included live central meetings, semi-packaged regional formats, and semi-or fully-packaged meetings for field use.

For over five years. his regular column for *Advertising & Sales Promotion* and *Sales & Marketing Management* magazines have created a new awareness of business standards and communications principles in what had been a complacent, glamor oriented field.

Lightning Source UK Ltd.
Milton Keynes UK
UKOW052145270612

195166UK00001B/3/A